Religion, Revolution, and the Future

Jürgen Moltmann

✛ ✛ ✛

Religion, Revolution, and the Future

TRANSLATED BY M. DOUGLAS MEEKS

CHARLES SCRIBNER'S SONS ✛ NEW YORK

IN MEMORIAM
MARTIN LUTHER KING, JR.

Translator's Preface

From September, 1967, to April, 1968, Jürgen Moltmann, Professor of Theology at Tübingen University in Germany, sojourned in the United States. While he was pivotally located as Visiting Professor of Systematic Theology at Duke Divinity School, he traveled widely to almost every major region of the nation and visited many of the large academic and urban centers. This book is comprised of a portion of the lectures and essays with which Professor Moltmann introduced himself and his thought to the American continent. A diversity of contexts occasioned the lectures. Some were written in response to specific topical requests of endowed lectureships or theological conferences, while one served to commemorate the centennial of a large university. Included is a lecture addressed to a world student symposium on revolution as well as a dialogical response to Ernst Bloch, which has become a milestone in the continuing conversation between Christian theologians and Marxian humanists. All the pieces, however, share the common, practical intent of re-Christianizing religion in terms of revolution and the future. Throughout, this theme is elaborated in a genuinely knowledgeable awareness of the intellectual, social, and political conditions of American society.

It is a pleasure to acknowledge my indebtedness and gratitude to a number of people who in varying ways have contributed to the translation of these essays. In particular, I must mention Professor Frederick Herzog, who, in addition to translating the essay "Resurrection as Hope," generously gave his counsel at difficult junctures of the project and made many suggestions for the improvement of the translation. Two friends and colleagues, Dale W. Cannon and Wilbur C. Benware, applied their adroit reading and critical skills to portions of the manuscript. My deep gratitude is also due Professor Moltmann for his unfailing encouragement and help from the time the lectures were first being prepared for delivery until the completion of their present form. I owe a special word of thanks to Mrs. Emma G. Repass and Miss Martha Duplissey, who are responsible for the various drafts of the typescript, and to my wife, who helped in innumerable ways, scholarly and otherwise.

It should be noted that New Testament quotations are usually given from the Revised Standard Version and occasionally translated directly from the German.

M. DOUGLAS MEEKS

Author's Preface

FREEDOM IN SPACE AND FREEDOM IN TIME

In place of an introduction, I should like to preface the publication of the lectures I gave in the United States during a guest professorship at Duke University, Durham, North Carolina, 1967–1968, with a few impressions of the New World and a few reflections on the "new age."

As John Steinbeck made preparation for his *Travels with Charley* with the intention of discovering America once again, he saw in the eyes of his neighbors something he was to find over and over in every part of the nation: "A burning desire to go, to move, to get under way, any place, away from any Here. They spoke quietly of how they wanted to go someday, to move about, free and unanchored, not toward something, but away from something."[1] But it is not only every American who hungers to be on the move, as John Steinbeck suggests. Even a poor European from the Old World has this dream of freedom and movement in his heart. And what is likely to impress him most about America is the seemingly unlimited freedom in space, the unfenced horizon, and the still inviting openness of this continent. In this regard he would be well advised by Sydney Mead: "He who would understand America

[1] John Steinbeck, *Travels with Charley*, p. 10.

ix

must understand that through all the formative years, space has overshadowed time—has taken precedence over time in the formation of all the ideals most cherished by the American mind and spirit."[2] If he travels through the land in all directions by plane or Greyhound bus, he will grasp just why the understanding of freedom as a freedom to move in space has remained dominant for Americans. But if he realizes that such a freedom is less and less possible in an overpopulated world which is increasingly becoming "one world" and everywhere the same world, he will be reminded of the European situation he left behind. He may then conclude with Sydney Mead: "Perhaps, then, the real hope lies in the thus far most inarticulate . . . —a hope for freedom based on the thought that, while space in this earth is obviously limited, time is less so and indeed may be infinite."[3]

This idea of Sydney Mead is excellent, though he has not elaborated the implications of this change from "freedom in space" to "freedom in time." Perhaps a comparison between the differing concepts of freedom in America and on the European continent can illuminate the consequences of this proposal.

In America, people found the "new world" in the wilderness of a country unlimited in arable land. Here nature was still almost undisturbed by human hands. Here there was room for everyone. If we compare the meager beginning of the Colonies in Jamestown and Williamsburg with the unbounded breadth of the continent and the superabundance of nature, we can gain a deep impression of the inviting and challenging character of the land. Even visiting Europeans hear, as it were, the call of "Westward ho!" and, along with their children, are inspired by Daniel Boone, who was always compelled to push further westward as soon as he saw the smoke coming from the chimney of a neighbor. Everyone could find an unsettled place for himself in the wide-open spaces. If anyone wanted a change, he could simply change his homestead. If his neighbors

[2] Sydney Mead, *The Lively Experiment: The Shaping of Christianity in America* (New York: Harper & Row, 1963), pp. 11f.
[3] *Ibid.*, p. 13.

ceased to please him, he could go to a place where he could lead his own life and follow his own whims.

In Europe, however, the close of the great migration of people before 1500 marked the end of freedom in space. The idea of a "new world" was useless for people longing for freedom on the old continent, for they could no longer find different and new worlds in space. To be sure, masses of emigrants debarked time and again for the wilderness of America or the expanses of Russia to find free and unsettled land. But those who stayed at home had to come to terms with the land and the place in which they dwelled. It is not correct to say with John Steinbeck: "The pioneers, the immigrants who peopled the continent, were the restless ones in Europe. The steady rooted ones stayed home and are still there."[4] The ones who stayed behind also dreamed of freedom. But since they had no desire to seek freedom in distant lands, they sought the freedom of the inner man. They dreamed of freedom in a world that transcended the narrowness and limitedness of their present situation. Among the mystics of the Middle Ages were the Brethren of the Free Spirit. Through their religious meditations the soul submerged itself in God and experienced a Godlike freedom from all conditions and limitations of this earth. The age of the Enlightenment witnessed the "free spirits." "Man is free, even if he is born in chains," they said. And Friedrich Schiller composed the song: "Thoughts are free, who can guess them. . . ." Nailed to a particular place, environment, and society, and ruled by the iron hand of princes and bishops, they found no opportunity for external, social, and political freedom. So they internalized the kingdom of freedom for which they yearned and made it the realm of the soul or of pure speculation.

But again and again, this inner light of freedom became the consuming flame of revolution and directed itself outward. "What was an inner light becomes a consuming flame turned outward," wrote the young Karl Marx. The mystical experience of the soul turned into revolutionary transformation of the

[4] Steinbeck, *op. cit.*, p. 103.

world. It was precisely out of this process that a peculiar, new idea of freedom was born in the Old World. Since the time of Joachim di Fiore in the Middle Ages, hope in the "new age" (*Neue Zeit*), the coming age of freedom, which must be ushered in, has influenced all revolutionary movements from the Renaissance through the Reformation to the English, French, and Russian revolutions. The term *Neuzeit*, probably used first by Heinrich Heine in the middle of the nineteenth century, is difficult to translate. "Modern times" is not a completely felicitous rendering because this expression does not connote the messianic expectations inherent in *Neuzeit*. What, in fact, is implied in this word *Neuzeit* is exactly the significance we find in the expression "new world," only it is thought with temporal rather than spatial conceptuality. This word *Neuzeit* is an expression for freedom, yet for freedom not in space but in time, not for freedom of moving from one place to another but of revolutionary transformation.

In this context freedom is no longer understood as movement through the open land of a "new world" but as movement into the open time of the future, into the "new age." Whenever one wanted a change in his life, he had to change the social and political conditions of the place where he lived. Whenever one was mistreated by his neighbors or superiors, he had to seek the transformation of these oppressive relationships; he had no alternative of escaping oppression by moving to another place. "Who will change the world?" pondered Bertolt Brecht, who gave his own irrefutable answer: "They who dislike it." In Europe, every unsatisfied man was thus a potential revolutionary. Nailed to his place, capsulated in his society and state, he could find freedom only in revolutionary, political, and social transformation, that is, in shaping a new future for his place. The emigrants left their traditions and authorities behind in the Old World. They found their utopia in the New World beyond the oceans. Like the Romans who stormed Carthage, they burned their ships behind them. Often enough, they cut off all family ties in attempting to begin a new life. Thus, their life in the New World was, and is even today, "without roots."

xii

Life in the New World therefore has been not only "the pursuit of happiness," as the American Declaration of Independence suggests, but also, on a deeper level, a desperate struggle for identity. But this New World with its pursuit of happiness and new identity has never been a field for the real conflict between the old and the new, tradition and progress, authority and freedom, and the past and the future. Between the powers of the Old World and the energies of the New World lay the ocean.

But for those who remained in Europe and sought the "new age" in the old place, the criticism of tradition, the destruction of authorities in church, state, and society became an inevitable task. Precisely the same place which people could not leave became the stage for the conflicts between the old and the new times. So, only from the perspective of America did Europe become the "old world." But for the Europeans themselves, Europe became the scarred battlefield of the "new age," the land of ever new revolutions, the place where the past and the future necessarily struggle over the definition of the present. From the Middle Ages to the present, Europe became the land of *Geschichte* (history). *Geschichte* is also a difficult word to translate because it is grounded in a peculiar experience which itself is not translatable. European *Geschichte* can be described at its important junctures as revolutionary history, as Eugen Rosenstock-Huessy has demonstrated.[5] Revolutionary history is a succession of attempts to realize freedom in time by creating a new future in the same place. Europe had no other land of freedom than the unlimited future. But men could enter this land only by breaking through the limits, the patterns, and the fences of the past.

With the possible exception of space travel to the planets, the idea of a "new world" and "freedom in space" has become meaningless today. Since the pioneers and trailblazers reached America's west coast, since the population explosion reduced the uninhabited land mass, and since an "American nation"

[5] Eugen Rosenstock-Huessy, *Die europäischen Revolutionen und der Charakter der Nationen* (3rd ed.; Jena, 1951).

xiii

developed out of the melting pot of immigrants, moving from one place to another no longer has its old significance. If one moves from one place to another, he will be simply changing places within a society whose advantages and ills are ubiquitously the same. Nothing really new will happen to a person for having simply changed his residence to the midwest or to California. Coca-Cola, General Motors, and Sears are already there before him. Moving from one area to another no longer makes any real difference. The external circumstances which molded America into a political unit as well as its emerging political and military traditions have buried the dream of the "new world." In this respect, America, like all other lands, is a living graveyard of utopias.

Immigration was stopped after World War I and is strictly controlled now. The effect has been twofold. On the one hand, in a way analogous to Europe, the universal idea of the "new world" and of freedom has produced only a new, particular nation. People left their homes to seek freedom in a "new world," but what they found was only the United States. This is not nothing, but it is also no fulfillment. On the other hand, the mobilizing utopia of freedom changed itself only too easily into the ideology of new power structures. Why fight in Vietnam? For the ideal of freedom, for the security of the American nation, or for the imperialism of *Pax Americana*? Freedom in space is now very limited and will become even more limited within the web of social structures. People can no longer emigrate. Today, the earth has no "new world." This is one reason why America stands on the threshold of a radical transformation of her ideals and visions. The descendants of the immigrants with their living heritage of inner unrest and rootlessness are now nailed to their place. Moreover, it is a place which is already determined by many unfree structures of society, a place which has not only a good but also an evil history. America no longer lives simply in the face of an unlimited future, but now, like many other nations, must learn how to live with her past.

What of the men who still have visions of a free world and the "burning desire to be on the move"—what will they do now? Perhaps they will kill their dreams with the help of social adjustment and psychological manipulation. Perhaps they are fed up with the restlessness of freedom and its inevitable loneliness and have no other desire than to strike some roots and remain "at home." Perhaps they will be conformists and adjust to middle-class standards. It may be that the feeling of social belongingness is enough for them now. So they will "belong" to a church, a club, or a "great society" and will unburden themselves of the destiny of freedom.

But those who cannot forget their original visions of freedom, those who cannot be satisfied with the trite compensations of an affluent society, must search for a new notion of freedom. If "freedom in space" has reached its limits, the notion of "freedom in time" is becoming a real option for those who love freedom. If spatial movements no longer make any difference, the temporal movement into a "new age" can make a difference for those who love freedom. They will realize that the very place they can no longer leave behind can be qualified by a new future. If people cannot move away from the conditions of the present, they can change them. The unlimited or infinite lies no longer in space, but in the future, in time. And it is through social transformation that we can now find it. It is no longer the open land which invites and challenges us, but the open future. The old so-called "frontier religions" moved westward into the open space along with the advancing pioneer settlements. They were thought of as the religion of the poor and the oppressed, of men hungering after freedom and new justice. They were future-oriented and characterized by a spirit-filled existence. Today, many of these awakening movements have reached their end, if not their goal, in the "paradise" of suburban captivity. But are there not already arising today new "frontier religions" in the underground of the cities, in the movements for social justice and racial equality? If we can no longer find "frontier religions" in space and in movement across the land, they are now appearing in time and revolutionary transformation. And it is there that underprivileged and nonadjusted groups must seek their freedom.

Into the "new world" which is yet also quite old, the conflict of the times intrudes. The Party of Hope raises its head and looks into a more just future. The Party of Anxiety flocks together in reaction and spawns acts of violence. John F. Kennedy, Martin Luther King, Jr., and Robert F. Kennedy had visions. They longed for the transformation of the status quo and asked sacrifices for the future of their country. Even if no conspiracy against them can be demonstrated, these men stood in the same ranks and gave their life as seed for a better future of America.

In all these respects, the situation in America is becoming very similar to the situation in Europe. In the nineteenth century, England could maintain its Victorian mode of life only because it could send its restless youths to the colonies. France could become bourgeois because it possessed a vent in its colonies for adventurous and critical youth. The European countries no longer have these vents today. They have their potential revolutions at home in the midst of their critical and freedom-loving youth. In Germany, as elsewhere, the skeptical postwar generation has been replaced by new rebellious youth. If there are no major wars, the United States and the Eupropean countries will be faced with a long revolutionary march through the outmoded, authoritarian structures of their societies. The "good old days" are gone. Now the future is our heaven or our hell and the present is something like a purgatory.

I dedicate these essays to the memory of Martin Luther King, Jr., whose summer dream at the Lincoln Memorial in 1963 is a spark of hope in a world without justice, and to young people who desire nothing more urgently than to rise up out of apathy and shape their own future.

Tübingen, Summer, 1968   JÜRGEN MOLTMANN

Contents

Religion, Revolution, and the Future

I · What Is "New" in Christianity:

The Category Novum in Christian Theology

1

"BEHOLD, I MAKE ALL THINGS NEW."

"Nothing new happens under the sun," says Ecclesiastes. "Hence all is vanity." In saying this he expressed that wisdom of resignation which can make man melancholy as well as serene. But if there can be nothing new in the world, there is also no real future. And if there is no future, there is also no real history. If there is no history, our world is not open, but shut in. Without history, man, too, is not a being who is open and full of questions and hopes for the future, but one who is enclosed and imprisoned in himself.

If we consider our contemporary situation, we find that in all areas of life the unique characteristic of modern times consists in the fact that we are everywhere asking for something that is "new." The modern world is modern precisely because men are fascinated by a future which so far nowhere has taken place and hence will be new. This is everywhere the case—with the exception perhaps of the church. Here hardly any-

This lecture was presented during the John XXIII Conference at St. Xavier College, Chicago, October 27–29, 1967, and occurs in a slightly variant form in a collection of the Conference's lectures, *The Future as the Presence of Shared Hope* (New York: Sheed and Ward, 1968).

thing new happens, and if occasionally we try to implement reforms, we are hampered by the anxiety of losing whatever of value we do have. Nowhere are men so conservative and so attached to the old as, of all places, in the church. There seems to be an unconscious desire in religion, at a time when everything is changing and is being renewed, to find one last bastion of continuity, tradition, and immutability. God is called upon not as the power of the new who creates the world's future, but as the power of eternity and everlastingness in the face of man's anxiety for the future.

Greek philosophy did not make the category of the *novum* a specific theme of its reflections. Plato and Aristotle use the corresponding terms (*kainos, neos*) only in passing. The *novum* is for them neither a category for grasping history and future ontologically nor a category for positing the openness of human existence anthropologically.

If we take up the basic writings of Christianity, we do not find a homogeneous document of revelation, but the antithesis of "Old" and "New" Testaments. Christianity is therefore obviously a matter of tension and conflict between "old" and "new." Now how can we have such an origin, without that conflict yielding a consciousness of history which seeks the "new" over against the "old"? On practically every page of the New Testament we encounter the word "new." A new heaven and a new earth, the new Jerusalem, the new wine, the new song, the new name, and finally the gathering up of everything ultimately new into the future of God who says at the end: "Behold, I make all things new" (Rev. 21:5). The new (*kainos, novum*) is here the essence of the wholly other, the astounding factor which the messianic future brings. In the midst of the life which has become old, hope is roused by the announcement of a new being. The new creation is the goal of this hope, and Christian hope recognizes that through Christ's resurrection from the dead this new future has become already present and effective for every being in misery. With Easter the future of God's new world shines into the present situation of the

4

old world and "into the sufferings of this time" (Rom. 8). Through this new element the believers recognize themselves. For in Christ, a new people of God, a new man, indeed, a new humanity is formed out of Jews and Gentiles. The proclamation takes place in new tongues. Life is placed under the new commandment of love. Through faith and baptism man becomes in Christ a new creature. A new obedience fills his life.

Even from this quite superficial survey of the use of the word "new," it is clear how much the New Testament joins together in its thinking God, the future, and the new. God is the power of the future and is believed in as the creator of a new world. Out of this qualitatively new future, new power already forces its way into the present so that man can find possibilities for rebirth and renewal, personal and revolutionary social change. We are confronted here with an eschatologically oriented faith. It is not interested in an event that took place at the beginning of time or in explaining why the world exists and why it is as it is. It is oriented, on the contrary, to a new future and hence wants to change the world rather than explain it, to transform existence rather than elucidate it. This eschatological attitude toward the world creates history instead of interpreting nature. For we speak of history where something that is new and has not yet taken place comes into being. This brief survey enables us to understand the New Testament as the "Testament of the new" and the new covenant in Jesus Christ as man's covenant with the new situation that God promises and desires to create. The category *novum* does not threaten faith in God. In Deutero-Isaiah *bara* signifies not so much creation out of nothing in the beginning, but more often God's power to create the new out of the old in his eschatological history.

If this is the case, then we may break into a lamentation over the condition of the church in our own day. From the beginning of modern times, hopes for something new from God have emigrated from the church and have been invested in revolutions and rapid social change. It was most often reaction and conservatism that remained behind in the church. Thus the Christian church became "religious." That is, she cultivated and apotheosized tradition. Her authority was sanctioned by what had been in force always and everywhere from the earliest times.

The modern world, however, thinks of the future in a progressive and revolutionary fashion and looks for the new things which now become possible. In religious tradition men turn into recipients of an old message. In the modern world they become pioneers of progress, trailblazers of the future, and discoverers of new possibilities. The church seems to live on memories, the world on hope. In theology one proves the truth by quotations from the Fathers, in the modern world by the success of experiments. We will overcome this present schism only if Christianity experiences a rebirth in terms of its origin in the "Testament of the new."

It is not true that new hope is born from a simple forgetting of the past or cutting off of the old world. Hope, too, has its memory; it recalls that past history in which the promises for the future were heard and in which the dawn of a new creation began to appear. Such remembrance of the past is not a "search for lost time" (Marcel Proust) but is fidelity to the promise incarnated in the past. "May my right arm wither if I should forget you, Jerusalem" (Ps. 137:5). We remember what has already been promised but has not yet taken place; we recall the claim of the past on the future. Wherever in history everything appears already achieved and completed, memory has no place. History forces itself on the present only where it has not become complete, where something obviously took place in it, which has not yet been fulfilled. It is in this sense that we now turn back to ask about the basis of a future which is in store for us today so that we may lay hold of it today. The new is never totally new. It is always preceded by a dream, a promise, an anticipation. "He who does not hope for the unexpected will not find it" (Heraclitus).

6

2

THE PROPHECY OF THE NEW

Yahweh, the name of God, was known in Israel through the stories of the patriarchs, the exodus, the making of the covenant, and the entrance into the Promised Land. Thus, in order to trust in Yahweh one had to remember his history of faithfulness in promises and fulfillments and to identify oneself with the exodus-generation. "In every generation a man is obliged to consider himself as if he had moved out of Egypt" (*Mishna Pesachim*, X, 5). But when, in the great wars of destruction from the eighth to the sixth centuries, Israel's existence was threatened and destroyed, Israel fell out with the God of her history. Prophet rose against prophet. In face of the threatening annihilation, prophets asserted the invincibility of Zion, for "here is the temple of the Lord." His name dwelt in his temple, and his presence, his power, and his fidelity were guaranteed by his name. But the great prophets of doom rose up and proclaimed the coming destruction as a new, unexpected action of God in relation to his disobedient people. For God is not only a "God close by" but also a "God from afar." Israel has broken the old covenant with God. Hence, God is no longer bound by this covenant. To be sure, God judges his people according to the law of the covenant, but in this new judgment the old covenant itself seems to change. The God of history, whom the people knew from the past in memory, becomes for Israel a hidden God. Therefore the prophets proclaim that with God's judgment of his people a new act of God is heralded and will come.

It is true that the prophets continue to interpret the old traditions of Yahweh. Yet, in view of these traditions, they bring something new to expression. A new future is to come from God, a future new and unexpected in relationship to these old traditions. The "God of history" is changing into the "God of the future." While Hosea stands in the exodus tradition,

Isaiah knows only the David—and Zion—tradition. With Jeremiah, Ezekiel and finally Deutero-Isaiah, the old desert tradition occupies center stage again. Nevertheless, the relationship of these prophets to their traditions is broken. The coming judgment puts an end to Israel's existence up to this point. The guarantees contained in the traditions of election were canceled by Israel's guilt. The only thing to which Israel could hold is Yahweh's new act in history, prophetically proclaimed. Thus the basis of salvation for Israel shifts from the past into the future. Israel's faith changes from a living memory into a living hope. The old dogmas of salvation history lose their effectiveness, since Israel's life and death are now being settled in terms of what is to come. In this process Gerhard von Rad has rightly seen the birth throes of biblical eschatology.

But how do the prophets proclaim the new thing which is coming? They do not expect a new God. Rather, they link the new reality, which God will create, with the memory of his fidelity. Thus Hosea prophesies a "new occupation of the land," Isaiah a "new David," Jeremiah a "new covenant," and Deutero-Isaiah a "new exodus." Isaiah views the old salvation history as still so forceful that God can presuppose it in his new deeds. With Deutero-Isaiah, however, the break is so radicalized that he has to demand: "Remember not the things of old and pay no heed to the former things. For behold I wish to create a new thing; now it must grow and you will experience it" (Isa. 43: 18-19). This does not mean that Israel no longer exists as the Israel of God. On the contrary, Israel has learned through the voices of the prophets to understand the catastrophes as the judgments of the same God who called Israel into being. Israel survived because she could recognize even in the judgment and in the holocaust the faithfulness of God, and through it all adhere to this God. In the discontinuity of history she found her own continuity in the transcending faithfulness of God. Therefore we can understand the Old Testament prophecy of the new as a new act in the promissory history of God.

From this prophecy of the new we can learn three things:

8

1. The new is proclaimed in judgment over the old. "God kills and brings to life." The new is preceded by the destruction of the old, that which has become guilty, and not by the development or evolution of the old. It is not out of the possibilities which we possess, but in the impossible situation which confronts us, that the new shows itself as God's creative act. God's new reality is always like a *novum ex nihilo*. When all hopes have died, there comes the wave of the future like a spirit of resurrection into the dead bones (Ezek. 37), creating hope against hope.

2. The first anticipation of the new future always takes the form of a recourse to the analogies of history. In the images of the "new Zion," the "new exodus," and the "new occupation of the land" the new is pictured as a renewal of the origin from which one has fallen away. But, in fact, as Gershom Scholem observes, the images of the new Jerusalem always convey more than ever took place in the case of the old Jerusalem. The new is more than the restitution of the old, since through guilt and judgment something has intervened which cannot be facilely eliminated.

3. This recourse to the analogies of history in order to understand the new reality of the future brings history back to life again. What once was, is now past and has its force only as a type or anticipation of the new.[1] Thus out of the past emerges a promise of what is to come. One sees in the past no longer a mass of completed facts; these facts, which are apparently over and done with, become real anticipations of the new future. In this way past history is understood as an advance promise of the future. We see that clearly in Deutero-Isaiah. He understands his own present message not as mere promise, but as gospel: "How precious are the feet of those who bring the news of joy, who proclaim salvation" (52:7). Here the word "gospel" appears for the first time in the Bible. It is not only an announcement of salvation (*Heilsankündigung*), but

[1] Gerhard von Rad, *Old Testament Theology*, Vol. II, trans. D. M. G. Stalkner (New York: Harper & Row, 1965), pp. 248ff.

is an offer of salvation (*Heilszusage*). It is not a statement about a distant future, but is the presence of this future as Wordpresence.

3
THE APOSTOLATE OF THE NEW

Easter is called the day of birth for the Christian church. Yet, faced with this event in which the crucified Christ had appeared to them anew, all the first Christian communities encountered it as a puzzle. These Easter appearances of Christ evoked a boundless astonishment and an open questioning. Who is this one who has been crucified and raised from the dead?[2]

As an initial reply to this question, certain patterns from Israel's tradition, namely, the faith in a Messiah (Son of David) and the apocalyptic expectation of the Son of man suggested themselves. Hence the earliest Jewish-Christian community gathered around Peter saw in the risen one the Son of David, the mysterious Messiah of Israel and, over and beyond that, the hidden Son of man. Consequently, the community understood itself under the leadership of the twelve apostles as the "renewed people of the twelve tribes" and as a Christian synagogue. Thus it remained within the "pale of Israel" and maintained law and circumcision. There were no evident grounds for a mission to the Gentiles. God would call the Gentiles only when Zion was restored. This community grasped the new reality which Christ brought only in terms of the memory of their Israelite history and hopes.

Another understanding of the new situation created by Easter developed—probably at first within the circle of the seven gathered about Stephen. They identified themselves with the apocalyptic prediction that the temple would be destroyed

[2] At this point I am following the interpretation offered by Ernst Käsemann in his New Testament studies.

and a new temple, not built by men, would come. For this they were persecuted. Moving to Antioch, they were astonished by the fact that the Spirit of Christ is bestowed upon the Gentiles. And, further, Gentiles become believers without having previously been Jews! If Christ is for them he is no longer merely Israel's Messiah, but indeed the Lord of the Gentiles as well. Thus arises a new community comprising Jews and Gentiles, a community in which the former distinguishing marks lose validity. This community can no longer call itself the old "renewed" people of God. It understands itself, rather, as "the new people of God" and adopts the political expression *ecclesia* as a name for itself. Thus the memory link with Israel's history is nearly severed. Something completely new becomes reality. The gospel of this community is announced in bold terms: "Here is neither Jew nor Gentile, neither Greek nor barbarian, neither master nor servant, neither man nor woman. All are one in Christ" (cf. Gal. 3:28; Col. 3:11). These Christians intend to proclaim "Spirit and freedom" in the whole world. As the Corinthian community understands it, "The Lord is the Spirit." For them, freedom means liberation from all obligations of the law, society, and the body. For them, Spirit is the supraearthly sphere of heaven. Whoever believes is already risen. But with this understanding, the memory of Jesus and his earthly cross is lost among these enthusiastic Corinthians. The Spirit assumes his place.

Yet another appreciation of the new situation initiated by Christ is found in Paul. He knows the universal scope of the Hellenistic Christian faith. But as a Jew he retains, nevertheless, the realism of the Old Testament hope, which can never be satisfied with merely an inner, spiritual fulfillment of the promises. For him then the new reality which has appeared with Christ is a new creation of God. In order to say what is, properly speaking, new, he goes beyond Israel's remembrance of history. The resurrection of Christ is an astounding miracle. There is nothing at all with which to compare it, except the world's creation out of nothing. The God who calls nonbeing into being and raises the dead has here acted in the case of Jesus (Rom. 4:17). Thus Christ's future is not the spiritualizing of man in an inner freedom, but the totally new creation of man and the world. What faith, Spirit, and joy do, above all, is herald the greater future of the world. The resurrection of the body is anticipated by the new obedience of believers in the everyday life of this agonizing world. Here and now the future of this new creation is present only in Christ's cross and with those who become disciples of the crucified one.

Thus with Paul the category of the new is still more radically understood than it was by the prophets. The new is not a mere renewal, but the entrance of the unexpected. The new thing of the future does not appear in the fact that the present is confirmed, or in some correspondence to the "good, old times," or even in the restoration of the original creation. "The old has passed away; behold the new has come" (2 Cor. 5:17). It is not out of the good factors which are at hand that God creates his new future, but it is out of the bad, the evil, and the Godless that he creates the new. God has chosen what is foolish in the eyes of the world; he has chosen what is weak and good for nothing (1 Cor. 1:27ff.). He justifies the Godless and only them; as the God of the forsaken he enters, in revolutionary fashion, a world where all take pride in themselves. He exalts the lowly and puts down the mighty from their thrones (Luke 1:52).

Is there thus for Paul no continuity between history and this new future? Yes, even for him there is continuity. But it does not consist in some human or immanent factor in perpetual process; it is, rather, the faithfulness of God who, in creating the new, remembers and brings back the old, which has turned away from him and been lost. The expression "resurrection of the dead" means that God brings back the dead in his new creation and gathers up the lost. The new creation therefore takes up the old creation in itself. Continuity is established by the future, just as all historical continuity is created by the future which takes up into itself what has been lost. Thus historical continuity distinguishes itself in principle from an organic or ontological continuity. If God creates a qualitatively new future, then he is not only the future of the present, but also the future *of* the past and *for* the past.

4

MARCION AND THE DESTRUCTION OF
THE NEW IN CHRISTIANITY

In an age which saw the rise of early Catholicism, Marcion, the most radical disciple of Paul, attempted once more to renew the church. The only work which we know he wrote is called *Antitheses*. From him comes the expression "New Testament" and the collection of Paul's letters. While the church of his time considered the Old Testament to be its Bible, it was through Marcion that what we still call today the "New Testament" came into circulation. It was directed antithetically against the Old Testament. It was only after Marcion that the church made the one canon out of both. If we recognize this, we can appreciate that this one canon comprising the Old and New Testaments contains dynamite. Marcion's *Antitheses* begins with a cry of astonished exultation: "O miracle beyond miracle, rapture, power and astonishment is it, that one can say nothing at all about the gospel or compare it with anything at all." For Marcion the new of Christ (*Neue Christi*) is without analogy. Everything which existed hitherto and was known becomes bad, evil, and pernicious in the face of the new thing which now comes. Marcion speaks no longer, as Paul spoke, merely of the new creation of God, but of a "new God" (*Deus novus*). Hence for Marcion the God of the Old Testament and of the creation of this world became an evil God. For Paul the history of the Old Testament was past, but not obliterated. He took it up as promise into his gospel. In the Epistle to the Hebrews the old covenant is seen as foreshadowing the new. But for Marcion the division of the old and new runs not only

13

through man, not only through heaven and earth, but also through God himself.

Thus the history of the new gives rise to a metaphysical dualism. The new, strange God of Christ succeeds the old creator of the world and destroys him. Redemption destroys creation, the gospel destroys the law, and faith becomes the enemy of every known reality. But in this antithesis the new cannot bring salvation. It means annihilation. As there is nothing on which it can be predicated, it becomes basically non-appropriable. But, in fact, the new is never wholly new. It is always preceded by a dream, a promise, an anticipation; otherwise we could not grasp and accept it, and it could not be effective in history.

When the universal church excluded Marcion as a heretic, it lost for itself the category of the new. As is always the case with the exclusion of heresies, the church became more united, but also poorer. Since then, God's revelation has no longer been proclaimed in terms of the claim of the new and of freedom for the future, but it has been proclaimed by the authority of what is old and always true. No longer is the *incipit vita nova* announced, but instead a *restitutio in integrum*. The lost paradise, of which even the sinner still has a fragmentary memory, is won back through Christ and the church. The original condition of creation is restored in grace. The old naturalistic notion of the eternal return of the same (*die Wiederkehr des Gleichen*) dominates Christian hope. We can recall the words of Augustine: "That which is now called the Christian religion was also there among the men of former times. Indeed from the very beginning of the human race until Christ appeared in the flesh it has never been absent. From then on the true religion which already existed began to be called the 'Christian religion'" (*Retractiones*, I, 12). Thus it is no longer "the new" but "the old" that now becomes the warrant for the truth of Christianity.

With Marcion, Paul also was lost for the church. It was only because she retained Marcion's "New Testament" in the canon, that the church stored up for herself her own permanent revolution. Today we must bring about this revolution. We have no right to postpone it further and to live on the basis of this delay. One can ask indeed whether or not Christianity became unfaithful to its origin in neglecting the category of the *novum*. In any case, we will have to go back quite far in order to discover the role of Christianity in the promissory history of God and to actualize it in the contemporary world.

5

PERSPECTIVES OF THE NEW
IN THE WORLD TODAY

It is surprising that the category of the new has for centuries scarcely been considered by philosophers and theologians, even though it should provide the chief concept for every philosophy of history and paraphrase the most valuable element in the Christian hope. It is only today that we find, in Ernst Bloch, a magnificent philosophy of hope,[3] in which the *novum* is made the central theme. Ernst Bloch is himself a modern *Homo viator* who has traveled as an exile through different lands and philosophies. In World War I he emigrated as a pacifist to Switzerland. During the era of Hitler he fled to Prague, to Zürich, and then to the United States. After the war he returned to East Germany. In 1961 as a Marxist he had to flee from a so-called Marxist country. Today he lives in Tübingen. Ever seeking for justice and freedom and ever disappointed anew, he sets before us a secular hope which has been sustained through many sufferings. He is a Marxist with a Bible in his hand, a Marxist who has hoped for greater things than socialism is able to fabricate. He is a messianic thinker for whom the philosophy of the younger Marx elicited a practical way to the fulfillment of prophetic promises. From him Christians can gain courage for their own hope.

For Bloch all reality arises from a sea of possibilities. From

---

[3] Ernst Bloch, *Das Prinzip Hoffnung*, 2 vols. (Frankfurt: Suhrkamp Verlag, 1959).

this sea of possibilities there emerges again and again a new fragment of reality. The world is not a prefabricated house, but an open process. Likewise, man does not yet have his true being in himself. He does not yet know what he properly is. Hence men seek in common the homeland of true humanity. The place where the future of men and of the world is decided is the present. This present is the front line of the future. Only by knowing what we hope for and desire, can we gain the future at the front line of the present. Otherwise we miss it and destroy it. The future can bring everything or nothing, heaven or hell, life or death. Thus the future is full of salvation but also full of danger.

How is the open world-process decided? Through the militant courage of present hope, Bloch insists. Bloch looks for men of hope, a "company of anti-nothing" who on the basis of their hope refuse to abandon the world to evil, inhumanity, and the powers of destruction, since they remain true to the utopian dream of complete salvation. This embodied hope is for him the dawn of the resurrection at the end of the world: death being swallowed up by victory. But for Bloch such a gleam of hope is maintained in its dawning only through human decision. This hope for salvation must be joined to what is now objectively possible in the world, if it is to become practical and to reduce militantly the areas of the negative and of evil death. In the new, which emerges at the present front line of the future and becomes possible, the ultimately new (*novum ultimum*) is always involved. Hence, in what is temporally and finitely new we must recognize what is eschatologically and ultimately new, seeing in the fragment the coming whole and in the potsherd the beauty of the perfect thing. Only if we aim beyond the present at this ultimate future do we hit the mark today. This power of transcending in hope gives us the freedom to do what is right in the present and will be the source of direction in the future.

For Ernst Bloch the eschatological hope links itself to the possibilities of historical activity in the sphere of that-which-

16

is-not-yet (*des Noch-Nicht-Seins*). This is a magnificent conception. Nevertheless, the question remains open: What does this hope accomplish in the sphere of that-which-is-no-longer (*des Nicht-Mehr-Seins*)? In Bloch's thought the hope for the new thing of the future is linked with what men can do. But do we not need also a hope which is connected with what we must suffer in sacrifice, in pain, and in dying? We naturally have hope when we are young. But do we not need hope also when we are old and incapable, when we can no longer help ourselves and when finally death robs us of all hope? Do we not need hope also for those who are gone, for the dead, in order to remain in love? Here the militant optimism of *Das Prinzip Hoffnung* is silent. There is for Bloch a hell on earth and even worse, a hell in which there is no Easter. There is a dying where the principle of hope can accomplish nothing. "Ever since Auschwitz, to fear death means to fear something worse than death," was the objection of his friend Th. W. Adorno who did not wish the principle of hope to become illusory in the face of that nihilism which we can suffer here on earth. Where then does Bloch's positive hope preserve the negative element? Where is the cross found in this hope?

Christian theology must go further; it discerns in the crucified Christ the deepest abyss of God-forsakenness and hopelessness on earth. But it also believes in Easter. Out of chaos, darkness, and flood God created the world. In the context of nothingness he revealed his creative power. Out of the humiliated, poor, and abandoned Jesus who was crucified in disgrace, God makes his Messiah of the future, of freedom, and of life. He justifies the Godless. He makes evil human beings his friends. He will raise the dead. If, for the sake of this God, Christians hope for the future, they hope for a *novum ex nihilo*. And because of their hope in God, the Creator of the future, they embrace all beings which are disappointed and hopeless. Out of that-which-is-not-yet something new can always come into being. That is fully possible. But can something new come to be also out of that which is nothing? This is the hope of

Christians, since they trust in a God who creates what is new out of nothing. Hence they not only join the "company of anti-nothing" and fight for the renewal of the world, but they enter as well into fellowship with the sinners, the poor, the abandoned, and the dying. If God creates what is new out of nothing, then the poor, the abandoned, and the dying are closer to him than are the efficient and militant heroes of revolution who help mankind. The rich and the powerful must take up the cause of the poor and the powerless, in order to effect for them a new future. But the rich and the powerful must realize that they are, in turn, represented by the poor and the repudiated, since it is they who are visibly handed over to the might of death, in terms of which God will show his power. We shall find the front line of Christianity in the present where the powers of nothingness are confronted by God's creation of the new.

II + Religion, Revolution, and the Future

Today in all dimensions of life we are searching for a future in which we can really hope. For only such a future can inspire our present work, give meaning to our present sufferings, and intensify our present joy. More radically than earlier generations we know that we live in history where everything changes and nothing remains in its place. We live "between the times." "The old times are gone" many say, "and the new have not yet begun." With the Industrial Age we have entered a period of culture which is as unstable as was the period of man's transition from nomadic to agricultural life in the Neolithic Age.

Thus we look back into the past in order to discover the promise and direction of the present. But in order to make urgent decisions at the opportune time, we have to look into the unknown future out of which flow possibilities for both good and evil. Today the future has become the problem of the whole of mankind, for we will either gain the future in a common struggle or lose everything in a common annihilation.

If in its present-day theology and practice Christianity wants

This lecture was given at the University of California at Santa Barbara during the Centennial Symposium, "The Future of Hope," April 1–3, 1968.

to offer a responsible contribution to the design and formation of the future, it must be prepared "to make a defense . . . for the hope that is in it" (1 Pet. 3:15). It must remember the incarnate promises of God in its biblical sources, while it demonstrates how men can proceed in dealing with the personal, social, and political problems of the present through hope in the coming God. The "eschatological conscience came into the world through the Bible," says the atheistic philosopher Ernst Bloch to the befuddlement of many Christians who evidently have no conscience with respect to the future. Reflection on God, future, and hope demands a revolution in the Christian way of thinking.

For a long time faith in God has been saturated more with anxiety about the future than with hope in a new future of the earth. Time and again Christians have searched in faith for the stability of eternity within the terrors of time. In the last century such a "faith without hope" elicited a "hope without faith." Because Christians believed in a "God without future," those who willed the future of the earth had no option but to join forces with atheism and seek a "future without God." That is the schism of modern times from which many Christians and many atheists are suffering today. And if one views as heretics those atheists who seek a "future without God" in a hope without faith, then those believers who hold fast to a "God without future" in a faith without hope wear just as clearly the stripes of heresy. After messianic hopes wandered out of the church and were invested in progress, rebuilding, and revolutions, the church was left with only a half-truth. But should the knots of history be so tightly tied against each other: Christianity with the past and the unbelievers with the future? I think that this present dilemma can be overcome, but only if Christians call again upon the "God of hope" of the Old and New Testaments and testify to him practically and concretely in responsibility for the present.

1

THE SYMBOLS OF THE ORIGINS AND THE PROMISES OF THE FUTURE

A ✦ *In Religion*

In Christianity's long "religious" epoch, Christian hope was fettered and rendered ineffective by the "myth of the eternal return."[1] Verification (*verum facere*) in history was not a matter of the inauguration of the new and unexpected but, rather, of the return to the origins and the repetition of antiquity. Christian faith was proclaimed not as *exodus* out of the bondage of the past and through the boundaries of the present into the freedom of a new future, but as turning back to the security of pristine origins. What is history? It is expulsion from paradise and the way into an alien land. What is salvation? It is return to paradise and the way back into the homeland. History is "paradise lost"; salvation, "paradise regained." The reason Christianity assumed these religious symbols of origin lies, to be sure, in the fact that it is threatening for man to open himself to the radically new and unpredictable future, leaving behind everything which guarantees stability and security. Confronted by hope's possible disappointments, one readily clings to the tradition, to the tried and tested knowledge of old. For whatever has been handed down from antiquity to the present has preserved itself in the past, and whatever has preserved itself must also have verified itself. Where else might one find the criterion for the good in the abundance of new possibilities for the future? So it happened that in antiquity Christianity assimilated the natural knowledge of man to its own origin and conceived the new which it proclaimed as the fulfillment, completion, and recurrence of the primordial origin of all men. What all men remembered in their vague longing for the pristine world of the primitive

[1] Mircea Eliade, *Cosmos and History: The Myth of the Eternal Return* (New York: Harper Torchbooks, 1959).

21

origins of things was to be regenerated and fulfilled through grace. The lost paradise, which man remembers insofar as he suffers in this world away from home, was to be brought back by church and faith.

With this schema, the old Judeo-Christian faith, whose essence is hope, was transformed into a mythical faith of remembering. The church condemned sin in the name of the very law against which the rebel had risen up and then re-established the law in submission to itself. The Christian church appeared as the "true religion" within the realm of appearanče. Disorder and enmity on the civil and social level were replaced by the peace of the original order. Thus Christianity became the religion which guaranteed the integrity of the Roman empire and even today functions in many places as the religion of national well-being.

These changes were accompanied by a shift in the center of the Christian life. Whereas for primitive Christianity *Easter* stood in the focal point and whereas that meant exodus out of this perishing world into the dawn of a new future world, now *Christmas* appeared at the center with its unmistakable emphasis on an original grace which came down blessing forsaken nature and revivifying it with heavenly gifts and virtues. The new in Christianity which had been considered the "resurrection of Christ from the dead" was now new only for men who had become daft or blind, but it was no longer new in reality itself. Grace was thus understood as the return of the ancient origin, the eternal source, and the beginning of history. The Christian hope in a new creation came back in terms of the ancient apocalyptic melody: *Ta eschata hos ta prota* ("The end is like the beginning"). Sin turns the good creation upside down. Grace places it back on its feet again. Consequently, what ultimately comes out of the history of human sin and divine grace is the creation as it was in the beginning and always is in the eyes of God.

Modern "dialectical theology" has not broken this spell of religious reflective preoccupation with primitive origins. For

22

the young Karl Barth, the synthesis in the primordial source takes precedence over the historical conflicts of thesis and antithesis. For Friedrich Gogarten, salvation is unity within separation: the unity of God and man is the reverse side of the separation of God and man. Whoever recognizes the separation is already at one with God. Finally, Rudolf Bultmann, in his demythologizing, constantly relies on the mythological model of the eternal return: "What does the forgivenness of sins mean? It means that the most primordial condition of creation is restored; . . . that the ancient revelation is made visible once again."

Only in one single, small, and often scarcely recognizable line of reflection was the Christian tradition able to formulate the newness of grace that is more than the restoration of the old creation. In the early church there was the speculative question whether man, once restored through grace, could sin again, resulting in an eternal cycle of apostasy and restoration. But if this were the case, nothing ultimately new and final would have appeared with Christ. Furthermore, a cycle of the world's origination and destruction would be set in motion unless there existed some additional factor. Irenaeus, Athanasius, and Augustine therefore maintained that grace brings so much more in the way of new being that a new fall becomes impossible. Grace brings a new freedom into the world, that is, the freedom no longer to have and also no longer to be able to sin and to die (freedom from the necessity of sin as well as freedom from its possibility). The inner ambiguity of creation in the beginning is, through grace, changed into the clarity of the new creation. Grace is therefore not only the overcoming of sin, but also the conquest of its very possibility. It is the completion of the incompleted and open creation of the beginning. Thus the "overtime" work of grace adds up over against creation: it is not only the renewal of original creation but also the birth of a new creation. Consequently, the future in which Christian faith hopes, brings forth "more" than can have existed in the old creation. For messianic hope claims to be in the end more than it was in the beginning; otherwise there would be no hope, but only memory.

B ✦ In Revolution

If, as we have done with the theology and religion of Christianity, we now examine the historical movements of political and social renewal, we will find that the "myth of the eternal return" was operative here as well. Ironically enough, all known movements for a new future were initiated under the banner of the category "re." We speak of renaissance, reformation, revolution, of revival, renewal, and restoration, etc. In all of these movements men sought not the new of the future but "paradise lost" or the "golden age," the primitive natural condition of men or the original order of things. They sought their future in the past. They connected the renewal of the present with a "dream turned backward." In these historical movements, hope was confined within the memory of history's point of departure.

The meaning of the concept "revolution," which is used today in all quarters to signify the breakthrough of something new, was, for these backward-looking movements, completely exhausted by this mythical conception of cyclical revolution. For Copernicus, to whom is ascribed a revolution of the world view in the West, revolution meant the return of a planetary system to the initial constellation. This astronomical conception of revolution became increasingly important for the natural sciences through his book *De revolutionibus orbium coelestium* (1543). In the Reformation, people often thought of themselves as restoring the golden age of primitive Christianity. The avowed intention of the Humanistic Reform was to discard the degenerated traditions on the way "back to the original sources" and the *bonae literae* of antiquity. The leaders of the French Revolution protested against the historically produced injustice in state and society by appealing to the idea of the primordial and inalienable natural rights of man. In light of all this we may quite justifiably say: Nothing is so conservative and reactionary as the idea of the revolution of history aimed

24

at and governed by the beginning point of history. It is typical of this view of revolution that many Russian poets and thinkers in the 1920's hypostasized the idea of revolution in terms of the myth of permanent revolution or revolution as the eternal principle of life.

The irony in the movements prefixed with "re" lies in the fact that they actually went forward with a "dream turned backward" and produced something new which was not in existence before. The hope which mobilized these renewals was only camouflaged by the "dream turned backward," for that paradise or golden age or natural condition of man before history has in fact never really existed. A misguided conviction doomed these movements. Man was to go forward in history, as it were, with his back toward the future and his eyes trained on the past which he wished to repeat. Proceeding thus in the fashion of a crab, revolutions always turned out to be something other than that for which they were specifically aiming. They wished to regain the primordial origin, but unconsciously brought about a new epoch in history.

With the beginning of modern times, mankind, for the first time, became future-conscious. The category *novum* assumed the status of the old category *re*. We see that happening clearly in two great movements. First, it is evident in ideas about a "new world." One emigrated out of the "old world" of Europe into America, the beautiful "land of freedom," in order to find a "new world." This world did not exist previously in the consciousness of Europeans. Thus the unknown continent could be felicitously conquered and colonized under the direction of a vision of hope whether it be the "new world," the "new Israel," the "new land of promise," or as the seal of the United States asserts, the *novus ordo seclorum*. "In any case, this feeling about America as really and truly the 'new order' of things at last established is the heart of the outlook defined by the American Way of Life."[2]

But the so-called "old world" did not remain old either.

[2] Will Herberg, *Protestant-Catholic-Jew* (Garden City, N. Y.: Doubleday Anchor Books, 1960), p. 80.

Another idea of the new became effective here. Since the time of Joachim di Fiore, hope in the "new age" has inspired all European movements for freedom. These movements broke the spell of traditions and criticized its authority in order, on the one hand, to free themselves from the dominance and tutelage of the past and, on the other, to find the "new age" in the future. "Enlightenment is man's *exodus* from his self-incurred tutelage. Tutelage is the inability to use one's understanding without the guidance of another person," exclaimed Kant. So Europe became the land where revolutions were propagated. One country after another sought to inaugurate the "new age" and, in so doing, stepped into history. There was no freedom in space. Therefore freedom could be realized only in time. In these revolutions one sought to emigrate out of an "old time" into the "new age." Thus "the future" became the theme of the history of European revolutions. They found freedom in the struggle of history between past and future.

Through the French revolution of politics, the industrial revolution of economics and the socialist revolution of society, mankind has today entered into a new epoch of history for whose form the prerevolutionary and preindustrial past has no ready models or prototypes in store. For the first time men and peoples throughout the earth are entering into one, common world history. For the first time they no longer have to endure history unconsciously but must consciously create and control history.

It is true that there was an *idea* of "world history" much earlier. It was born out of the faith in the one, transcendent God whom all men at all times confronted. Likewise, there was much earlier an idea of the conscious lordship of men over their own history. It was born out of the belief in the image of God in men. But there was not yet the reality of a common history in danger and hope.

Today the possibilities of consciously controlling the evolution of nature and the progress of history are proliferating immeasurably for the first time. The increasing solidarity of all

men, and thus the synchronization of the various histories out
of which they come, is the process we are undergoing now. Our
world situation contains the past in the plural: every country
has its own national history; every culture has its own cultural
history; every religion and every church have their own religious and church history. But our present is becoming more
and more one single, common present, for we have the future
only in the singular: nations, cultures, and religions all share
in the common distinction of possible extinction. It is obvious
that none can survive except insofar as all participate in a new
community. Therefore "world history," which is conceived at
present in terms of the origination of a common world, leaves
the various pasts and traditions behind. Memories still have
worth precisely insofar as they prepare the way for the
common, new future. But their preponderance in the particular
and provincial dimension, i.e., their preponderance in that
which divides men, must be broken. The new far-reaching
world situation is so new and so dangerous that all histories up
to this point must be considered, at most, prehistories of this
new future. Particular memories find their value only in their
contributions to the universal hope against the universal death.
Thus, what is past is at best a prologue to this future.

The concepts of a pristine origin, of an order of creation and
an original natural condition of the world, no longer have anything to say to us about the future which we must realize now.
Yet if we relinquish these ideas of the good, the true, and the
beautiful, we seem to lose any orientation in history whatsoever. Whoever claims to orient himself *in* history by orienting
himself *to* history is like a shipwrecked sailor who clings to a
wave. He is going to sink. Therefore, the crucial question is
whether the future can afford us an orientation within the ups
and downs of history and a criterion for the meaningful realization of new possibilities, now that the past can no longer provide them.

If we start from the future which becomes present today,
we come in the first place to a new interpretation of reality as

history. What we call the past today was at one time a present which wrestled with the future. Thus what we find in the way of reality in the past are those possibilities for the future which have been both realized and impeded. Future is not only the agony and the problem of our present; it was also the agony and problem of those presents which have already passed away. Thus, conversely, our present is a new present of the future, and the past consists of the fleeting presents of the future. Notwithstanding all the differences of time and circumstance between our present and the past, we can still recognize a common direction toward the future, with which, like those before us, we have to struggle today. The ruling category for a historical understanding of reality is therefore the future (Jan Huizinga).

The future realizes itself in history and as history and by transcending all its historical realizations becomes the future once again. What we call history is the "element of the future," the experimental field of the future. We find in the past, on the one hand, realizations of the future and, on the other hand, hindrances of the future as well. Everything past can be understood as future begun or as future aborted. So with the French Revolution a new democratic freedom made its appearance in history, but at the hands of Napoleon and the bourgeoisie this freedom was simultaneously hindered. Likewise, a new social freedom was introduced into the world by the socialist revolution only to be shortly denied by Stalin and the bureaucratization of the Russian Revolution. Israel sought its promised future in the "land flowing with milk and honey," but found only Palestine. Jesus preached the Kingdom of God, but what came was the church (Alfred Loisy). "In the citizen of the French Revolution the bourgeois was hidden: God have mercy on us, we cannot tell what may be hidden in the comrade," said the Marxist Ernst Bloch. It is presumably the functionary.

By all this I wish simply to say that there is a difference between future and reality, between hope and experience, between exodus and arrival, and it is precisely in this difference

28

that we experience history. The hopes which we connect with the future always shoot over the mark and are not able to redeem themselves in history. It is not true that we experience nothing on the way into the future, but neither do we experience perfect fulfillment. If we remain at a standstill on the way and are surfeited with an already achieved reality, we are soon overwhelmed by the "melancholy of fulfillment" (Bloch). Yet, if we scorn what might be an achieved reality for us, we are overwhelmed and incapacitated by believing that our hopes are out of reach after all. Our hopes lead us into new experiences which in turn necessitate the revision of our hopes, since the situation of their conceptualization has changed. If we are really acting in history in this way, we approach the old Israelite way of thinking. "Here everything is in motion, the accounts never balance, and fulfillment unexpectedly gives rise in turn to another promise of something greater still. Here nothing has its ultimate meaning in itself, but is always an earnest of something still greater" (Gerhard von Rad). All historical events of the past indicate this difference between an emerging future and a submerging reality. Therefore, whoever wants to appropriate the inheritance of the past and understand his own present in the historical process can neither simply assume the ideas and visions of tradition nor regard the past as a great garbage heap of dead facts. He must translate the ideas and visions of the fathers into his own, new situation and seek new realization in his own present, which has been largely determined by the failures and oversights of the fathers.

What men essentially expect and hope for from the future is articulated not only in their dreams by day and night but even more in their suffering because of what they lack and because what they have is not that which they seek. The consciousness of misery in history is, of course, quite varied, but in our pain and suffering we are nearer to reality than in our visions and dreams. The future is realistically conceived not so much in positive terms of that which is not yet, but much more

29

in negative terms of suffering in the present. Undergoing suffering in the present and criticizing the evil conditions in the present, men seek another and better future. What "freedom" really is, is difficult to say inasmuch as we have not yet experienced the "kingdom of freedom," i.e., freedom in a truly free world. But if we seek this freedom and take it to be our future, then we begin to suffer in the chains of the present. Thus we can analyze what is oppression, slavery, dependence, and humiliation because we have experienced each one of these a thousand times. On the one hand, what true humanity is can be comprehended in a positive affirmation only with extreme difficulty. On the other hand, what inhumanity is—from Nero to Hitler and from the hell of Auschwitz to the hells of our own day—can be designated with moderate precision from our experience.

Theoretically expressed: the positive, the new, the future which we seek can be historically circumscribed in the process of the negation of the negative. The obverse side of the positive knowledge of the future is accessible for us, as it were, in negative knowledge. Hope in the positive is alive in suffering from the negative. Hope in the happiness of the future is realistically present and effective in the criticism of present misery. This critical negation of the negative affords the anticipated positive the freedom to prove itself and does not define the future by means of historical prejudices. Beyond that, it permits a man to define freedom, the positive, his happiness, and his freedom for himself and does not dictatorially prescribe what his happiness and freedom should consist of.

How then can we take the initiative for the future? In a community of suffering and rebellious men we can struggle against the common evil and eliminate the underlying causes and massive hemorrhages of human unhappiness in the conditions of social, political, and racial estrangement. The future upon which mankind is entering today comes into our consciousness first through the common and reciprocally inflamed threat to mankind in the form of atomic war, famines, racial conflicts, and class struggles. A new international solidarity in the common repression of this evil is the *conditio sine qua non* for a new, common future of men. Theory and praxis are bound up in a unity in such thoughts about the future. All efforts which are directed toward the approach of truth can be called reasonable. "Reason is the access to future truth" (Jürgen Habermas). If in historical and practical thinking we link up the search for truth with the search for future, there results a transformation in the historical method of effecting the truth from the well-known definition of Spinoza: *Veritas est index sui et falsi* to the definition of Ernst Bloch: *Veritas est nondum index sui, sed jam falsi.*

Under the presupposition of this critical influence of the future on the present through the "negation of the negative," we can also appreciate the reverse way of defining the future, that is, the way of analogy, of prefiguration, and of anticipation. The perpetually limited and inadequate reality of the past begins to speak positively concerning the as-yet-unrealized future. It no longer addresses the present from the viewpoint of guardianship and prejudice, of burdensome tradition and oppressive authority but from the viewpoint of promise and hope, of process and liberation. To be certain, no past has already embodied the "kingdom of freedom" in a "golden age." But this is no justification for contending that the past is nothing or only the "old world." No present begins with the year zero despite the fact that every revolution has sought for it there. Along with errors and violence in the past, there have always been, also, origins and beginnings, anticipations and prefigurations of the truth to come. In the midst of the history of slavery and humiliation there is also, though always ambiguous, a pioneering history of freedom.

It is absurd to surrender already achieved fragments and institutions of freedom for the sake of gaining new freedom in the future. It is senseless to nullify the past for the sake of one's future. One does not gain a new future by forgetting the past but only by freely appropriating the positive fragments and hopeful tendencies of the past. The revolutionary terrorism directed against the old order always turns into the absolutism of the new order, which is revengefully directed against its critics and thus against its own future. To give further theoretical expression to this line of thinking, one might say that the anticipations and analogies of the future become manifest in present reality through the historical dialectic of the negation of the negative. The dialectic of thesis and antithesis is the presupposition by which one can recognize in the thesis the prefiguration of the future synthesis. Effective revolutions begin with the criticism of the present because the conditions and institutions of the present are no longer capable of coping with the problems of the future. But revolutions are able truly to realize themselves only when they are able to control and propel the process of history. If the concept of "revolution" is to lose its reactionary "re" and become a concept of the realization of the future, then we must replace it with the concept of "provolution." In provolution, the human "dream turned forward" is combined with the new possibility of the future and begins consciously to direct the course of human history as well as the evolution of nature.

What does all of this portend for religion and for the Christian faith? By the forced alteration of a single syllable, we can replace the word "religion" with "proligion," in order thereby to interpret the connection of the present in faith to the future. After many long centuries in which Christ was considered the incarnation of the eternal God or was viewed as the reparation of the lost paradise, today we will begin with the question of the *future* in order to see what *new* thing it was that came into the world through Christ. With this query we return to the old messianic question: "Are you he who is to come, or shall we look for another?" (Luke 7:20). If we ask in this way, we will find that Christ has manifested in the world a new future which makes this world the history of an experiment of salvation and fills human life with hope while simultaneously charging it with responsibility. This new reality was conceptualized in primitive Christianity by an apocalyptic image of hope, the "resurrection of Christ." By "resurrection" the earliest Christians did not mean a return of the dead Christ into mortal life or a restoration of the fallen creation. They meant, rather, the entrance of something completely unexpected, the inbreaking of a qualitatively new future and the appearance of a life which is no longer "life toward death" but "life out of death." In the historical *novum Christi* they saw the anticipation and the already effective promise of that which was ultimately and universally new. But what is this ultimate and universal new thing of the future which they believed to have recognized in Christ? I think it is the vision of God himself, about whom it is everywhere and at all times reported that no one ever saw him. It is God himself in the kingdom of his identity. It is the earthly and visible presence of God, which is called *kabod* in the Old Testament and *doxa* in the New Testament. It is the earthly and visible inhabitation of God in a new creation.

If what they saw is the new future of the world, then the resurrection hope implies the transformation and fundamental revolution of the world. As is contended in older theological wisdom: To know God, i.e., to be able to endure God's presence, means to die and be born anew. A world which is capable of enduring the earthly and visible presence of God must be a world completely transformed. It is a world which no longer stands over against God in endless disparity but now has God dwelling in it. It thus participates in the boundless creating power of God himself. It is a new humanity which will be no longer only the creature of God or no longer only a child of God but will be "like God" and participate in God's infinite creativity.

What new thing has come into the world with Christ? The vision of God along with the vision of a new creation and the vision of the new man. But what actually was seen in Christ of this new future of God, of the world, and of man? At first only the negation of the negative and the *index falsi*. It be-

33

came apparent in the crucified one what God-forsakenness, what alienation, what misery really is. The new future of Christ becomes effective historically by exposing the negative, the past, and transitoriness itself and by overcoming them. We can discern the future glory in the present only by viewing the crucified one. We can anticipate the future only as the present becomes obsolete. We experience freedom for the first time as we begin to suffer in unfreedom and no longer apathetically submit to slavery as our destiny. There are no pictures of the resurrection which represent its new humanity and its boundless freedom. The resurrection pictures, which have been attempted, are pitifully inadequate because the colors for painting the future must be taken from the already spoiled palette of life in the here and now.

On the other hand, in the pictures of the crucified one we find the accumulative misery of every epoch reflected. Thus we can also say here that the coming truth of the resurrection and of life and of God is realized first in the critical negation of the negative. What is the abundance of life? The death of death. What is complete freedom? The elimination of every rule, every authority and power. What is God? The elimination of nothingness itself, which threatens and cajoles everything that exists and insults everything that wants to live but must die.

If we perceive the new future for the first time in the resurrection of the crucified one, we can grasp the new in the dialectic of the negation of the negative. If Christianity orients itself on these grounds, it can no longer be the "honey" of an antagonistic and repressive society or the one who pronounces the benediction on the way things are. It must become the salt of the earth and join itself in a provolutionary way with what is foolish in the world, what is weak in the world, what is low and despised in the world, even with things that are not, in order to shame the wise and the strong and to bring to nothing the things that are (1 Cor. 1:26-30). I believe that Rauschenbusch was right when he said: "Ascetic Christianity called the world evil and left it. Humanity is waiting for a revolutionary

34

Christianity which will call the world evil and change it."[3] For this purpose, however, we need positive visions and concrete utopias so that we will not end in pragmatism and reaction.

Can Christian hope provide us with such visions which are *extensive* enough to grasp the whole present misery and *concrete* enough to give the present necessary initiatives both meaning and power?

2

THE VISION OF GOD AND
THE NEW CREATION

History's field of experimentation in which we move about has certain obvious conditions and presuppositions. Everything which is, wishes to be and to remain and yet may come to nothing and vanish. In this possibility, to be or not to be, lies the other possibility of its transformation. Everything which exists stands in suspension between being and nonbeing and every conscious being has hunger for being and dread before nothingness. Over against the theses of Greek ontology, *What is, is* and *Out of nothing, nothing comes*, was advanced the ontological thesis of the biblical creation faith: Everything which is, is *creatio ex nihilo*. A creation *out* of nothingness is nevertheless simultaneously a creation *within* the sea of nothingness. A creation *out* of chaos is an order of life *within* chaos. Thus it is figuratively expressed in the Genesis account that the creation is a creation composed of being and nonbeing. Day and night, land and sea are separated from each other, but, in the form of "night" and "sea," nothingness towers up out of chaos and the original deluge into the creation. The creation is therefore an open creation. It is open for its own destruction as well as its redemption in a new creation. It is not perfect but perfectible. It is good, but that does not exclude the possibility that it can become worse or the possibility that it can become

[3] Walter Rauschenbusch, *Christianity and Social Crisis*, ed. R. D. Cross (New York: Harper Torchbooks, 1964), p. 91.

better. We cannot understand it therefore as the golden state
of affairs before history; instead, we must conceive it as the
laying of the foundation and inauguration of history. The process is inaugurated. The experimental field of destructive and
constructive possibilities is laid out.

This experimental field of world history also has a goal and
a future which can likewise be described ontologically. The
conception of the restoration of the old creation or the return
of history to its point of departure is not depictable in the
images of the new creation. Omega is more than alpha. Only
if the "end is good" can all things be called "good." The vision
of the new creation is the vision of the successful world experiment. The new creation is to be a creation without the
penetrating shadows of the "night" and without the threatening
"waters of the flood." It is no longer to be only a *creatio ex
nihilo* and a *creatio in nihilo*, but a new being which participates in the infinite creative being of God.

The original creation was created out of the will of God. But
in its future God will dwell in it with his essence. This is to
say that the new creation corresponds to the essence of God
and is illuminated and transfigured by God's earthly presence.
It will be a creation without the necessity of religious mediation or sacred zones. It will be not the Garden of Eden but the
City of God. The first *creatio ex nihilo* will be taken up into
a new *creatio ex gloria Dei*. Out of this new creation will arise
a new being that will put an end to the ambivalence of all
created beings between being and nonbeing. In such a new
being God himself will come to his rest. If God himself dwells
in the midst of this new creation, all beings will take part in
his creativity. Therefore, the future new being with which
history experiments here cannot be tediously repetitious. Also,
if affliction, pain, and work are overcome, the eternal play before God and with God will comprise the infinite richness of the
new. The deadly antagonisms of present history will be transformed into the dialectic of eternal life according to the
analogy of the transformation of work into play.

The all-embracing vision of God and of the new creation is

36

for Christian hope anchored in the resurrection of the crucified Christ. In the resurrection of Christ we can know a new freedom in history which is not only liberation from the tyrannies within history, but also a liberation from the tyranny and agony of history itself. In the resurrection of Christ there can be seen a glimmer of the glory of the coming God and of his new creation. To be sure, according to the Christian faith, only Christ has yet been raised. Only in him has this future of a new being really begun, whereas we are not yet in the reality of his new being. But in faith and in hope we participate here already in the "power of the new world." For this reason Christ becomes for believers the focus of an all-embracing hope for the new world in which God dwells. Therefore, in the midst of the open experimental field of history, the future, as understood by the Christian faith, attains predominance over the past and hope enjoys ascendency over anxiety. The power of the past, which drags everything that exists into its wasteland where things cease to exist, is broken by hope which draws the new future into the sufferings of the present. Thus the evening and its farewells is a poor symbol for historical life, which is more like the morning with its greeting of a new day. But this means that in this faith the historical future is linked up with the ultimate future of history, and the quantitative future of tomorrow is infused with the qualitative future of the new creation. If, as is said, "his grace is new every morning," the anticipation of the ultimately new lies hidden with the historically new.

3

THE VISION OF THE NEW MAN AND
OF THE NEW COMMUNITY

From this all-encompassing vision of God against the threatening nothingness that surrounds us, we come now to the concrete utopias which can inform our initiatives against the historically experienced negative. The all-embracing vision of

37

God, on the one hand, imbues concrete hope with an urgent and ultimate character and, on the other hand, makes it versatile enough to encounter effectively the unprecedented situations of the present.

We experience the historical negative today in the definite estrangements of man from his true essence and his future. Although real misery appears different in different times and in different situations, we can still identify the definite alienations which confront us today with a common peril.

There is on the first level the *economic alienation of man.* Over half of mankind lives under conditions of minimal existence. This is unworthy of man and it is intolerable in a time which has, on the other extreme, developed affluent societies. If we wish to set humane goals in the modern industrial systems and if it is to be humanly significant to live, to work, and to invest for their realization, then the concrete utopia for the first level means to hold in view a future in which hardships and burdens cease and all men can live free from hunger and anxiety. That is easily said, but accomplished only with great difficulty. For the present tendency of the history of industrial development is to increase the already great distance between preindustrial, industrial, and postindustrial societies. The present capitalistic and nationalistic industrial systems give proof of the possibility of overcoming hunger and misery on the earth and yet, by the same token, create increasingly deeper divisions between peoples. Even within an industrial system the disparity between the progressive classes and the lower classes of the population is becoming not less, but greater. Thus the concrete utopia of a human world community of nations and men must, in an economic sense, unite the highest capability of economy and government with the victims of economic injustice, the underprivileged and the ones who are left behind. There can be no humanity without the end of need. There is no humanity without solidarity.

There is on another plane the *political alienation of men* through authoritarian political systems, through dictatorship of a privileged elite over the unprivileged, and through the imperialism of the powerful peoples over the weak. The happiness of men achieved through economic means can never replace political liberation and independence as a definition of the future for which men yearn. Today many revolutions in the throes of birth are directing themselves not only toward economic liberation, but more passionately toward independence and the freedom of self-determination. Peoples have the right to determine their own future. They can be humiliated and offended by imperialistic exploitation as well as by paternalistic aid for development. Even in an industrial society men are humiliated and enslaved by the careers which are the prescription of a repressive establishment. Therefore we will find both outside and inside the progressive industrial societies more and more rebellions, protests, and revolutions.

There is no human dignity without the end of economic want. But there is no human happiness without the end of submissiveness and dependence as well. Therefore industrialization must be carried forward in conjunction with the democratization of society and of international relationships. There is no longer a question of priority with respect to industrialization and democratization. Whoever neglects one creates the very misery which he sets out to overcome.

The concrete political utopia, then, is the transformation of nationalistic foreign policy into the beginning of a worldwide domestic policy. The primary question is not "What is good for my land and my standard of living?" but "What is good for the peace of the world and the building of a coming world community?" To act in accord with the expectation of this coming community, one must have the courage to act against the so-called justified interests of his own nation and to declare solidarity with the victims of the national policy of his own land. It is evident here also that the tendency of history is the increase and in no way the reduction of the spirit of growing nationalism and imperialism. The means of political and military power, however, have long ago outgrown the efficacy of

39

national institutions and can no longer be adequately controlled on the national level. This tendency of history, therefore, portends only disaster for all men.

Finally, we find on a further plane the racial alienation of man. If a man is judged and acknowledged according to his skin color, whether black or white or yellow, he has in effect no human identity. In all candor, however, we must admit the fact that the progress of the white has been purchased with the regress of the nonwhite man. The white superiority complex has systematically bred an inferiority complex in the nonwhite man. The nonwhite man was reduced to "his place" where as menial "helper" and servant he was obliged to serve white progress and, only within clearly delineated boundaries, to share in it. This political humiliation of man to a condition of unfreedom is hardly distinguishable from the human humiliation of man to a condition of inhumanity. Here man is offended in the very core of his person. It is therefore inevitable that the victims of white racism will rebel and sue for their lost humanity. As a result of the racial revolution during the coming decades, the present world could very well sink into oblivion. Only in a humane society where man no longer identifies and differentiates himself racially, where each group receives and assumes an equal share of responsibility for the whole, can the future be attained. The concrete utopia must, in this instance, envisage a new identity of man which overcomes, relativizes, and destroys all racial identifications. The present deadly antagonisms must at the very least be transformed into no-longer-deadly, i.e., productive, antagonisms.

In conclusion we may summarize in this way:

1. The all-embracing vision of God and of a new creation is to be realized in concrete utopias which summon and make sense out of present initiatives for overcoming the present negatives of life.

2. We find these present negatives in the economic, the political, and the racial alienation of man.

3. Therefore the all-embracing vision of God must be linked

40

with the economic liberation of man from hunger, with the political freeing of man from oppression by other men, and with the human emancipation of man from racial humiliation. It will thereby give these initiatives a power for prevailing over the world—a power which is necessary in order to go forward persistently against resistances and in face of disappointments. It will infuse these movements with that inner freedom which makes it possible for them to endure the sight of their own failures and sins.

What until now we called "religion" becomes through the messianic vision of Christianity a kind of "proligion," i.e., the joining of faith in God with hope in the liberation of man on a new earth and under a new heaven.

What until now we called "revolution" becomes a concrete provolution which, set over against the present misery of man, will produce the initiative for destroying this misery.

In both we find the combination of the past and the present with a "dream looking forward." That prepares us to take up the conflicts of the present and to seek their resolution in our common future.

III ✦ Resurrection as Hope

1

THE RESURRECTION OF CHRIST:

TRADITIONAL QUESTIONS

The resurrection of Christ is controversial. It does not fit into the modern world of things calculable and manipulable. Is it a historical event among other historical events that took place or that are still taking place? Is it a symbol of the language of times past?

For many Christians as well as for non-Christians the meaning of "resurrection," talk about the resurrection of Christ and hope for the resurrection of the dead, has become clouded. They do not find grounds for such hope in reality. "Resurrection" does not afford them experienceable meaning. It does not tell them anything about the future on this earth, at which mankind is presently working. The inability to understand is not caused by an intellectual deficiency. It goes deeper. The questions the traditional doctrine of the resurrection tried to answer can no longer be our questions. For this reason, the Christian tradition of the resurrection hope as well as the idealist teaching of the immortality of the soul has been caught

This essay, translated by Frederick Herzog, was first presented as an Ingersoll Lecture at the Harvard Divinity School, October 30, 1967. It was printed in *Harvard Theological Review*, 61 (1968), pp. 129–147.

in the frustrating situation of offering a heap of superfluous answers no one is interested in in the first place. The answers are not wrong. At least no one has proved them wrong thus far. But they have lost the character of open questions. They have dried up like fish in a drained pond.

Thus it is inevitable that theology descend from the lofty realm of traditional dogmatic answers to the foothills of present-day critical inquiry. Community in the form of answers always turns out to be divisive and partisan. But the community of open questions affords a universal solidarity among men who have nothing of their own, except perhaps the hope sometime to find an answer.

The Ingersoll Lectures of the past few years by and large have been concerned with the historical aspect of the resurrection faith and the immortality of the soul. Systematic theology is now challenged to say whether or not it can still represent the hope for resurrection in the modern world and how this might be done. I accept the suggestion of Krister Stendahl in his Introduction to the four essays by Oscar Cullmann, Harry A. Wolfson, Werner Jaeger, and Henry J. Cadbury in the volume entitled *Immortality and Resurrection*, and I ask together with him: "What question(s) did or do the belief in immortality and resurrection answer? How do or did these concepts function in the minds and lives of men?"[1]

If in the history of the Christian hope we look for this correlation of answers and questions, we find a great variety of options. In primitive Christianity, as documented by the New Testament, the "resurrection of Jesus from the dead through God" was the center.[2] The Easter event was the origin of the various Christologies of the church.[3] It was the foundation of

[1] Krister Stendahl (ed.), *Immortality and Resurrection*: "Death in the Western World: Two Conflicting Currents of Thought" (New York: Macmillan, 1965), Introduction, p. 6.
[2] Cf., on the exegetical historical and systematic discussion of the resurrection of Christ in Germany, the excellent collection of essays by B. Klappert, *Diskussion um Kreuz und Auferstehung* (Wuppertal: Aussaat Verlag, 1967).
[3] Cf. H. Anderson, *Jesus and Christian Origins. A Commentary on Modern Viewpoints* (New York: Oxford University Press, 1964), pp. 185ff.; W. Pannen-

salvation. For in this event one saw constituted the eschatological character of Jesus' total person.[4] One remembered and proclaimed his words as the words of the exalted one. One remembered and proclaimed his miracles and healings as the miracles and healings of the risen one. His historical appearance and activity were made present in the light of his Easter presence. His dying on the cross was interpreted and proclaimed as the suffering and dying of the eschatological person exalted through the Easter event.[5] His end for primitive Christianity was his real beginning. His historical life was therefore interpreted in view of his eschatological end in the resurrection. Jesus' future *in* the coming God and *for* this passing world became the key for the understanding of the lasting significance of his past.[6]

But what did "Easter" mean, and what did they mean when they spoke of God as the one "who raised Jesus from the dead," and when they proclaimed Jesus as "the resurrection and eternal life"? In order to understand, we must descend to the realm of the open questions.

---

berg, *Grundzüge der Christologie* (Gütersloh: Gütersloher Verlagshaus G. Mohn, 1965; Eng. trans.: *Jesus: God and Man* trans. D. A. Priebe and L. L. Wilkins [Philadelphia: Westminster Press, 1968]; J. Moltmann, *Theology of Hope* (New York: Harper & Row, 1967), pp. 139ff.

[4] The resurrection was not so much seen as a further event in the history of Jesus after his death, which was added to the events of his life and death, but, rather, understood as a new eschatological qualification of his life and death. The systematic question of whether it is a matter of a new "constitution" or only of a "confirmation" and revelation of his eschatological person cannot be stated theologically in the double formulation: God gave him for this dead was surely understood as a new unexpected event. The basis for his resurrection, however, is found in his obedience in living and dying. For this reason, his life and death on the cross and his resurrection from the dead can be stated theologically in the double formulation: God gave him for this purpose—God raised him from the dead.

[5] Cf. W. Kramer, *Christos, Kyrios, Gottessohn* (Zürich: Zwingli Verlag, 1963), p. 32: "Since then, the resurrection constituted (or confirmed respectively) the eschatological status of Jesus, ὑπὲρ ὑμῶν is thus the interpretation of the death of this eschatological person."

[6] A Christology of resurrection and a Christology of the life of Jesus are then not really opposed to each other, although they have been placed in opposition repeatedly in modern times.

The vision of hope pertaining to the resurrection of the dead developed in late Jewish apocalypticism. The basic question, from which the apocalyptic images of the future arose, is the *theodicy* question: When will God's righteousness triumph over this world of evil and pain? When will God show himself in his divinity and fulfill his promises?[7] The resurrection hope did not arise from an anthropological debate between Jew and Greek, as Oscar Cullmann seems to emphasize.[8] It can therefore also not be made accessible for contemporary understanding in terms of a modern anthropology of the "world-openness" of man, as Wolfhart Pannenberg tries to do.[9] "The approaches to a belief in an individual resurrection found in the Old Testament are due to a demand for the accomplishment of justice."[10] Because of his being God and because of his faithfulness, God must be proved right. This is the basic tenet of Jewish apocalypticism. Death can thus be no limit for the realization of God's justice. Following Deutero-Isaiah, its spiritual father, apocalypticism developed the idea of a twofold resurrection of the dead: one of "shame and everlasting contempt," and another of "everlasting life" (Dan. 12:1-3). And for IV Esdras the basic theodicy question is: Why is Israel offered to the Gentiles for contempt, thy beloved people to the godless tribes?" (4:23). The answer does not explain and justify anything, but points to the hope of God's coming: "Why do you not take the future to heart, but only the present?" (7:16). The theodicy

---

[7] Cf. P. Stuhlmacher, *Gerechtigkeit Gottes bei Paulus* (Göttingen: Vandenhoeck und Ruprecht, 1965); L. Mattern, *Das Verständnis des Gerichtes bei Paulus* (Zürich: Zwingli Verlag, 1966), and especially E. Käsemann, "Die Anfänge christlicher Theologie," and "Zum Thema urchristlichen Apokalyptik," *Exegetische Versuche und Besinnungen*, II (Göttingen: Vandenhoeck und Ruprecht, 1964), pp. 82ff., 105ff.

[8] O. Cullmann, "Immortality of the Soul or Resurrection of the Dead," in *Immortality and Resurrection, op. cit.*, pp. 9ff. Cf. also the criticism of H. A. Wolfson, "Immortality and Resurrection in the Philosophy of the Church Fathers," *op. cit.*, pp. 54ff.

[9] W. Pannenberg, *Was ist der Mensch?* (Göttingen: Vandenhoeck und Ruprecht, 1962); *Jesus: God and Man.*

[10] J. Pedersen, *Wisdom and Immortality*, Suppl. to *Vetus Testamentum*, III (1955), p. 245. Also G. von Rad. *Theologie des Alten Testamentes*, I (München: Chr. Kaiser Verlag, 1957), p. 404.

45

question, at first in the more narrow sense of the sufferings of Israel, and then in the universal sense of "the suffering of this present time" (Rom. 8:18) covering all of creation, was the open horizon. The resurrection hope for the individual was part of the universal hope for God and the coming of his new creation in righteousness, in which the theodicy question would be solved.

In the New Testament it is especially St. Paul who interprets the Christ event of Jesus' cross and resurrection in view of the horizon of the coming victorious righteousness of God.[11] The righteousness of God for which one must "wait" (Gal. 5:5) is now revealed in the word of the cross for everyone who believes (Rom. 1:16), and it will become real when death is destroyed and the body is redeemed and "life from the dead" (Rom. 11:15) will show God's presence. The resurrection of the dead, of which St. Paul speaks in 1 Corinthians 15, is thus not wishful thinking, longing for immortality, and also not an answer to man's quest for happiness, but a consequence of faith in God's divinity and in the victory of his righteousness. It is an answer to the theodicy question. Not because of the consummation of their salvation, but because Christ "must reign until he has put all his enemies under his feet," the dead shall live and this mortal nature must put on immortality.[12] God is vindicated because of himself. This is the basic tenet of St. Paul's theology. And therefore God justifies the Godless. Therefore he creates hope against hope. Therefore the dead shall live. These are the corollaries. St. Paul draws the basic tenet from the Christ event, which for him is the preview or the dawning of God's future in this world.

St. Paul sets himself apart from the old apocalypticism in at least two important points. (1) He no longer awaits the consummation of God's righteousness only from the future, but believes that from the cross of the resurrected Christ this righteousness begins in Word and Spirit its creative course

---

[11] Cf. to the following, E. Käsemann, "Gottesgerechtigkeit bei Paulus," in *Exegetische Versuche und Besinnungen*, II, pp. 181ff.
[12] *Ibid.*, p. 127.

46

through the Godless world. (2) For this reason, he no longer speaks of a resurrection of the unjust for judgment. "Resurrection" is for him, just like "God's righteousness" and "predestination," an unequivocal concept of salvation. He understands resurrection as a new creation of God, a creation which is good and no longer equivocal.[13] The apocalyptic theodicy question was raised by St. Paul on grounds of the cross of Christ and in the midst of "the sufferings of this present time," and was answered in the proclamation of the creative righteousness of God. It was faith pointing toward hope in conscious solidarity with the entire creation still "groaning in travail" (Rom. 8:22).

In the time following the primitive church, the church-teaching of the resurrection remained oriented toward the theodicy question, although one no longer fully grasped the meaning of the Pauline view of God's creative righteousness that comes in the Word. One combined the apocalyptic expectation with the ancient view of a *justitia distributiva*, which allots everyone his own.[14] The "general resurrection of the dead" became the ontological presupposition for the realization of the final divine judgment over the good and the evil. "Christ the kingly world judge" replaced, as Byzantine pictures show, the evangelical memory of "Jesus, the eschatological conqueror" of a world of suffering and guilt. Even so, one must see that the early Catholic Church's expectation of the resurrection of the dead for the purpose of divine judgment of the world initially does not belong to the anthropological debate about the salvation of the soul or the body, but serves the realization of God's righteousness. The coming judgment makes man responsible for everything he does or fails to do. It com-

[13] Cf. to the discussion of this in opposition to the surprising state of affairs in the doctrinal tradition of the church found in H. Molitor, *Die Auferstehung der Christen und Nichtchristen nach dem Apostel Paulus* (Münster i. W.: Aschendorf, 1933); H. Schwantes, *Schöpfung der Endzeit. Ein Beitrag zum Verständnis der Auferweckung bei Paulus* (Stuttgart: Calwer Verlag, 1962); L. Mattern, *op. cit.*, pp. 76ff.

[14] Evidence for the following exposition can be found in L. Atzberger, *Geschichte der christlichen Eschatologie innerhalb der vornizänischen Zeit* (Freiburg: Herder Verlag, 1896); W. Haller, "Die Lehre von der Auferstehung des Fleisches bis auf Tertullian," *Zeitschrift für Theologie und Kirche*, 2 (1892), pp. 274–342; H. A. Wolfson, *op. cit.*

pels him to identify himself completely with his present existence. For he will be judged according to his life here on earth. Since a man will have to give account of his life in its totality, this is why he will be raised from the dead in his totality, body and soul. Without a personal resurrection a man could not identify himself in the transcendent judgment with his earthly life. From the juridical logic of judgment, responsibility, and self-identification, the Fathers drew the conclusion of the resurrection of the dead, and from this resurrection in turn the anthropological unity of man—body and soul. In the anthropological debate of antiquity between the idealism that teaches man to identify himself completely with his soul and the materialism that teaches man completely to identify himself with his body, Christianity introduced a new definition of man: he is a person in view of the coming judgment. Since he must give a total account of his life, he is compelled to identify himself completely with his life on earth. Body and soul are like "cohorts" of a gang brought to court. Therefore both can in turn also become coheirs of salvation.[15]

It is indeed strange to see how the juridical conceptualization of God and his coming just judgment, in the theology of the early Catholic Church, breaks through the extant ontological, anthropological, and experiential concepts and seeks for new ontological and anthropological ideas. When Tertullian declared, "The whole body will rise, the same body, the total body," he apparently thought of the total accountability and the limitless self-identification of man before the judging God. The physicians of the school of Galen, who debated with him, understood this to mean the decaying bones of man and found doctrines of the resurrection absurd. Since modern man in our present scientific civilization has the same problem, we must take care to discover in which horizons and dimensions of thought faith in resurrection can become meaningful and how the directions of its questing can be related to those of our scientific age.

We will therefore first examine the foundation of the resur-

[15] Cf., especially for this, Tertullian, *De resurrectione mortuorum*, chaps. 55–56.

48

rection hope, turning to the *historical problem* of Jesus' resurrection. From here we will move to the present personal, social, and political meaning of the resurrection hope and deal with the *anthropological* problem. Finally, we will consider the destiny of the resurrection hope and discuss the *eschatological* or *futuristic* problem.

2

THE FOUNDATION OF THE RESURRECTION HOPE:

THE HISTORICAL PROBLEM

If we turn to Jesus' resurrection with the tools of historical research and criticism, there are two aspects to be considered. Questionable is Christian *resurrection faith* and its reality content. But questionable is also the *world* which for historico-critical research has become the only access to reality. The inquiry has, therefore, two sides.

Historico-critically we first ask whether or not there lies a historical datum behind the resurrection faith which entitles it to its hope. If we ask in this fashion, we will find that the witnesses indeed claim that Jesus was crucified and buried and that the crucified one appeared to them in an amazing light so that they could identify him. But no one claimed to have witnessed what had happened between the two experiences. The tradition of the empty tomb is secondary. In order to say what had happened and who he was who appeared to them in such a contradictory way, they turned to the vocabulary of the eschatological future hopes and spoke metaphorically of "the resurrection of Jesus from the dead." What they had in mind apparently was that the future for which, in God-forsakenness and fateful death, one can only wait had manifested itself in the crucified one. They claimed to have witnessed in and through Jesus the *dawning*, the *anticipation*, the hidden *representation* of a future never possessed before.

Is this a historical event, for whose reality content one can

49

vouch historico-critically? The Christian proclamation of Easter points indeed to a historical *person*, namely, Jesus of Nazareth, and to a particular *time*, namely after his crucifixion and before his appearance to his disciples, and to a particular *place*, namely Jerusalem. Under the aspect of the Easter event, only Jesus, the crucified, and the Easter faith of the disciples are tangible. Along with Martin Dibelius one will be able, in an unbiased way, to point out historically that "something" happended between the dead Jesus and the disciples which generated the faith of the disciples.[16] What this "something" really was escapes historical verification, since there are no historical analogies. Here the historical question reaches not its objective limit, but its categorical limit.[17] We can verify historically who is involved in the alleged resurrection event but we cannot verify the event itself. Thus we have available a historically ascertainable *framework* of the Easter event. But beyond it there is nothing we can "check out," either positively or negatively.

At any rate, the New Testament witnesses of the Easter event themselves do not claim that the crucified had appeared to everyone in glory, but only to particular persons, who thereupon, in hope of his coming and everywhere-visible glory, indeed tried to fill the whole world with the gospel. We must therefore state that the act of the raising of Jesus is not a historically observable and ascertainable event. We would already have to live in the world of the resurrection and no longer in history dominated by death, if the resurrection should have become for us an observable and measurable event. Jesus' resurrection is in itself an eschatological *novum*. It is the foun-

---

[16] Martin Dibelius, *Jesus* (3rd ed., Berlin: W. de Gruyter Verlag, 1960), p. 118: "Something must have taken place which, in a short period of time, not only called forth a complete reversal of attitude, but also enabled them to new activity and to founding the Christian congregation. This 'something' is the historic kernel of the resurrection faith."

[17] Cf. the discussion of the notion of the "historical" (*Historischen*) between G. Ebeling, *Theologie und Verkündigung* (Tübingen: J. C. B. Mohr/Paul Siebeck, 1962); W. Pannenberg, *Jesus: God and Man*; J. Moltmann, *Theology of Hope*, pp. 172ff., 230ff.; and B. Klappert, *Diskussion um Kreuz und Auferstehung.*

dation of the Christian kerygma and the Christian hope, for it qualifies the historical and crucified Jesus as the eschatological person, in whom the future of God is dawning. The historically tangible aspect of the risen one is the crucified one, and, moreover, that which St. Paul calls "the spirit of resurrection," the gospel vindicating the Godless, and the hope which can hope against all worldly hope.

The Christian resurrection faith is thus historically unverifiable. But since the historian cannot work with the world as a whole as his subject matter, but only with that part of the world one calls the past, we could add that this resurrection of Jesus is not historically verifiable "as yet." According to the nature of its appropriation thus far in Word and faith it is subject to *eschatological verification.*[18] This means that something has happened which in its significance and meaning is not universally visible "as yet." Historical proof and certainty in this instance mean an anticipation of the end of history in which all historical events and persons stand still, as it were, and can be valued in terms of their significance for history as a whole.[19] But within history we do not live by such valuations, but by hopes and fears, since all things are still in a complete flux. Only at the end of history might one change from a man of hope within history into a historian of history.

The positive function of historical research lies, therefore, not so much in the effort somewhere to position ourselves in the process of history on the safe foundation of fixed facts, but, on the contrary, in the permanent criticism which dissolves all facts in open processes and therefore all certainties and all ties in expectations and liberties. Historical criticism of the Christian Easter message joins here the iconoclastic power of the Christian hope itself. For if the Christian hope understands the resurrection of the crucified one as the touchstone of its expec-

---

[18] I. M. Crombie and John Hick have spoken similarly of an "eschatological verification" of God's existence. Cf. Hick's *The Existence of God* (New York: Macmillan, 1964), pp. 252ff.

[19] Cf. R. Bultmann, *Glauben und Verstehen*, III (Tübingen: J. C. B. Mohr/ Paul Siebeck, 1960), pp. 113ff.

tation, in the contemplation thereof it is reminded of the future and is thus unable to file it away among the data of the past. One cannot cast anchor in the tradition of the Easter kerygma. On the contrary, this tradition is like a following wind in one's sails that drives the boat into an unknown and yet hoped-for future. If a "miracle" happens, one is placed in the category of the *novum*. If one only looks back upon it, it is merely a puzzle or a stupefying event. It did not change its environment at all. In its secular context the "miracle" lost its aura. It therefore belongs to the category "future," which is an "unhistorical" aura, as Nietzsche said, a dimension not yet historical.[20] "Miracle" in the past exists only insofar as in certain events or words a future has appeared which gives meaning to the present sufferings of transience. Therefore the Christian resurrection hope is itself interested in the historico-critical iconoclasm against the fetishism of religious facts.

If this is true, how can we grasp the foundation of the Christian hope? The Christian hope is not founded on the isolated event of Jesus' resurrection, but in his total person and entire history—which through the resurrection became eschatologically qualified. Cross and resurrection therefore inseparably belong together and interpret each other. In confessing Jesus' resurrection, faith does not imply that Jesus has been removed to heaven or has been eternalized in God, but that he has been received into the future of the "kingdom of heaven" and the coming glory of God. Faith therefore saw in Jesus "the first fruits of those who have fallen asleep," "the first to rise from the dead," and "the Author of life." In him the old promises of God became effective. In him that future appeared in which God is God, man is man, and peace and justice reign on earth. Jesus' resurrection signifies a new factor which opens our world locked up in guilt and death toward the future. This new factor is not a mere renewal, but the entrance of the unexpected, for it opens the future of a qualitatively new.

[20] F. Nietzsche, *The Use and Abuse of History* (New York: Liberal Arts Press 1949), p. 15.

The Christian hope, however, is not a one-way street on which one leaves the present behind in order to flee into the future. It has two-way traffic, as it were. For it draws the future into the sufferings of the present. This implies for Christology that Jesus' resurrection is by no means only an arrow pointing to the hitherto unknown future of God and man, but that this future has become flesh in Jesus, the crucified, and thus has become involved in the present. Resurrection, life, and freedom did not merely *dawn* in Jesus, so that we would now have some reason to hope for these things. They were also mediated through Jesus to those who live in darkness and in the midst of death. This is the meaning of the cross of the risen Christ. The prolepsis or anticipation of the future that was seen in his resurrection was embodied in his existence for others and in the vicarious mediation of freedom, justice, and salvation that one had seen in his cross. Jesus' resurrection may have been understood as a *sign* of hope for a God-forsaken mankind. But only his cross was the real mediation of this hope for the hopeless. Thus the cross is the present form of the resurrection. The coming glory of God is mirrored in the face of the crucified one. We are therefore able to say that Jesus' resurrection is only *indirectly*, but the meaning of his cross is *directly*, the foundation of the Christian hope for justice and life.

The memory of Jesus' cross in the primitive church was its protection against enthusiastic hopes and their inevitable disappointments, and will continue to function as such. A hope born of the cross is a "hope against hope," is hope tested, is *docta spes*. And again we can say: the historico-critical destruction of all illusions of hope stands in the service of the crucified hope of the Christian. It is a kind of negative theology, which clears the road for the coming God, removing all images and representations of the fantasies of hope. Thus, in historical criticism we can find the iconoclasm of hope turned backward.

Looking at the matter from a different perspective, we can

also say that the Christian faith in the resurrection questions that modern world for which historical research has become the only access to the reality of history. A few pointers must suffice in this context. Do we not find in every historical examination of a historical movement or of a tradition the tendency toward objectification and thingification of a living process? "History regarded as pure knowledge and allowed to sway the intellect would mean for men the final balancing of the ledger of life," said Nietzsche.[21] Thus, in the attempt to know history and to make it calculable, there develops, consciously or unconsciously, the consequence of terminating history and of robbing human life of its real character as history. For history moves for human perception out of the *mode of being* into the *mode of having*. We always *have* history more, since we always can have and comprehend the past more. But then we are no longer historical in the open processes of the present. "Whenever philosophy paints gray in gray, the form of life has become old, and through gray in gray it cannot be rejuvenated, but only known," said Hegel.[22]

The historical objectification and thingification of history in facts of the past therefore results dialectically in a nonhistorical present. But the truth of Jesus' resurrection balks at this category of *having*. Its certainty cannot be translated into some form of security according to which we control things or facts. Only in a transformation of our own being is its meaning unlocked for us. It does not enrich the past we have with the other facts, but in new ways makes us new historical beings. Here we find the justification for existential interpretation and its necessity.

Yet, the problem of *having* and *being* is not only a personal problem, but also, and even more so, a social one. We can very well characterize the society in which we live as a "society of having." Principally in this society one can have and can leave

[21] *Ibid.*, pp. 19f.
[22] G. W. F. Hegel, "Vorrede zur Philosophie des Rechtes," *Sämtliche Werke* (Stuttgart: Fr. Frommans Verlag, 1952), pp. 36f.

54

all things. If, however, there is connected with the recognition of the resurrection of Christ the experience of new historical being, there evolves from this the claim and the expectation to transform the "society of having" into a "society of being." This implies that historical scholarship is compelled to reflect on its role as to the totality of history. For it is not only reflection about history, but also participation in history. The last great philosophies and theologies of history, from Bossuet (and Voltaire) to Hegel and Droysen, among others, were at their core always *theodicy* projects. After the catastrophes of our century we know that history writing is incapable of a theodicy. But even though we are unable to come up with a justification of God from the processes of history, the question of the meaning of history continues to remain open in spite of the failure of our attempts at justification. To raise the theodicy question, and along with it to question the future of history, does not already mean to be able to answer it. But suffering and evil, on the one hand, and the indelible memory of hope, on the other, raise this question for us. In a Godless world we hunger for righteousness upon the earth, that is, for a world which we can recognize as God's world. If the world, the way it is, would proffer a theodicy, we would need no faith. But if there were no theodicy question, where would the risk of faith be? (Martin Buber).

3

THE MEANING OF THE RESURRECTION HOPE:

PRESENT ANTHROPOLOGICAL PROBLEM

For an analysis of the contemporary human condition, we resume our reflection on the "society of having."[23] Triggered

23 The distinction of this category was first introduced into social anthropology by Moses Hess. Cf. his *21 Bogen aus der Schweiz*, which was published by Georg Herwegh in Zürich in 1843. See also E. Silberner, *Moses Hess: Geschichte seines Lebens* (Leiden: E. J. Brill, 1966). E. Thier has shown the influence of Moses Hess on Karl Marx in his work, *Das Menschenbild des*

by Platonism and Cartesianism, the category of *having* was infinitely broadened in our scientific and technological civilization. Man regards his body as his *possession*, but he is no longer identified with his *bodily* life. His bodily and social life is something that he *has* and that represents him, but it is not he himself. An environment takes shape in which all things are replaceable and all human relationships interchangeable. Pathology analyzes disease configurations and cases. Often enough the sick person remains unnoticed. This leads people to play it cool in everything and to enter human relationships without love and their jobs as though they were roles of an actor in the theater. In love we identify ourselves with our bodily and social existence. But that makes us vulnerable. It is therefore a self-defense to play a role with one's life, while at the same time, as it were, holding back one's soul. Identification of the self with bodily and social existence has been replaced by the category of having and of possessing, affording an increasing differentiation between man and the reality of his life. One can therefore understand that in the reactionary movements against this "society of having," in protests, rebellions, and revolutions, man's passion somehow really to be man is revived time and time again. "The children of protest" seek their social and bodily identity in the battle against the repressions of this society, even in view of the danger of losing the battle.

In the background of this conflict between *being* and *having* there lies an even more profound difficulty: How can one identify with one's bodily life, seeing that one must expect bodily death and that one experiences it daily in suffering and disappointments? And yet we also must ask conversely: How can one live at all, if one does not identify with one's transient and mortal being? Either one must accept death as belonging

---

jungen Marx (Göttingen: Vandenhoeck und Ruprecht, 1957). The anthropological evaluation of the dialectic of being and having is carried out by H. Plessner in *Die Stufen des Organischen und der Mensch* (Berlin, 1928), *Lachen und Weinen* (Bern: Franke Verlag, 1958); F. J. J. Buytendijk, *Das Menschliche: Wege zu seinem Verständnis* (Stuttgart: K. F. Koehler, 1958); G. Marcel, *Being and Having* (New York: Harper & Row, 1965).

to life, or one must renounce this life from the start. In this respect life and death cannot be harmonized in human existence.

Apparently the Christian faith, precisely in the midst of suffering that appears whenever finite life is expected to be the locale of infinite bliss, evolved the resurrection hope. In other words, the love in which we fully identify ourselves with this transient, vulnerable, and mortal life and the resurrection hope belong together and interpret each other. The Christian resurrection hope does not deny the importance of our earthly life by making us dream of heaven. If rightly understood, it makes us ready to accept our mortal life and completely to identify it. This hope does not differentiate between body and soul like the Greek concept of immortality, but makes us ready to animate the mortal body and thus also to humanize the repressive society of having. The resurrection hope is thus not an "opium of the beyond," but a "power of worldly life." The resurrection hope claims paradoxically: *Caro est cardo salutis* (Tertullian).[24]

Probably from the mouth of Jesus himself we received that strange eschatological principle of life: "He who finds his life will lose it, and he who loses his life for my sake will find it" (Mark 8:35). We often rediscover this thought in a secularized form. "If you don't risk your life, ne'er will you win it," said Friedrich Schiller. And Hegel wrote: "Not the life that shuns death and keeps itself pure from destruction, but the life that bears death and keeps itself in death, is the life of the spirit."[25] In the modern "society of having" and in the institutional escapes from the battle of life, boredom often raises its ugly head, since life appears meaningless and one no longer finds anything for which one could take a stand. Man, however, does not find identity in this life, in remaining isolated and in keeping his soul for himself, but only in going out of himself and becoming personally, socially, and politically incarnate.

---

[24] Tertullian, *De resurrectione mortuorum*, 8, 2.
[25] Cf. G. W. F. Hegel, *Phenomenology of the Mind*, trans. James Baillie (London: George Allen and Unwin, 1910), p. 93.

Which hope is strong enough to make this incarnation and the identification and the commitment of one's life meaningful beyond all frustration, which finally means beyond death? Man always regains his identity from that to which he gives himself. If this is mortal and transient, he will die and perish himself. In the early church it was said that man finds himself again in eternity, if he gives himself to something eternal, namely, God. Today we perhaps should say that man finds himself again in the future, if he risks his life for a coming future that will not pass away. He will find himself again in the Kingdom of God, if he risks his life for the coming of this Kingdom, and if he takes his cross upon himself, as the Word of God would have him do. The resurrection hope readies one for a life in love without reservation. Therefore we can say conversely that creative and self-giving love mirrors future resurrection under the conditions of this present life. The resurrection into life and freedom is here anticipated in the reverse movement of the incarnation, of self-oblation and faithful labor. Love, creating new life out of nothing, is resurrection in this life. Not the corpse that we can dissect objectively, but the body with which we identify in love, stands in the horizon of the resurrection hope. There is no meaningful hope for the body we have, but only for the body we are. In love we break through the deadly category of having and arrive at the category of affirmed being. Herein alone lies resurrection hope in accord with the Christian faith. In this acceptance of the body and this identification of our self with the body we experience an anticipation of the final liberation and redemption of the body. The body is being liberated from the repressions of fear, as it is liberated from the law and the repressions of the law. It enters into the sphere of influence of the gospel and of the freedom of faith.

This "prolepsis" of the resurrection of the body has psychological implications. I am thinking, for example, of the book by N. O. Brown, *Life against Death*.[26] But it also has socio-

[26] N. O. Brown, *Life against Death: The Psychological Meaning of History* (Middletown, Conn.: Wesleyan University Press, 1959).

political consequences. What did Moses Hess and Karl Marx want in their earlier writings? They wanted to break the domination of the category of having over the category of being and they looked for social conditions in which the inhuman and artificial world of things, goods, and money is replaced by a world of true humanity, in which one can "exchange love for love only, and friendship for friendship only," but cannot buy either one or capitalize on both.[27] Of course, such a world of true humanity is a dream. Man is obviously subjected to both having and being, and cannot manage to live in fealty to one category only. But he must search in each situation for a meaningful and live balance between the two. Man always *is* body, but simultaneously he *has* this body as his very own. He must be able to identify with the reality of his life, and yet at the same time to transcend it and to reflect on it. Spontaneity and reflection both belong to man's very being. And yet one will have to look in the *culture of reflection* in the modern world for the necessary humanization of a new personal spontaneity and a satisfactory social identification. Dietrich Bonhoeffer thus emphasized the passionate "worldliness of the Christian faith," for which the "knowledge of death and resurrection are ever present."[28] For this reason there are also many who today in the resurrection hope find the power for social and political revolt against a world of death, fear, repression, and alienation. In the *anastasis* is contained the *stasis*, and in the resurrection, the revolution. Jesus' resurrection can be understood as the protest of life against death, and the life in the spirit of the resurrection pertains to the "making alive of the dead conditions" (Hegel) and the humanization of the human condition as a whole.[29]

This makes for a change in the ancient and troublesome *theodicy* question. Nature with its orders and its chaos does

[27] Karl Marx, *Die Frühschriften*, ed. S. Landshut (Stuttgart: Alfred Kröner Verlag, 1964), p. 301.
[28] D. Bonhoeffer, *Letters and Papers from Prison*, rev. ed. by E. Bethge, trans. R. H. Fuller (New York: Macmillan, 1962), pp. 225f.
[29] Cf. W.-D. Marsch, *Gegenwart Christi in der Gesellschaft* (München: Chr. Kaiser Verlag, 1965).

not give an answer. History, this "mishmash of error and brute force," in Goethe's terminology, does not give an answer either. The theodicy question must become a questioning of the future, and from the future we can expect the advent of a new creation of God, and in this expectation we can actively try to change the present, so that our world becomes transformed into the recognizable world of God, and our sinful humanity into the recognizable humanity before God.

4

THE FULFILLMENT OF THE
RESURRECTION HOPE:

THE ESCHATOLOGICAL PROBLEM

In a time when God was questioned, the Christian faith saw, in Jesus, God's incarnation. Not the resurrection, but the incarnation; not Easter, but Christmas stood at the center. In a time when man began to regard himself as questionable, faith saw in Jesus the true man, the creative archetype of the divine man. Today the future is becoming more and more the pressing question for a mankind that is now able to destroy itself. Thus Christian faith discovers today in God the power of a future that stems itself against the destruction of the world. The God of the exodus and of the resurrection is the "God of hope" rather than the "God above" or the "ground of being." He is in history "the coming God," as the Old Testament prophets said, who announces his coming in his promises and his lowly Messiah. He is "the absolute future" (Karl Rahner) or, figuratively, the Lord of the future, who says, "Behold, I make all things new."

If we simultaneously begin to think of God and future, faith and hope, we move in a new way close to the primitive Christian Easter message. We are able to understand it again eschatologically. We can recognize in the inexplicable *novum* of Christ the anticipation and the incarnation of the ultimately or

60

universally new, which in the coming of the recreating God can be hoped for. God is the power of the future. God is the power of the new. Jesus himself has been translated into the future of the new. He represents this future and at the same time mediates it. Following the emphasis on divine Sonship and the emphasis on true humanity, the old titles for Jesus, "Messiah" and *ho erchomenos*, the "coming one," seem quite timely again. In him, who from cross, God-forsakenness, and hell was raised, we become certain of a future which will conquer God-forsakenness and hell. But this is not everything: The fulfillment of the resurrection hope must now be joined with the expectation of a future which has not existed before, with the expectation of the presence of the God who announces himself in Word and Spirit. The ultimately new lies in the promise: "He will dwell with them, and they shall be his people" (Rev. 21:3). The resurrection hope can fulfill itself only in the future of God in which God is really God and will be "all in all" (1 Cor. 15:28).

The hope for such a presence of God can be fulfilled, however, only if the negatives of death, suffering, tears, guilt, and evil have disappeared from reality, that is, in a new creation, which, figuratively speaking, is no longer a mixture of day and night, earth and sea, and in which, ontologically speaking, being and nonbeing are no longer intertwined. The hope for the future, in which God is God and a new creation his dwelling place, the expectation of that home of identity in which man is at one with God, nature, and himself radically anew confronts the unfulfilled present with the theodicy question. Where freedom has come near, the chains begin to hurt. Where life is close, death becomes deadly. Where God proclaims his presence, the God-forsakenness of the world turns into suffering. Thus the theodicy question, born of suffering and pain, negatively mirrors the positive hope for God's future. We begin to suffer from the conditions of our world if we begin to love the world. And we begin to love the world if we are able to discover hope for it. And we discover hope for this world if we hear the promise of a future which stands against frustration, transiency, and death. To be sure, we can find certainty only in complete uncertainty. To be sure, we can hope for God only in the pain of the open theodicy question.[30] But it does not take more, in terms of George B. Ingersoll's question, to make man immortal.

[30] John Hick, *Evil and the God of Love* (New York: Harper & Row, 1966). This work can be noted as the resumption of a theology in the horizon of the question of theodicy.

IV ✦ The Revolution of Freedom:
Christians and Marxists Struggle for Freedom

The dialogue between Christians and Marxists in Europe has completely changed during the past few years. Recently, on my way to give lectures in Prague, I bought a copy of *Time* magazine in Frankfurt and read a long article on the "God-is-dead movement" in the United States. When I arrived in Prague, a series of articles by the Marxist philosopher Gardavsky on Jacob, Jesus, Paul, and Augustine was given to me. The title was: "Buh neni zcela mrtev" ("God Is Not Quite Dead"). This is symptomatic of the changing fronts between Christians and Marxists. When the Paulus Society met last year in the Czechoslovakian city of Marienbad, this realignment was recognized openly[1] The Christians—Catholics and Protestants—attempted to demonstrate the relevance of the Christian faith for this world. They accentuated the engagement of the church with society, the hope for the earth, and the necessity of a Christian critique of unjust social conditions. The Marxists, on the other hand, revised their well-known "critique of religion" and asked for a new openness of men for transcendence. It was expected that the theologians would be assigned the care of

This was originally presented as an Alden-Tuthill Lecture at Chicago Theological Seminary, January 23, 1968.
[1] Cf. "Marienbader Protokolle," in *Neues Forum: Zeitschrift für den Dialog,* XIV (1967), pp. 162–163.

transcendence, while the Marxists would assume responsibility for the formation of this world in a revolutionary way. However, paradoxically enough, we found it to be exactly the reverse.

Professor Prucha from Prague, a scholar of the Lomonossow University of Moskaw, confronted his comrades with this query: "Our Christian friends have awakened in us the courage for transcendence. For a long time we Marxists have tried to criticize and retard the Christian striving for transcendence. Should it not, rather, be our task to encourage the Christians to be even more radical in their striving for transcendence?"

Professor Machovec, philosopher of religion in Prague, supported the view that after the solution of the economic problems, the "searching for the meaning of life" would become more and more the crucial problem of the future.

Roger Garaudy, the chief ideologist of the Communist Party in France, said to the audience: "What would your [i.e., the Christian's] faith be like if it bore not in itself the latent atheism which prevents you from serving a false God? What would our atheism be like if it would not learn from your faith the transcendence of a God of whom we have no living experience?"

Lastly, there was Dr. Gardavsky from Brünn, whom I have already mentioned, asking: "Can the Marxian atheist expect of a Christian the same responsibility for the future of mankind as he himself is willing to bear? Can he assume for himself co-responsibility for that idea which is meaningful to Christians, namely, to work for the coming of God's Kingdom?" And he said Yes to both questions. Owing to recent Christian achievements, such as the Second Vatican Council, the encyclical *Populorum Progressio*, and the Geneva World Conference on "Church and Society," Christianity looks different to a sensitive Marxist today from the way it did to Karl Marx and Friedrich Engels. On the other hand, Christians also have to acknowledge that Marxism in Europe has changed since the time of Stalin. The humanists lift up their heads. Their Marxism is no longer a dogmatic ideology but a critical philosophy. Under these presuppositions a new dialogue can begin today. For today we are *both* struggling with new problems that were not encompassed in our traditional doctrines.

Some men base their community on answers alone. Such communities are always biased, factious, and confessional. They cannot be universal. However, there is also a community of men based on asking. This is the community of the seeking and hungry, neither biased nor confessional. It is a community pervading all parties and churches, uniting men in their common experience of deficiency and not-knowing. Such a community of questioning and seeking can today unite Christians and Marxists. Formerly, the Marxists appeared to us as dogmatists who had the right answer to all questions. Today Christian theologians appear to be possessors of an unquestionable and incontrovertible truth. Often they have answers to all human questions and are astonished that people are unwilling to pose questions to them any more. Bertolt Brecht wrote in one of his "Calendar Tales": " 'I have noticed,' said Mr. Keuner, 'that we scare away many people from our doctrine because we know an answer to everything. Couldn't we, in the interest of our propaganda, comprise a list of questions which seem to us to be completely unsolved?' "

It seems to me that Christian theology of today should turn away from a dogmatic theology to a critical one, from beginning with answers about God to the unsolved asking for God. The tense of asking is the future. In the process of asking persistently and eschewing the satisfaction of trite compensations, man becomes open to the future and thus exists in time and history.

By way of asking he goes, as Abraham once did, from his country and his kindred and his father's house. By way of asking he opens himself up for the unknown future. By way of asking for God and ultimate freedom he enters into worldwide solidarity with the whole "waiting creation" of which Paul is speaking in Romans 8:18ff. A "theology of hope" is a theology of questions that can be answered only by the coming of God through the kingdom of his freedom. It can therefore be ecumenical if, behind the conflict between different answers of the churches and ideologies, it detects and brings to awareness the deeper community of asking and seeking, a community bonded by man's poverty and existing for the sake of a wider future.

I shall now attempt to outline some of the characteristic points of a theology of freedom as it is possible in the new dialogue between Christians and Marxists, Liberals and Socialists.

1

THE RELIGION OF FREEDOM[2]

The Christian faith understands itself authentically as the beginning of a freedom that was, hitherto, unseen to the world (John 1:18; 1 Cor. 2:9). Christian faith not only believes in freedom but is already freedom itself. It not only hopes for freedom but, rather, is in itself the inauguration of a free life on earth. However, it is just a historical beginning and not yet the universal fulfillment.

There is an inexorable difference between the "realm of freedom," which we hope will ultimately free the whole creation from its misery, and the beginning of freedom here in the midst of a world full of bondage and slavery. Christian faith is freedom in struggle, in contradiction, and in temptation. The realm of freedom, however, of which the present beginning is faith, is freedom in its own new world—that is, God's free world. The difference between freedom in faith and the realm of freedom is the motor and the motive power for our work of realizing freedom in history.

Is Christianity a religion of freedom? At the starting point of the biblical faith, we see the creative symbols of freedom:

[2] Cf. my article, "Die Revolution der Freiheit," in *Evangelische Theologie*, XXVII (1967), pp. 595–616.

the exodus of Israel from bondage in Egypt, and the resurrection of the crucified Christ into the coming Kingdom of God—a deliverance *in* history and a deliverance *from* history.

The future for which Christian faith is hoping is a new creation in which the whole groaning creation shall be set free from the bondage of evil and death. Christians who believe in God believe in the coming, creative God, who will create out of the misery of the living creatures the Kingdom of his glory, a new being in which he himself will dwell. Through their faith, Christians participate in the creative freedom of God. Thus, faith should no longer be described, in the terms of Schleiermacher, only as a *schlechthinninges Abhangigkeitsgefühl*—i.e., as the "feeling of absolute dependence" in religious submissiveness. Faith can, on the contrary, be described as a *schlechthinninges Freiheitsgefühl*, as the "feeling of absolute freedom" in spiritual communion with the creative God. As the Gospel puts it: "All things are possible to him who believes" (Mark 9:23); "with God all things are possible" (Matt. 19:26). "For all things are yours, whether . . . the world or life or death or the present or the future, all are yours; and you are Christ's; and Christ is God's" proclaims the apostle Paul (1 Cor. 3:21-23). Thus, Christian proclamation is actually the religion of an exceedingly great freedom, even though the Christian church has often concerned itself more with authority and order than with this freedom.

This freedom in faith must be made clear to the atheist as well as to the religious man of today, for the former is still thinking: Either there is a God, in which case man cannot be free; or man is free, in which case there cannot or may not be a God (cf. Marx, Engels, Bakunin, Sartre, N. Hartmann, and others). Those are actually the alternatives in the mythological world of religions. For in that world the half-god Prometheus becomes the hero of man's freedom over against the gods. He is still the philosophical saint of Marxism. Here, God and man are considered to be one and the same essence. Thus what you grant God, you must have taken away from man, and what you grant man, you must have taken away from God. But when will we stop measuring God and man with the same yardstick?

In the Old Testament, however, things are different. Yahweh is here the God who leads his people out of the house of bondage. Thus he is the God of freedom, the God "ahead of us." One acquires social, political, and world-surpassing freedom from God, not against him.

In the New Testament, Jesus is believed in as the Messiah of freedom because he sets sinners free through his word and liberates the sick by his wondrous works. Those who labor and are heavy laden, the humiliated and offended, the poor and hungry find freedom and justice in him. In his resurrection from death on the cross we can see freedom dawn, freedom from the power of death and from the misery of the eclipse of God. In Jesus we can see the Messiah of God's freedom on earth. For he did not seek to be master of mankind but took the form of a servant. His suffering works as the unburdening of man in order to set man free. For freedom is always born out of unburdening. Freedom of faith is born out of his serving, joy out of his suffering, life everlasting out of his death. Kings and emperors have called themselves God's representatives on earth, founding their authority in the supreme authority of God. However, if we believe the crucified Christ to be the representative of God on earth, we see the glory of God no longer in the crowns of the mighty but in the face of that man who was executed on the gallows. What the authorities intended to be the greatest humiliation—namely, the cross—is thus transformed into the highest dignity. It follows that the freedom of God comes to earth not through crowns, that is to say, the struggle for power, but through love and solidarity with the powerless.

Therefore, in spite of Romans 13, Christians are hoping for a future in which "every rule and every authority and power" will be destroyed (1 Cor. 15:24) and the crucified shall reign, "the first among many brethren." Already here in history, they will strive for neutralizing and destroying the differences between the powerful and the powerless, master and slave. The community comprised of Jews and heathen, of masters and slaves, becomes the prototype and sacrament of men's hope for a world of brotherhood (1 Cor. 1:20-29).

Therefore, Christian freedom is not a special one, different from that freedom for which all mankind is longing. Nor is it a partial one that is exhausted in the practice of a certain religion or cult. If it really is the beginning of the realm of freedom in the midst of all the misery of this world, then Christians can only demonstrate this freedom by using their own freedom for the actual liberation of man from his real misery. Privileges are always the perversion of freedom. If religion induces not new freedom *for* the world but only new chains, then according to the dictum of Karl Marx, the liberation *from* religion would bring about more freedom than would religious liberty.

Which aspects of concrete freedom do Christians claim for themselves? They do not seek the liberties of liberalism, in which each one may go to heaven according to his own fashion if only he does not impede the fashion of others.

Freedom is no private affair, but is always freedom *for* others. Therefore, the Christian faith cannot acquiesce in the liberties of individual people. To believe is no private hobby, but hope for the whole, for society, for mankind, for the earth. On the other hand, Socialism cannot be the heir of Christian freedom, for neither a social nor a political system of life is able to realize already, here and now, that future of freedom for which the Christian faith is hoping. The Christian faith will find its peace only when it rests in the realm of God's freedom. Until then, however, it remains a troublemaker in every society which is content with itself and coerces its people to regard themselves as happy and fortunate. Thus Christians must seek the freedom for their own original mission in every form of society. Specifically, they must search for (1) the freedom of proclaiming God's liberating power publicly, (2) the freedom of assembling a new congregation of brothers out of

Jews and heathen, masters and slaves, black and white, and (3) the freedom of critically cooperating in the process of community according to the criteria of creative love. But Christians will also always seek possibilities of working together with Liberals, Democrats, and Marxists for the sake of the realm of freedom. For the hope for an all-embracing and ultimate freedom and the belief in a creative future have inspired all of our freedom movements. But in none of them has it been materialized until now, for every revolution of freedom has evolved new unfreedom in the world, too. Let us now survey briefly the history of the revolutions for freedom.

2

THE HISTORY OF REVOLUTIONS FOR FREEDOM

All of those whose struggle for freedom commits them to participation in dialogue—namely, Catholics, Protestants, Liberals, and Communists—stem from particular historical revolutionary freedom movements. Therefore, they understand freedom differently. But since all of them stand in one and the same history in which people have searched for freedom, they find a deep community existing among themselves.

Today the Marxists criticize Christianity by pointing to a historical distinction. For them the history of Christianity is the continuous conflict between a Constantinian wing, in which the state church is linked with the ruling powers, and a chiliastic wing, which is united with the humiliated and oppressed in a revolutionary way. This distinction is correct to a large degree. But it flings back to the Marxists like a boomerang, for we must equally distinguish between a Stalinistic Marxism, showing the symptoms of a Byzantine or bureaucratic state ideology, and a humanistic Marxism which is, in a self-critical way, allied with those who are humiliated and disappointed in Socialist countries as well. These mutual self-distinctions are very helpful, for they indicate that in our present day the front in the struggle for freedom runs right through the

70

churches and parties. The nonconformists of all countries and parties recognize each other in order possibly to form a new alliance. But the history of freedom reaches further, as one may suppose, than these very important alternatives.[3]

Freedom out of Christ

When the Christian faith came into being in the ancient world, a new kind of man was born. For him the act of existing no longer meant entering into a relationship with the eternal rules of polis and cosmos, but now meant to be set free through Christ for a life of free decisions. Thus life in history was made meaningful for the first time. The past was considered to be the power of sin; the future, the dynamics of grace; and the present, the time of decision.[4] This was the pattern of the Christians' struggle against the idolatry of nature, of fate, and of political power. They did away with the idolatry of nature because they believed in God the Creator. They did away with the idolatry of fate in history because they hoped for the kingdom of freedom. They demythologized the cult of Caesar because they worshiped God in the name of the crucified one. Christianity always took a stand for the coming theocracy of freedom; otherwise it would not have been persecuted. Christianity was thus to some extent historically justified in participating in the Constantinian effort to Christianize the world of that time, for Christians considered Constantine to be the emperor of peace over the expected kingdom of freedom (Eusebius of Caesarea). However, out of this realization of freedom there grew, at the same time, its well-known disappointment. Out of this situation was born the next task in the history of freedom: the liberation of the church from the power of a Christian Caesar.

The Freedom of the Church

The spell of the Constantinian age—that is, Christian faith in terms of the ancient Roman religion—was not broken until

---

[3] Cf. Eugen Rosenstock-Huessy, *Die europäischen Revolutionen und der Charakter der Nationen* (3rd. ed., 1951).
[4] Cf. Rudolf Bultmann, *Theology of the New Testament* (New York: Charles Scribner's Sons, 1961), chaps. 38–40.

the great revolution of the papacy and the church reform of Cluny in the Middle Ages. In the struggle between Pope and Caesar concerning "ecclesiastical investiture," the church recovered her autonomy and, with it, the possibility of acting freely. But there was more in it than meets the eye: The Kingdom of God on earth was now embodied in the power of the keys of the Pope and the church rather than in the government of an anointed Christian Caesar. *Libertas ecclesiae* became the slogan for the "realm of freedom" in the Middle Ages. However, this new Christian freedom had its price: the clericalization of the church. Clericalization marked a bad consequence of the magnificent liberation of the church from the emperor. Everybody could see that this church was not yet the "realm of freedom" itself.

The Freedom of a Christian Man

The Reformation was not simply a protest against the clericalization of Christian freedom. Here the birth of a new kind of man took place once again. According to Luther's treatise, "The Freedom of a Christian" (1520) and Calvin's chapter "De libertate Christiana" (*Institutes*, III, 19), freedom is born out of the justifying gospel in everyone who believes. If Christ himself is the ground of freedom in everyone's life, everyone becomes "a perfectly free lord of all, subject to none." However, if the ground of this freedom lies in the crucified Christ, every believer voluntarily becomes "a perfectly dutiful servant of all, subject to all." In the congregation of brotherhood without hierarchy everyone becomes "Christ" to his fellow man. The privileges of the clergy are liquidated for the sake of the "common priesthood of all believers." Every worldly work is understood to be a divine calling into the liberation of the world from the realm of Satan.

The Reformation of the Christian freedom, however, has brought forth its perversions, too. The redresses of the princes and landed nobles who truly loved to fight for *religio et libertas* finally developed into a Protestant form of Constantinianism, a new particular religion of the national well-being, oppressing the enthusiastic wing of the Reformation and dividing the unity of the church. And here can be found the origin of the well-known resignation on the Continent which no longer seeks the Kingdom of God and man's freedom outwardly in social and political change, but inwardly alone, deep in the ground of the individual's soul.

These new chains of freedom were effectively broken first by West European reformations. In the name of the common "kinghood of all believers," Calvinism struggled against the absolutist sovereigns. In the struggle for the freedom of conscience the state was neutralized in England. The Presbyterians succeeded in establishing the right of free congregations against the state church. The congregation consists of free people who are all born to be rulers, not slaves, because they all exist in the image of God, said John Milton. Therefore, the crown rests upon the democratic constitution of the free and not upon the head of a divinely appointed person. The freedom of being created in God's image was thus maintained over against the sinful supremacy of men over men. The perversions of this freedom movement originated from the fact that freedom and the right of lifting up one's head was limited to the "Christian man." This is the reason why this movement was soon taken over and surpassed by the humanism of the Enlightenment, for the realm of freedom is characterized by universality and breaks up all limitations and barriers created by man.

The Freedom of the Citizen

In the definition of human rights in America and France, freedom finally becomes a secular phenomenon. Man is born free. This freedom of man is not to be denied or abandoned. It has to be the irreducible basis of civil rights in society. Everybody has the right to determine freely and to seek his fortune and happiness as long as he respects the same freedom of others. Therefore everybody has the right to criticize all kinds of "happiness" imposed on him "from above" or by his peers. These personal liberties are unforgettable once they are articulated.

The free development of the humane in every single person

73

is the presupposition of the humanization of society. But these liberties have also brought forth their inevitable disappointments. There was, first, the disillusionment of the French Revolution. People had stormed the barricades for the sake of "human rights" with the despicable result that political rights were disposed of by the propertied citizens. On the other hand, there is the general misery of the bourgeois society, which "does not permit man to find the realization but rather the barrier of his freedom in the other person," as Karl Marx rightly pointed out.[5]

The Socialism of Freedom

The civil revolution had not done away with the difference between "man" and "citizen." This became the starting point for the next, the Socialist revolution, which wants to liberate men from economic slavery. Its way thus leads from the propertied bourgeois society and its private men to Socialism and its "men in society." From the political emancipation of men it turns to the social emancipation of men, from which the "human emancipation of every person" is expected—"an association, in which the free development of every person implies the free development of all men" (*The Communist Manifesto*). This represents a change from the society of *having* to a society of authentic human *being*. The starting point of this Socialist revolution lies in the disillusionary experiences of the French and capitalistic revolutions. Its goal of making man free from his economic misery is a new and significant step toward the universal and eschatological hope of freedom for the whole suffering creation, which is the Christian hope for the salvation of the body.

Nonetheless, this movement of freedom has its perversions too, and has also added its own chapter to the history of the disappointment of mankind. This disappointing experience is not simply represented by Stalinism, which is horrible to many people. It lies, rather, in the foreboding that the expected "hu-

[5] Karl Marx, *Die Frühschriften*, ed. S. Landshut (Stuttgart: Kröners Taschenausgabe, 1953), p. 193.

man emancipation of man" will not come automatically when the economic liberation of men in the Socialist industrial states has taken place. This disappointment will certainly become the motor of post-Marxist revolutions. The relation between the "realm of freedom" and the "realm of work" remains ambiguous even in Karl Marx. On the one hand, he describes the "kingdom of freedom" as a sudden transition or change of quantity into new quality. The realm of freedom suspends all labor, changing all work into absolutely free "self-activity." "In a communist society, there will no longer be any painters but, at most, people, who among other things, like to paint," he says in his early writings.[6] On the other hand, in his later writings Marx described the "realm of freedom" as the outcome of the "realm of work." If this is the case, however, the "realm of freedom" will be forever combined with the "realm of work" and can move forward only in the leisure hours of men guaranteed by automatization and the shortening of working hours. Everybody knows, however, that a man with more leisure time does not necessarily become a free man. "Should it be the effect of the great revolution that the number of French sportsmen and anglers is being enlarged?" Jules Romain asked incisively. Consequently, we must make clear whether and how men may become children of freedom so that they may engage in free work. Are we, here and now, children of freedom or is freedom the reward of our good deeds? If freedom is nothing more than the reward for, or success of, our deeds, then men will always remain unfree. This is the question of the Reformation to Marxism. This is the question of freedom through faith to the modern form of justification by works.

The disappointment that in the last analysis Marxism has only advanced industrialization without bringing about the longed-for humanization frustrates the young working people of today in the East, just as competition frustrates their counterparts in the West. The disappointment that the demanded "abolition of the state" has only strengthened the bureaucracy

[6] *Ibid.*, p. 475.

of the ruling elite is today also agonizing Marxists. "In the citizen of the French Revolution the burgeois was hidden. God have mercy on us, we cannot tell what may be hidden in the comrade," said the Marxist Ernst Bloch in 1930.[7] In struggling against the freedom of competition in the capitalist society, Karl Marx is, in a deeply Christian sense, right when he says that true freedom means "for me to have been the mediator between you and the species, so as to be known and experienced by you as a completion of your own nature and as a necessary part of your self and therefore for you to know me confirmed in your thought as well as in your love."[8] But what is the "true essence of the species of men" and which group is authorized to determine it? Have not certain groups in society used such collective categories as the "true essence of the human species" and the "universal moral code" in order to mask their claims on power? Truly, it is contradictory to the freedom of man to be made happy "from above" and to be put under categories of his essence represented by a party or a church. That is contradictory to his history which is open to the future. Is there not also a personal freedom of man which is not the freedom of profit-making wolves but which presupposes human progress in science and culture? Today we find exactly these basic ideas of a liberal Socialism in the Polish Marxists Adam Schaff and Leszew Kolakowski: It is impossible to make people happy by force. But you can eliminate the enormous causes of misfortune (A. Schaff).[9] Whoever defends personal freedom defends human progress (Kolakowski).

[7] Bloch, *Spuren* (1930), p. 32; rev. ed. Frankfurt: Suhrkamp Verlag, 1959.
[8] Marx, *Mega*, Vol. I, No. 3, p. 546.
[9] Adam Schaff, *Marxismus und das menschliche Individuum* (Frankfurt: Europa Verlag, 1965), p. 236: "If one begins to construct definitions of happiness and to derive out of them obligatory norms of conduct for man—naturally for his own welfare!—then even in socialism the danger of 'making men happy' 'from above' can suddenly emerge. The attempt to make men happy through coercion and according to the currently accepted models of happiness can become the cause of an enormous unhappiness. . . . Since there is not such a thing as a happiness which applies to all, one should not seek to create a uniform model of a happy life for all." The real foundation for the activity directed toward human happiness lies not in the understanding "that we make men happy but that we eliminate the exceedingly offensive causes of his unhappiness."

Integration of Freedom Movements

The freedom movements based on Christian faith, on the church, on the conscience, on the citizen and Socialism have succeeded one another in such a way that the one caught fire in the disappointing consequences of the preceding one as each strove for greater freedom. So far, no one of them has brought about the "realm of freedom" itself, but each one has opened a new front in the struggle for freedom. None of these revolutions was as yet the "last battle," although everyone set out under this apocalyptic sign, be it the struggle against Antichrist, against the beast coming out of the "bottomless pit" (Rev. 17:8), or against the class-enemy. Therefore, these movements have always corrected each other. The older brother on the road to freedom must warn his younger brother lest the younger give up liberties already won for the sake of a new liberty.

A revolution has to assimilate the tradition of the former revolutions, otherwise it achieves not more freedom but simply another liberty. On the other hand, tradition must adapt itself to revolution, otherwise it will not prevail over its own disappointments. Such an integration of Catholics, Protestants, Liberals, and Marxists is possible once all of them learn to look beyond their own systems forward to the future of the realm of freedom.

3

THE REALM OF FREEDOM

Until now, Christians and Marxists were involved in a struggle of different ideological positions which excluded and limited each other. Today we have come *de l'anathème au dialogue* (*From Anathema to Dialogue: A Marxist Challenge to the Christian Churches*, by R. Garaudy). We are criticizing each other in order to help each other to realize the best of both our positions. We shall be able to go beyond the dialogue forward to a cooperation if both sides comprehend that they do not constitute "positions" or "standpoints" but are, rather, ways directed toward a yet unknown human future. In many respects these ways could run parallel and supplement each other. In the first place, it is common to Christians and Marxists to suffer under the real misery of mankind. This suffering is always the negative form of hope for the future of men. The Marxists see the misery of man represented in his political dependence, in his economic slavery, and in his being tied up with nature and fate. Thus freedom implies to their understanding the abolition of the dominion of men over men, the ending of exploitation of men by men and, finally, the exaltation of a united mankind in which man will be the creator of his own history.

Christians understand that the misery of men does not simply lie in their not-yet-realized possibilities, but even deeper in man's real impossibilities or his lost possibilities. He is enslaved under the dominion of sin, that is, the failure of life because of selfishness and fear. He is handed over to death, transitoriness, and nothingness. Finally, he is exploited by law, which commands him to live in freedom without giving it to him. Hence freedom implies to them liberation from the curse of the evil deed through grace; it implies freedom from death and fear through hope in the coming God, and freedom from the law of works through faith.

When we compare both sides, we do not find them simply to oppose each other. What Christians call the misery of man includes, by all means, political, social, and natural misery and does not exclude these forms, as *Christianity Today* does: ". . . man's problem lies in his sins against the creator, not in domination by capitalistic economic forces."[10] The real possibilities after which Marxists are striving to overcome this misery are also possibilities for the Christians' struggle for freedom.

Nevertheless, the two sides are not exactly identical. Wherever freedom from misery and inhumanity can really be achieved, socially and politically, there Christians discover the

[10] "The Danger of the Christian-Marxist Dialogue," *Christianity Today*, XII (1967), p. 27.

immanence of their hope. But wherever in the necessary struggle against evil in the world new dependencies are being produced, there Marxists discover the transcendence of hope. For the realm of freedom is always more than the fragments of a free life which we may accomplish in history. Immanence and transcendence of freedom are not divided dichotomously into two realms like earth and heaven; rather, they form dialectically two aspects of freedom's history. The immanent significance of hope for salvation is visible wherever the emancipation of men from the chains of slavery takes place in history. On the other hand, hope for salvation from this hostile world of history is the transcendence of all attempts to make this world the homeland for all people. If we conceive that salvation be the transcendence for the immanent emancipation movement of men, then the Christians' "beyond" is not a compensation or "the opium of the people" any more, but is the power and the ferment of emancipation here and now. Traditionally we have always combined reconciliation with God with the conservation of the earth. But there is no reconciliation without transformation, that is, without personal repentance and social revolution.

Since Feuerbach and Marx, Christians and Marxists have readily "divvied up" "heaven" and "earth." Heinrich Heine mused: "We relinquish heaven to the angels and the birds."

Today we find an attempt to combine both again. Marxists are pleased to quote the sentence of Teilhard de Chardin: "The world will not be converted to the heavenly promise of Christianity unless Christianity has previously been converted to the promise of the earth." On the other hand, theologians are delighted when Roger Garaudy says: "The Christian can open the Marxist to the idea of transcendence."

I think we can overcome this kind of division and combination if we begin to take notice of the eschatological category *novum*. Why do Christians seek their salvation in heaven and why do they feel redeemed by heavenly promises, if the first heaven will pass away and be replaced by a new heaven? (Rev.

79

21:1). Even "in heaven" Christians will not be safe from the future of the God who judges and creates everything anew. On the other hand, one can ask why the Marxists seek their salvation on the earth and feel secure in earthly promises, if it may be likewise true that "this" earth does not endure but will pass away. Neither heaven nor earth, neither history nor transcendence are, in the last analysis, secure places. There is salvation only in the new creation of heaven and earth, history and transcendence. The "powers of the future world" are historically effective in the "criticism of heaven" just as in the "criticism of earth," i.e., in the liberation from religious and ideological superstition as well as in the liberation from the anonymous and repressive powers of society and from the obstinacy of human work.

We need this power of the new and of the future in order to act with certainty in the midst of the ambiguities of history and of human activity, even our own. All struggles for freedom are ambivalent: How can alienated people struggle against alienation without, in their struggle, producing new alienations? That is the question for the Marxists who see the guilt of Stalinism. How can sinners struggle against sin without producing new sins? That is the question for the Christians who suffer under the guilt of the church. How can the kingdom of nonviolent brotherhood be won without using violence? That is the open question on both sides. For the most part, moral and revolutionary enthusiasm has overlooked this "cross of reality" (Hegel). Therefore, enthusiasm quickly turns into resignation. By believing only in the "hereafter" the church has tried to view this cross of history as a tragic "vale of tears." In this posture, it was simply waiting for a far-off salvation, while in the meantime stabilizing conservative and repressive powers. Both ways of thinking are one-sided. Revolution of freedom is alive where people hear the categorical imperative "to overthrow all circumstances in which man is a humiliated, an enslaved, a forsaken, and a despised being." Karl Marx is completely right in this. And if his critique of religion ends with this categorical or eschatological imperative, it is better than all demythologizing of Christianity by theologians too well adjusted to the social, economic, and political status quo. This revolution of freedom, however, attains its end only if we find the certitude that future and freedom do indeed gracefully meet us in our revolutionary struggle.

While Bertolt Brecht was in exile during the era of the Third Reich, he wrote his most thoughtful poem. It says:

> We who wished to prepare the soil for kindness
> could not be kind ourselves.
> But you, when at last it will come to pass that
> man is a helper to man,
> remember us with forbearance.

In a secular way, he has taken up what the continuous plea for reconciliation means to the Christian faith.

It is time now for all the different freedom movements to cooperate in a brotherly way, for the misery of mankind has not become less urgent. The disappointments are growing.

I think it is impossible to reduce Christianity and Marxism with their divergent positive conceptions to a lowest common denominator. But a Christian–Marxist cooperation in the present necessary negation of the negative is indeed quite conceivable. In the first place, there can be created a common future only out of the common averting of common threats by evil, such as atomic war, catastrophes of famine, and so forth. This method has the advantage (1) of solidarizing very different men and groups, and (2) of leaving open to them the freedom of shaping their own future. We may not know what true humanity is and how a just order of the world looks. But what mankind should not be and which order of things is false we can know by consideration of the past and also by consideration of the future's possible development. Only in the concrete negation of the negative is the other, the positive, open to us. *Solidarity* in suffering and in struggling against evil, *lib-*

81

erality in goods of the positive and the *future* belong inexorably together.

None of the freedom movements mentioned above has already brought freedom itself, but we find roads leading to its future in all of them. The realm of freedom is greater than all of them. It inspires all our endeavors, but it also condemns all our presumptions, and comforts us where we become guilty. At all frontiers of life the summons of the prophet Isaiah (61:1) is to be heard:

> to bind up the brokenhearted,
> to proclaim liberty to the captives,

for these are the opportunities of the messianic age, in which, because Christ is born, we live.

V ✦ Toward a Political Hermeneutic of the Gospel

1
THE ORIGIN OF THE PROBLEM

The modern historical consciousness can be characterized as a crisis consciousness because with the beginning of modern times the traditions and the institutions which regulate life have become uncertain and insecure. New experiences of history compel critical revision of the former structures of life. And, on the other hand, historical criticism of traditions and ideological criticism of social and political institutions produce a revolutionary freedom which undermines prejudice against novelty in the future.[1]

At the beginning of modern times historical criticism was directly bound up with revolutionary criticism. It began by unmasking the authoritarian myths of the contemporary powers of church and state. Then in the name of the comprehensive and many-faceted truth, it turned its attention to the Scriptures

This lecture was delivered at Vanderbilt Divinity School, February 2, 1968, and at School of Theology at Claremont, February 19, 1968. It appeared in *Union Seminary Quarterly Review*, XXIII (Summer, 1968), pp. 303–323, in a slightly different form.

[1] The "sole historical-empirical foundation of all these institutions and the stripping away of all of their absolute validity is taken care of today by sciences which are thoroughly historicizing in their methods. They are therefore shaken by the most emphatic and complete of all revolutions that there could be. This is also true of all authorities and norms" (F. Gogarten, "Historismus," *Zwischen den Zeiten*, 2/8 [1924], p. 8).

in order to undermine the church's claim to authority. As Wilhelm Dilthey has written: "The historical consciousness breaks the last chains which philosophy and natural science could not rend asunder. Now man stands there completely free."[2] Thus, in the hands of the historical critic, history becomes a kind of judgment upon every metaphysical or dogmatic claim to absolutism. Two problems have arisen out of the combination of crisis consciousness and historical criticism:

1. When the historical basis of a tradition is subjected to criticism, a gulf develops between the past, from which it emerges and to which it belongs, and the present, in which it claims validity. In the first phase of the Enlightenment, this distance between past and present meant the liberation of man from the guardianship of tradition and from the burdens of the past. Historical reflection on a present power, be it the state, the social order, or the church, serves to set free one's own experience and one's own creative powers for the future.[3] This relationship of the historical critique of tradition and the sociological critique of institutions to our freedom in the present for the future needs to be vividly brought back into our consciousness to counteract the increasing haziness in the notion of historical criticism. Historical criticism produces freedom, and freedom, in turn, manifests itself in historical criticism of all repressive powers.

This does not mean that modern, historical critical research is a child of the Protestant freedom of belief. This "renowned page" in history also bears ideological traces of later adoption.[4]

---

[2] Wilhelm Dilthey, *Gesammelte Schriften*, VIII (Stuttgart: B. G. Teubner Verlagsgesellschaft, 1960), p. 225.

[3] Thus, on the contrary, in the course of the restoration in the nineteenth century, the revolutionary spirit of Democrats and Socialists was reproached again and again for its lack of tradition. Cf. e.g., A. F. C. Vilmar, "Kirche und Welt," *Gesammelte Aufsätze*, I (1872), p. 17: "Of course it appears that the calling of the German people for a thousand years will in the not too distant future come to a perhaps ignominious end, because . . . . For their part, a very great mass of people have purposefully and consciously turned their backs on all former times."

[4] This must be maintained, in all honesty, against the familiar and oft-repeated assertions of A. Schweitzer and P. Tillich about the "act of truthfulness" of Protestant historical criticism.

For when the historical basis of one tradition is uncovered, other traditions simultaneously appear once more. That which has been forgotten is retrieved and the historical horizon of the present extends backward. History no longer merely binds one to a particular tradition that he may call his own, but it becomes the broader field of past human possibilities. When the compulsive character of the present is broken critically by the tradition of one's own past, this past loses its claim to absolutism and becomes relative to other truths in history. Historical criticism supports freedom *of* the Christian faith as well as freedom *from* the Christian faith. And historical criticism's mirror image, the pluralistic society, functions in the same way in relation to the church.

2. With the consciousness of the distance between the present and a diverse past, the other problem of the appropriation of history arises. In the last phase of the Enlightenment the romantic philosophy of history took up this question. It recognized the peculiar character of traditions as they are at home in their own original place and time. The historical gulf was bridged with the help of the idea of organism. Through this idea each epoch of history could be understood in its uniqueness, and simultaneously, as a constitutive element in world history, each epoch could assume its unique value in relation to the present.[5] For the critical consciousness of freedom in the initial period of the Enlightenment, however, the manner of appropriating the past with the help of the idea of organism was nothing more than the old heteronomy of the tradition dressed up in new garb. In fact, the romantic philosophy of history mustered the historical traditions against the spirit of the Enlightenment, and the powers of the "holy alliance" against revolution in order to conquer the terrors of freedom. It still performs this function even today. Therefore, the question is one of how the past can be brought into the consciousness of the present, so that the freedom of the present for the future can be maintained or increased without being limited or de-

[5] Cf. W. Maurer, *Aufklärung, Idealismus und Restauration*, II (1930), esp. pp. 115ff.

stroyed by the prejudices of tradition or by subordination to an ideology of history.

There is a special problem for the Christian tradition and for Christian freedom: Within the framework of the free and undetermined understanding of the Christian tradition and proclamation, how can we come to an understanding of the necessity of this proclamation? And how can we arrive at the necessity of understanding and appropriating precisely *this* tradition? Even if the hermeneutical dialogue between the Christian text and the present is opened, the question still remains for the most part unheeded and unanswered: Why dialogue precisely with *these texts* and with *this past*? As long as hermeneutical theology does not answer this question, it still lives on the interest of that churchly tradition which the texts present to it. And it is thus a continuation of traditionalism by other means. But behind this question, *How* can and should we understand the Christian tradition today? presses the even more radical question, Why are we compelled today to preach precisely these texts, to understand and to believe them?

2

THE HERMENEUTIC OF WILHELM DILTHEY

From Wilhelm Dilthey comes the famous definition, "Hermeneutic is the art of understanding written expressions of life."[6] Life and expression of life and understanding of life constitute here the nature of the historical world. They indicate both the distance and the common factor in history. Between the written expressions of life in the past and those who try to understand today lie the distances of history; nevertheless, there also lies here a common communication with unfathomable life itself. Dilthey calls "life" this ground out of which all historical manifestations originate, insofar as they are "expressions of life." On the one hand, it is unfathomable and inexhaustible; on the other, it is objectified in ever new histori-

---

[6] W. Dilthey, *Gesammelte Schriften*, V (Stuttgart, 1957), pp. 332f.

cal expressions of life. "Only through the idea of the objectification of life do we achieve an insight into the nature of the
historical. . . . What the spirit projects today of its character in
its expression of life, is tomorrow history as it stands before
us."[7] Still, this expression of life would be quite foreign and
inaccessible if we ourselves did not participate in life and did
not have to form objectifications of our own lives. "We are first
of all historical beings before we become observers of history
and because we are the former, we become the latter."[8]

So against the obscure background of the common flow of
life, there is the possibility of understanding the historical expressions of life. Presupposition for the interpretation of strange
texts is therefore the previous relation of the interpreter to life
itself, through whose objectification he can understand the
phenomena of history. But when there are innumerable objectifications of life, how can they be understood in their individual and peculiar significance? How can they, in their incon-
gruence and their lack of simultaneity with the present, be
shown to be meaningful, without becoming immediately
swallowed by the presupposed, dark flow of life for which
they are only signs, expressions, and manifestations?

Dilthey attempted to evade the obvious pantheistic, historical relativism and struck against a deeper aporia: The real
meaning of individual historical phenomena can only be disclosed in their associations with other such phenomena and
this means only in view of the whole of history. This totality
is, however, not available and cannot be surveyed because we
do not yet stand at the end of history. "One has to wait until
the end of the course of his life and he can only survey the
whole in the hour of his death. Only from this vantage point
would his part of the relationship be ascertainable. One has to
await the end of history in order to possess all of the material
necessary for the determination of its meaning."[9] This necessary view of the individual case from the vantage point of the

[7] *Ibid.*, VII (Stuttgart, 1958), p. 147
[8] *Ibid.*, p. 258.
[9] *Ibid.*, p. 253.

whole, which is not really accomplishable by historical beings, would be the deductive method. But, on the other hand, re-membered phenomena of the past can become quite meaningful for us insofar as they open up possibilities of the future and thereby direct the present to a responsible determination of goals. A moment of the past becomes for us "meaningful inso-far as in it a bond with the future is effected by a deed or through an external event. Or to the extent that the plan of the way life is to be conducted in the future is conceived. . . . What we set as the goal of our future serves the determination of the meaning of the past."[10] The individual's view of the greater whole and his view from the past upon the future, for which he is to be responsible, is the other, more inductive side of understanding. Nevertheless, only the end of existence and the end of all things conclusively opens up history in the signifi-cance of its parts and moments.

Let us set aside here the fact that death need not in any way be identical with the consummation of life, but is the disintegration of what cannot be completed. Let us set aside, too, the fact that the end of history need not be the consum-mation of the whole but, rather, the conclusion of the imperfect, incompletable, and ambiguous. Yet, the reflections of Dilthey make it clear that hermeneutic need not end in historical rela-tivism, but that the meaning of past expressions of life, to-gether with the present's responsible determination of goals for the future, can be attained. In these determinations we ac-cept responsibility for the whole and, simultaneously, respon-sibility for the past.

3

EXISTENTIALIST HERMENEUTIC

For the existential thinker the actual meaning of particular historical events does not lie in the speculative association of

[10] *Ibid.*

the objectifications or manifestations of history. Therefore Kierkegaard objected against Hegel: "Demoralized by too assiduous an absorption in world-historical considerations, people no longer have any will for anything except what is world-historically significant, no concern for anything but the accidental, the world-historical outcome, instead of concerning themselves solely with the essential, the inner spirit, the ethical, freedom."[11] In Heidegger's existentialist analysis, history is no longer viewed as the self-development of the absolute spirit as it was with Hegel. Neither is it seen as the expression of the life of the unfathomable life but, rather, as being grounded in the "historicity of existence." "And because Dasein, *and only Dasein*, is primordially historical, that which historiological thematizing presents as a possible object for research [that is, world history], must have the kind of Being of *Dasein which has-been-there*."[12] The totalization of all particular moments and parts of history is therefore not to be sought in a future end of world history, but is to be decided in one's historical ability to be integral in the face of death. Accordingly, history is no longer questioned about its actual developments and tendencies, but about the possibilities of existence which have always been inherent in it.

Rudolf Bultmann also brings the biblical texts to present understanding with this general presupposition. On the basis of the questionableness of being, they disclose possibilities of human existence. If a certain self-understanding expresses itself in the texts, then a genuine understanding must engage the question it answers and the claim it makes, the claim which summons one to the responsible acceptance of one's own existence. This general approach, however, insofar as it has any validity at all for the understanding of texts from the past does not yet grasp the special claim of the New Testament texts,

[11] S. Kierkegaard, *Concluding Unscientific Postscript*, trans. Swenson and Lowrie (Princeton: Princeton University Press, 1941), p. 121.
[12] Martin Heidegger, *Being and Time*, trans. Macquarrie and Robinson (New York: Harper & Row, 1962), p. 445.

for in biblical hermeneutic there is something unique. This unique something is the *kerygma,* which is not identical with the foundation of the historicity of being but constitutes something like its own history of proclamation, the history in which Christian faith occurs.

Of course, this existential event of the kerygma can be understood only in the framework of existentialist analysis and existentialist interpretation. But it is not identical with this. The appeal of the existentialist interpretation of the event of word and faith lies in the intelligibility of the new existence it promises to the believer. Its limitation lies in the undemonstrable nature of the ground of kerygma and faith. Is it enough to be constantly aware of the significance of the Christian kerygma in the correlation of claim and decision in one's being? Must not the meaning of the proclamation, rather, be perceived, for its own sake, in the historical horizon of total being? In this way the unique Christ event can be conveyed as the ground of the kerygma with its own goals of the Kingdom of God and freedom. And the history of proclamation, inclusive of the new existence in faith, is grasped as the means of this conveyance. This does not mean replacing faith with an idea of world history, but bringing faith to its historical self-consciousness.

Here we must mention another line of Bultmann's thinking which corresponds to what Dilthey emphasized. It is known that the modern problem of historical distance determines certain alternatives for Bultmann: either objectification or personal encounter and decision. But Bultmann also intimates a third perspective, which is adapted to overcome that new form of the subject-object scheme (as Wilhelm Kamlah calls it), without suppressing it. At this point the alternative between "the historical fact in itself" and "the historical event for me" is finally bypassed and relativized with respect to "the future," for which historical events and persons are open. Therefore "to each historical phenomenon" belongs "its future, in which it first shows itself for what it is; more exactly, in which it *in-*

creasingly shows itself for what it is."[13] Also, one's own present
is related to the future insofar as it is accepted in responsibility.
With this, the relationship between past and present, between
event and existence, falls into a framework of "the end of history"
insofar as the future which will finally reveal the significance of
history will be "the end of history." The dualism in the dialogue of historical understanding becomes a dialectic including
a common third factor or shared middle term. The "future,"
which belongs to historical phenomena and brings out their
meaning, is also the future for which the present, if it wishes
to be a historical present, must assume responsibility. For this
reason, the "future" mediates between past and present, making the dialogue of historical understanding necessary. For
Bultmann, however, this line of thought soon breaks down. For
him knowledge of the end of world history is "presumptuous."
Therefore the question of the sense of the whole course of
history is already meaningless.

This resignation, however, does not appear logical to the
impartial reader. When a question cannot be answered because
all of the previous answers prove inadequate, must the question therefore be meaningless? Does it not then become an
open question? In this case, it has its basis in the openness of
history. In the openness of history alone can the future give a
judgment about the meaning and significance of the past and
the present.

For the quest for sense and purpose of world history, Bultmann substitutes the search for the meaning of the history of
existence, i.e., the search in the individual case for one's own
being.[14] Only he who is moved to participation in history, he
who accepts responsibility for the future, can understand the
"language of history." This is evident, but his qualifying post-

---

[13] Cf. "Wissenschaft und Existenz," *Glauben und Verstehen*, III (Tübingen,
1960), pp. 113–115.
[14] Cf. R. Bultmann, *History and Eschatology* (New York: Harper Torchbooks,
1957), p. 155: *"The Meaning in history lies always in the present*, and when
the present is conceived as the eschatological present by the Christian faith,
the meaning in history is realized."

script is not: "Only he who is moved by the question of his own existence is able to hear the claim of history."[15]

Participation in history is participation in the history of mankind, in political, social, and scientific-technical history. This participation, however, leads far beyond the search for the meaning of one's own being. There arises from it a responsibility for the future of the whole and for the future of that which is held in common. In this responsibility one inquires after the goal, purpose, and significance of the course of history in its entirety. A universal historical understanding of the past does not develop out of a speculative interest in unburdening but out of this responsibility for the future itself. Bultmann replaces this universal historical quest for the future with the quest for existence, and thus replaces the theodicy question, which is the search for a just world, with the quest for the identity of one's own existence. But it need not necessarily be taken as a "substitute." The totalization of history in one's striving to be integral can also be understood as an anticipation of the future of world history. On this basis, what Bultmann would like to establish could be meaningful, namely, the responsibility of the present for the future of history. The meaning of a historical phenomenon for one's own existence in the present, then, would be a prolepsis of its meaning in its own future at the end of history. Thus, existentialist interpretation falls into the larger framework of a world historical-eschatological interpretation.

In a certain manner "the end of the world" is actually present in the existence which has come into its freedom over against the world, namely, in present, responsible decision. This is not hampered, however, by the fact that "the end of the world" is still to come: if it had already come, man would no longer have any responsibility for the social and political history of his present which stands before that future. Theologically speaking, the solution of the question of the identity of

15 R. Bultmann, *Glauben und Verstehen*, III (Tübingen: J.C.B. Mohr/Paul Siebeck, 1960), p. 115.

man through word and faith is not the solution of the question of the whole suffering creation waiting for freedom. But the universal solution does come into view for the first time with the appearance of the freedom of the believer. "The end of the world" practiced in the freedom of belief is then the end of the world and the goal of history only when faith understands itself as the anticipation and the representation of the not-yet-realized end of all things and when faith understands itself as the beginning of the liberation of the whole enslaved creation from the power of transitoriness. Faith, as an anticipation of the salvation of the whole, thus opens up a future for the mortal body, for society, and for nature—in short, for everything which still lies in anguish.

In the horizon of the theodicy question the resurrection of the crucified Jesus by God is understandable as the beginning of the new creation of God's righteousness, which corresponds only *provisionally* to faith but *conclusively* to a new world. In effect, this transforms faith from deliverance from the world into an initiative that changes the world and shapes those who believe into worldly, personal, social, and political witnesses to God's righteousness and freedom in the midst of a repressive society and an unredeemed world. In this conception, faith comes to historical self-consciousness and to the recognition of its eschatological task within history.

4

REVOLUTIONARY HISTORICAL HERMENEUTIC

On the way to a political hermeneutic, we cannot neglect Karl Marx. His purely political analysis of religion is intended as "irreligious critique" of religion. This is literally what Bonhoeffer set out to do in the inception of his "non-religious interpretation of biblical concepts." Still, for the young Marx it is a matter neither of an *interpretation* of the transmitted Christian tradition nor of a rationalistic *enlightenment* of the "essence of Christianity" (Ludwig Feuerbach). Rather, he is

93

concerned with the historical, which means social and political, *realization* of religion: "What was an inner light becomes a consuming flame turned outward."[16] If the beginning of the critique of religion lies with Feuerbach's referring all religions back to mysticism, the reversal of mysticism into revolution[17] becomes the spear point of the Marxist criticism of religion. If we take this aspect into hermeneutic, the historical work in tradition and proclamation is radically altered. Rather than mere interpretation of past history, it becomes an effort to realize what is announced historically under present circumstances.

Religion for the young Marx is the illusory expression of the alienated man because this expression is held captive in a "perverted consciousness of the world." It is the "fantastic realization of the human essence, because human essence does not have a true reality."[18] Religion is thus a realization of human existence, but only in fantasy. Its conceptions of the true nature of man are correct, but as mere conceptions they remain incongruent with the reality of the "vale of tears." While Bultman criticizes the conceptions of religion as myths in order to interpret them existentially on the basis of man's self-understanding, Marx criticizes the evil reality which forces man to deceive himself by representing his happiness and his true nature in illusory religious conceptions. While with Bultmann the existentially interpreted myths still remain myths, Marx seeks a way of overcoming myths in a changed and new reality. Religious conceptions are determined by three factors. They are the *expression* of real misery; simultaneously they are *protestations* against real afflictions; and taken as mere conceptions, they are the *opium* of suffering people.[19] Religion therefore originates in the concrete experience of the difference between

---

[16] K. Marx, *Die Frühschriften*, ed. S. Landshut (Stuttgart, Kröners Taschenausgabe, 1953), p. 17.
[17] Cf. K. Mannheim, *Ideologie and Utopie* (3rd ed.; Frankfurt, 1952), pp. 184ff.
[18] K. Marx, *Die Frühschriften*, op. cit., p. 208.
[19] *Ibid.*

existence and essence. It will be placed on its feet when its conceptions are no longer an escape from this painful difference into another world and when it no longer serves to promote resignation to these afflictions. Religion must, rather, be conceived of as direction for the overcoming of this difference in a revolutionary manner. The "protestation against real affliction" is the unmythological kernel of religion. So the revolutionary realization of human happiness enters into the real inheritance of religion. Revolutionary criticism does not pull the flowers off man's chains so that he will accept his chains, but so that he will throw off his chains and pick the living flower. To this extent this "irreligious critique" is an interpretation of religion through the realization of what was merely conceptualized by religion.

If we admit this, then in no religion is the "character of protest" so vital as in the messianic faith of Christianity. We cannot grasp freedom in faith without hearing simultaneously the categorical imperative to serve through bodily, social, and political obedience for the liberation of the suffering creation out of real affliction. If we grasp only the promise of freedom in faith and forget the realistic demand for the liberation of the world, the gospel becomes the religious basis for the justification of society as it is and a mystification of the suffering reality. It results in the "easygoing flesh" of old and new "realists" when the criticism of religion leads only to criticism of the heavens in demythologization and not simultaneously to the criticism of the earth, to the criticism of politics and of law. The radical consequence of the criticism of myths is not existential interpretation, but revolutionary realization of freedom within present conditions. As long as mythical conceptions are considered to be simply "expressions" of human self-understanding and not agonizing protests against real misery, demythologizing interpretation remains in the dimension of the "fantastic" and does not approach the messianic kernel of the Christian proclamation.

The criterion for the criticism of Christian myths cannot

95

simply be the changing of modern man's world-views. It is the cross of Christ. When we understand the cross of Christ in this connection as an "expression" of real human affliction, then the resurrection of Christ acquires the significance of the true "protest" against human affliction. Consequently, the missionary proclamation of the cross of the resurrected one is not an opium of the people which intoxicates and incapacitates them, but the ferment of new freedom. It leads to the awakening of that revolt which in the "power of the resurrection," as Paul expresses it, follows the categorical imperative to overthrow all conditions in which man is a being who labors and is heavily laden. Paul has done this for his time, when religion and idols repressed mankind, with the gospel of free justification. Today the misery of men is no longer determined by a coterie of idols to which they are subjected. How, then, must religion's character of protest against the present affliction of humanity appear today? Religious Christianity has preserved the "inner light" down through the centuries. Again and again it has become the consuming flame directed outward. How must the inner light force its way out today?

Within hermeneutical reflection this development of the question of understanding into revolutionary transformation is possible as soon as the horizon of understanding for the possibilities of human existence is extended to the "horizon of concern" (W. Pannenberg) for the possibilities of history. The biblical texts outline a horizon of concern between the Christ event, on one hand, and the future of Christ and the kingdom of freedom, on the other. But if one is aware of this, then in the horizon of the present personal, social, and political lack of freedom, he must surely ask how the biblical horizon of freedom can be mediated to the oppressions of the present. From this vantage point, then, textual exegesis is no longer merely a peculiar concern of self-understanding which upon occasion wishes to correspond in understanding. It is more a matter of a special understanding which strives for practical congruence between the biblical tradition's horizon of concern and the conditions of the present. It is therefore an understanding which perceives the needs and the opportunities of present social reality. The desire for practical correspondence cannot get bogged down in endeavors at understanding. Then it would only be the mystification of the present. The effective, revolutionary transformation of the present state of affairs is much more the consequence of an understanding intimacy with the biblical proclamation.

With this in mind, it will also be clear *why* exactly this Christian tradition and proclamation necessitates understanding and cannot, as with other traditions of the past, be appropriated arbitrarily or simply forgotten. If the biblical texts present a horizon of concern which encroaches upon the whole affliction of the present and indicates for it the new possibilities of a future open to God, then out of an indeterminate historical observation will come a passionate understanding captivated by the future. Proclamation, through its annunciation of new freedom, becomes the denunciation of the bondage and fettering of the present to the past. Just as the "inner light" in Marx's image forces its way outward as the "consuming flame," so the understanding of the biblical proclamation turns from the inner harmony of faith to embodied obedience and political action for the liberation of mankind from present misery. This obedience is no longer the old heteronomy which had to bear the yoke of an authoritative tradition. It is, rather, an understanding obedience that answers the concern of hope and freedom, as represented in the Christian tradition, in the conditions of the present.

5

POLITICAL HERMENEUTIC

Hermeneutic falls into the danger of formalism when it merely seeks in retrospect for an understanding of the past under the conditions of the present. A material hermeneutic, however, must seek the transformation of the present condi-

97

tions. It therefore finds a parallel with the Marxist coordination of theory and practice which is kindled by the conviction that philosophy must be overcome in order to be realized.[20] "The unity of theory and practice designates the truth, which is produced by, and at the same time, is the highest standard of reason; to the extent that within estrangement anything which advances efforts toward the establishment of truth can be called reasonable—reason is the entrance to future truth."[21] Correspondingly, theological hermeneutic is abstract as long as it does not become the theory of practice and sterile when it does not make "the entrance to future truth" possible. Theology serves future freedom to the degree that it prepares the way for it in historical criticism, in ideological criticism and, finally, in criticism of institutions. This criticism must always initially be directed toward its own hindrance to freedom. If we find in the Bible the written promises of freedom and in proclamation the mission of this freedom, then it is the peculiar responsibility of a historical hermeneutic to outline the means and the methods of practical liberation. This hermeneutic can therefore be called a political hermeneutic because it apprehends politics, in the Aristotelian sense of the word, as the inclusive horizon of the life of mankind.

If we analyze the scriptural texts from this viewpoint, with the help of the form-critical method, we come upon the language of apostleship. We find this language among the missionized and missionary groups, in congregations of the assailed and persecuted. In their worship, their proclamation, and their disputations they were concerned not only with an interpretation of the world and a self-understanding, but they also desired to bring something new into the world. Through his gospel, Paul wanted "to bring about the obedience of faith" in all lands (Rom. 1:5; 16:26) and to extend the freedom of faith as the vanguard of the liberation of the world in the future of

[20] *Ibid.*, p. 215.
[21] J. Habermas, "Zur philosophischen Diskussion um Marx und den Marxismus," *Theorie und Praxis, Politica,* II (Berlin: Luchterhand, 1963), p. 316.

Jesus Christ. The content and forms of kerygmatic language are not understandable without consideration of this concrete, missionary initiative.

"The scriptures arose in the service of God, hence there is also appeal to and direction from them," Adolf Schlatter said.[22] The common ground and the common direction of the different proclamations and theologies in differing situations is that social initiative which we most correctly describe as "mission." They all stand in the movement of the apostolate of Christ in an un-redeemed world. If we take account of this alignment, we can no longer read the Bible as "the charter of our religion" or tra-dition; it must, rather, be understood as the creative witness to our call and commission in the world. Only then does he who understands, stand in the same alignment with these texts. If he stands in the same alignment, however, it will be necessary to investigate critically the conceptions of the kerygma in every period of history. But to do this alone would be to remain on a superficial level. One must go deeper and consider the afflic-tion from which the kerygma liberates man in his time. Then one will be in a position to see how the kerygma stands out of joint with his time and how timely it really is. One sees that it does not correspond to his time, but that it brings the Christ of God to expression in a way that frees men and changes their conditions. This contemporaneous noncontemporaneity is the thorn of the gospel which is deeply embedded in history. In it there is expressed a future which has not yet been gleaned from any historical present.

When we find the gospel in the garb of the cosmological metaphysics of another era, there is no sense in describing this as mythological and childish as seen from the plateaus of modern times. Behind this theistic representation of the world into which the kerygma entered stands a real affliction of man-kind: his suffering in the chaos and the absurdity of history and the threat of transiency against him. The doctrine of the two

[22] Adolf Schlatter, *Der Dienst des Christen in der älteren Dogmatik* (1897), p. 69.

natures was not ontological speculation, but the Christian answer of freedom to the agony of transiency. Behind that cosmological representation of the world stands the question of theodicy, the question of suffering in expectation of God's just world. If today the theistic representations of the world are outdated, this interrogation of God about evil and pain is not at all outmoded. The question has merely lost its old cosmological form. It has become more of a political and social question. Therefore, this cosmological theology can be changed into a political theology, because "politically," in the broadest sense of the word, mankind suffers and struggles against, but also brings forth, evil. One can, of course, demythologize the answers of the Fathers; but he cannot demythologize the foundation of the painful question which they wanted to answer. The old apocalyptical, world-historical eschatology has lost its cosmological language, but its lasting horizon is the theodicy question. It is precisely within the range of this question that one has to speak in a secular way of the righteousness of God. Here the proclamation of the resurrection of the crucified one, i.e., of the righteousness of God which creates anew, attains its understandable as well as its revolutionary meaning.

Since the beginning of modern times, the advance of the gospel clothed in an anthropological metaphysics has had its real basis in the changed conditions of human misery. If man has become the master of his world, then he no longer finds grandeur and misery in the powers of nature, but in himself. Behind the theological turn to anthropology in the "consciousness theology" of Schleiermacher, the "existence theology" of Kierkegaard, the "ethical theology" of Kant and his followers, man's identity question is hidden as the concrete experience of misery. Man's identity question has become so agonizing for him that he connects it to the God question and often considers them to be the same question. The "Christology from below," "the doctrine of faith," and "existentialist interpretation" were and are not only accommodations to the modern representations of the world, for which anthropology has become the central problem. They were and are, as well, the kerygma's concrete initiatives for liberating man from his modern afflictions. We must see the real agony behind man's search for himself. Christian proclamation does not enter into this quest only to make itself understandable and to adjust its own tradition to the present. It enters into it for the sake of liberation. Today the limitations of existentialist interpretation come into focus because the real unredeemed state of mankind looks different. Therefore, we must arrive at an ideological critique of this existentialist interpretation,[23] while keeping in mind the concrete experiential content behind the outline of existence theology.

The question of man's identity becomes more and more pressing the more man becomes a historical being. But he becomes a historical being only in connection with the social changes of world history. Therefore, this agonizing and impelling identity question is, in fact, the reverse side of the theodicy question which seeks the meaning of history. Practically speaking, this means that persons and groups of men are to find their identity in history—not apart from it. Their identity is to be found only in concrete historical identification with projects directed toward overcoming human misery and enslavement. Even Christians and Christian churches can lose their identity in social changes if their traditions can no longer cope with the new situations of distress in the present. But they can be regenerated from their origins if these origins present themselves and can be presented as something indispensable in the present distresses.

Christian hermeneutic cannot concern itself exclusively with proclamation and language because they themselves stand in the larger political and social forum of public life. Therefore, the political configuration of the church and the ethical form of the Christian life are the proper subject matter of Christian hermeneutical considerations. If the totality of Christian expressions of life or charisms must be considered in the herme-

---

[23] T. W. Adorno, *Jargon der Eigentlichkeit* (Frankfurt: Suhrkamp Verlag, 1964).

neutical significance of the Christ event, then it becomes clear why one can no longer derive hermeneutic from a principle. Hermeneutic is then not simply the "act of understanding written expressions of life," but of understanding all historical expressions of life within their political context. In kerygma, koinonia, and *diakonia*, the spirit of freedom and of the new future of God is brought into the total misery of the present. Thus we arrive at a method which is not a principle, that is, at the method of historical effectiveness in the form of a project, the experience and then the criticism of this project. Preaching needs the text as its basis and the dialogue of the congregation as a check. The church needs the Bible as its foundation and the public discussion as a check. Obedience and love need the discipleship committed to Jesus as their ground and the working-out of present experience as a control. This is a hermeneutical process which encompasses the whole history of Christianity. From it arises the method of the realization of faith, community, and free life under the changing conditions of misery in the present.

In this process one must take into account the following factors:

1. *The constant* in the changing situation of history is the relation of spirit and faith, of freedom and life to Jesus, the crucified one. Content and manner of proclaimed and lived freedom must be legitimized by reflections on their ground in the crucified Christ. The cross of Christ is the criterion for distinguishing between the spirits, i.e., for the separation of faith and superstition. The church is the Church of Christ only as the brotherhood of the crucified one. This is its criterion. The new life in freedom and for freedom is the discipleship of Jesus. This is his criterion. Where this fundamental connection is lost, proclamation, church, and life lose their Christian identity.

2. *The invariable* is the alignment of proclamation, church, and life toward the future of the crucified one, i.e., toward his parousia in bodily, political, and cosmic openness. No one can conserve our forefathers' conceptions and representations of

hope. They arose out of the misery of their time and were directed against that misery. For this reason, we must go beyond them, but always in the same direction and with the same intention. The conceptions, images, and words are variable because they are determined by their time. Invariable, however, is their orientation toward the future of Christ and the coming freedom which he reveals to the afflictions of the present situation. Whoever abandons this orientation does not demythologize any more—he breaks off the transmission of the gospel.

3. *The variables*, then, are exegesis and application, because new forms of alienation, sin, and affliction are continually produced. Nevertheless, throughout all periods of history there is a solidarity of afflicted men in their common lack of freedom and glory, as Paul says. This means that as one exists through changing world-views and social orders, he can understand himself in the partnership of deprivation. And in this solidarity, the freedom of the "coming one" becomes the common future for all periods of history, until the kingdom of freedom overcomes the conditions of alienation in history. Therefore, figuratively expressed, the "wandering people of God," who go from affliction to affliction and from freedom to freedom through the course of history, can better represent the continuum in history than institutions which vacillate between orthodoxy and modernism, between fundamentalism and accommodation. Finally, this is shown in a practical outline for the witness of the Christian in the modern world:

a) *The Kingdom of God comes to those who labor and are heavily laden.* If Jesus, the Messiah of the Kingdom, came to the poor, the wretched, and the sick, he made plain by this action that poverty, hunger, and sickness rob a man of all dignity and that the Kingdom of God will fill him bodily with riches. The Kingdom which Jesus preached and represented through his life is not only the soul's bliss but *shalom* for the body as well, peace on earth and liberation of the creature from the past. "The body is meant . . . for the Lord and the Lord for the body" (1 Cor. 6:13). If, however, the body be-

103

longs to the Lord, the task of the Christian is to await and anticipate his dominion in the emaciated and exploited bodies of the poor. This is not just Christian *caritas*, but a practical proof of hope in the redemption of the body in this world.

The social revolution of unjust conditions is the immanent reverse side of the transcendent resurrection hope. Only because the church limited itself to the soul's bliss in the heavenly beyond and became docetic did the active hope of bodily salvation wander out of the church and enter into social-change utopias. In them, circumstances are represented in which those who labor and are heavily laden cease to be so, as Ernst Bloch correctly asserts with an unmistakable biblical emphasis.[24] Therefore, the church and Christians should recognize in the movement of changing social relationships a spirit which is of the Spirit of Christ. It is, of course, not so much a matter of a "latent church" or an "anonymous Christianity" that appears here. It is, rather, much more the latent Kingdom, for which the church, in its own way, exists, that proves itself effective in these movements. Through a critical analysis of the compulsion and possibilities of "one-dimensional" (H. Marcuse) humanity in modern society, hope for the Kingdom can be joined to present possibilities and thus become practical.[25]

b) The Kingdom of God comes to the humiliated and abused. If Jesus, the Messiah of God's righteousness, came to those who had no rights, to sinners and tax collectors, he indicated in this way that not only through poverty, but even more by deprivation of rights, is man held in humiliation. With those who had no rights, he celebrated the eschatological banquet. His resurrection from the humiliation of the cross can be understood as the revelation of the new creation of God's righteousness. In view of this, Christians are commissioned to bring, with the gospel and with their communion, the justice of God

[24] Ernst Bloch, *Naturrecht und menschliche Würde* (Frankfurt: Suhrkamp Verlag, 1961), p. 13.
[25] Cf. W. Rauschenbusch, *Christianity and the Social Crisis*, ed. R. D. Cross (New York: Harper Torchbooks, 1964), p. 91 and *passim*.

and freedom into the world of oppression. Men do not hunger for bread alone, but also in the most elementary way for recognition and independence.

Since the church limited itself to the forgiveness of moral and spiritual sins, the hope for justice departed the church and entered into revolutions for freedom. Many of the revolutions which today go through Africa, Asia, and the Americas are declarations of independence. They embody the right to be free and to determine one's own destiny so that one can live in a truly human way and find his own identity. One of the most difficult tasks today lies in the attempt at mediation between economic progress and democratic freedom. Foreign aid in terms of patronizing economic gifts is in continual danger of making men economically dependent. The "great leap forward" out of poverty and affliction is, on the other hand, too easily purchased with dictatorship, i.e., with renunciation of freedom. All kinds of protests and rebellions indicate that the compulsion for economic advancement encourages continual conflict between freedom and social accommodation in industrialized countries as well. Here there is an open front for the commitment of Christians who should actualize the freedom of faith in an unfree world and justification in a repressive society.

c) God himself comes to mankind. Finally, it is not to be overlooked that Jesus forgives sins as only God can forgive. In him who was crucified and resurrected, the coming God is himself present. The social and political commitment of Christians errs if there does not stand behind and within it the vivifying expectancy of God's own presence. It would be false if Christians expended all their energy in political activity because of a bad social conscience. If there were no hope against guilt and life's susceptibility to emptiness, i.e., if there were no hope for the coming of God himself, everything else would be only a renovation of the prison, but not a real break from the prison into the land of freedom.[26] Luther called the

---

[26] The social-gospel theology knew this quite well and in no sense did it idealistically overlook it. Cf. W. Rauschenbusch, *Christianity and the Social*

scale of human affliction sin, death, and the devil. Leibniz translated this philosophically into the scale of a moral, physical, and metaphysical evil. In the nineteenth century the distinction was made between the economic, moral, and religious spheres of man's life. But if there were no hope against the devil, against the metaphysical evil of nothingness, and against the religious anguish over the pain of mortality, whatever remains in human existence would not be of much value. Hope for the coming of God himself is described in Revelation 21 in the cosmological conceptions of the new creation: In the city of God the succession of day and night ceases because God himself and the Lamb are "the sun." The first earth has passed away and the new earth is no longer threatened by the waters. If we translate this into ontological concepts, it would mean a new being which is a participation in the pure being of God beyond the ambivalence of being and nonbeing in the first creation. The ontological ambivalence determined through the *creatio ex nihilo* is overcome in the *participatio in Deo*. Hope for the coming of God himself is directed against the nothingness at whose boundary everything that is exists. We do not find this hope in social revolutions and wars for independence. We find the sacrament of this hope in the church. The newness which the church of Christ advocates, and without which there is no advocate, means, "Behold, the dwelling of God is with man. He will dwell with them, and they shall be his people and God himself will be with them" (Rev. 21:3). Here lie hopes and powers for mankind for a future in which contradictions wholly other than social, political, and personal ones shall cease. But, on the other hand, these hopes can become the inexhaustible source for social imagination and for legal and political visions in the name of freedom. Religion dare not make these hopes relative and irrelevant. It must intensify and strengthen them against every defeat and disappointment.

Crisis, p. 47: "When the question of economic wants is solved for the individual and all his outward adjustments are as comfortable as possible, he may still be haunted by the horrible emptiness of his life and feel that existence is a meaningless riddle and delusion. . . . Universal prosperity would not be incompatible with universal *ennui* and *Weltschmerz*."

When, finally, everything should come to pass and God himself comes, when his presence changes the ontic condition of all things and relationships, then the interpretation of scriptural promises will take place not just for the sake of the salvation and freedom of mankind but for the coming glory of God himself. This is also a doxology—of course, here in the form of the calling out of the depths, but still a doxology—the proclamation of God for God's own sake.

VI + New Frontiers of Christianity in Industrial Society

There are two ways of inquiring about the future of Christianity in industrial society. From an external viewpoint we can consider Christianity as we know it historically and ask about the chances of survival for this entire complex composed of church and social order, faith and thought, proclamation and tradition. Since the Enlightenment, prognoses of this sort have been attempted frequently and for the most part concluded negatively. But the question can also be posed from within Christianity. From this vantage point the question would be: For what future does Christianity exist in its faith and action, in its proclamation and social involvement in the present? For what future and for whose future does it bear responsibility in its hope and action? If this is our mode of inquiring about Christianity's future, the question is no longer limited to the external historical forms of the past and its traditions. Rather, it is asked in openness to the Lord's summons to a missionary task. Whether or not Christianity has a future does not depend upon the maintenance of its well-known status in society. It depends, rather, upon whether or not it can credibly present in a changing world the future placed before it by its origin and Lord. Here we are concerned only with this second question, for we must recognize that the answer to the first question depends upon whether Christianity can recover the power of its own peculiar hope.

If we speak of Christianity in this context, it should be obvious that it is not simply identical with the church in her institutions and public functions. Nor are we speaking exclusively about the congregation or the gathering of Christians to receive the Word and sacraments. Christianity appears publicly in the church as a whole, in the individual congregation, but in secular vocations as well. Focusing on Christianity we thus think not only of the forms of preaching, sacrament, and organization, but also of the concrete historical expressions of the life and obedience of the believers as they are dispersed throughout the everyday world. Christianity is singularly significant in this context precisely because it is here that new frontiers become visible, new and unusual decisions are demanded, new possibilities emerge out of history, and old possibilities become impossible.

When we speak in this connection of the industrial society, we mean that society and that social commerce which arose as the result of the industrial revolution and the scientific-technological civilization, and which is in the process of establishing itself throughout our world. Therefore, we are not initially referring to the state or the family but, rather, to that area of public life which is shaped by production, consumption, and economic transaction. Our interest is that dimension in which human relationships are mediated through objects and with objectivity and in which human beings encounter one another as bearers of achievements and demands and, therefore, cooperate with one another according to fixed structures. This social, object-mediated, and functional intercourse naturally invades the political sphere, whether the government be subject to the control of economic complexes or whether it be in a position to regulate the economy from above. It also invades the family whether in terms of removing production from family management or of making family life increasingly inhuman by introducing consumer advertising into the intimacy of the home via television and other media. But the unique characteristics of the modern society do not arise out of the spheres of government or family but, rather, out of the proliferating possibilities of technical civilization and the rapid growth of its productive potential. Here all traditional human relationships are transformed. This society, which is so dominated in its economic dynamics by the "myth of the growth rate," has this additional characteristic: It is constantly emancipating itself from tradition and inherited historical patterns of behavior. It is no longer shaped by history and custom but by its own progressiveness and the possibilities continually opening up before it. Consequently modern society eliminates the influence of what until now has been known as "religion." Now the question is: To what social role does this society assign the Christian faith?

1

THE TRANSFORMATION OF SOCIETY'S CONCEPTION OF RELIGION

A ✚ *Christianity as the Religion of National Well-Being*

From the days of Emperor Constantine to our own century the Christian church has always possessed through all historical changes a clearly outlined public and social character. The place of the church in the social order was fixed. One knew what to expect from the church, and the church in premodern society knew what it could expect in terms of respect and influence. It was not until the rise of the industrial society and the accompanying Enlightenment that the old symphony of church and society was interrupted.

Viewed from the perspective of the history of religions, this premodern public position held by the church originated with the inheritance of the public claim of the Roman state religion. This claim, in turn, originated with the ancient notion of society in which the first necessity and the highest duty—*finis principalis*—of the body politic was to grant the gods the worship due them. Peace and welfare depended upon the favor of the state gods. Thus the purpose of religion was the worship of the powers upon whose favor the welfare of the state depended. First with Constantine, and then further consolidated by the laws of Theodosius and Justinian, Christianity became a public cult and the guardian of the *sacra publica* of the social order. The public state sacrifices came to an end. In their place arose the prayers for Caesar and state. Christianity assumed the role of the "religion of society" and, as such, fulfilled the highest purpose of the state.

So, the ancient and premodern conception of society always included a religious goal for that society. Assuming responsibility for the realization of that goal, Christianity can present itself as the "crown of the social order," as the "redemptive center" and "inner life principle of the social order." If Christianity accepts such a task, however, it must take this form and no other. And this has always led to a scandalous estrangement of Christianity from its own origins and task.

As modern society has emerged from the industrial revolution, it has freed itself from this ancient conception of society. It has gained its own dynamic and progressive power through a declaration of independence from such a "religious center" and such religiously oriented social goals. It has unchained the earth from the sun (Nietzsche) and in so doing, it has uncovered the unexpected possibilities for good and evil which are now appearing before it.

For a brief analysis of the peculiarities of this new society, one might profitably refer to Hegel's description in his *Philosophy of Right*. It seems to me to be the most objective. He calls this society a "system of needs." According to its fundamental principle, this society contains nothing that does not arise out of "the mediation of a man's needs and his satisfaction through his work and through the work and the satisfaction of the needs of all others."[1] What he is saying is this: For the first

---

[1] *Hegel's Philosophy of Right*, trans. T. M. Knox (Oxford: Clarendon Press, 1952), p. 126 (slightly altered).

time in history a society has been established upon the uniform nature of man as a creature of needs. A man associates with other men necessarily, irrevocably, and solely as the bearer of needs and the producer of that which satisfies them. In contrast to earlier societies, men are here related to one another by social necessity, that is, only as they are producers and consumers and participants in the appropriate corresponding activities. Everything of which a man's life may otherwise consist—his background, culture, nationality, religion—is removed from the sphere of necessary social intercourse and relegated to the sphere of individual freedom.

It makes no difference whether a man is Italian or English; Protestant, Catholic, or Jew; married or single; old or young. As a worker or consumer he can live anywhere. Only the power of his labor and his capacity to purchase goods are of any social consequence. Everything else that he is, thinks, believes, and loves is irrelevant so far as its social necessity is concerned and becomes a matter of individual freedom. In earlier times, the religious unity of a country was necessary for the cohesion of the country. Today such religious unity is superfluous. Even unity of language and national history increasingly loses its character as a social necessity. And it may well be that the ideological base of social organizations will become superfluous as a uniting element. The affect of such rationalization and objectivization of public social intercourse is through and through ambiguous. On the one hand, there is the threat of an age of the "lonely crowd" and the "organization man," conformity and anonymity in all aspects of public life. However, these nightmares are very one-sided. For, on the other hand, a society appears in which the conformity and adjustment of all elements of production, consumption, and commerce creates in a peculiar fashion new convivial space for personal freedoms: freedom of religious choice, freedom to change vocation and residence, freedom to shape a personal culture of one's own. Both conformity and individualism of the new age have their roots in the fact that social relationships are looser, more objective, and functional.

The adjustment to specific patterns of relationship in work and consumption also makes easier the achievement of a private sphere of intimacy which one can shape according to his own liking. This is something easily observable in every large city. If this modern society has been emancipated from any religious center, it is equally true that Christianity for its part is now free of the burden of that social role in which it is expected to provide a religious integration of society. But, specifically, what status has it attained?

B ✦ *Faith as the Religion of the Personal*

"Religion is a private matter." With this shibboleth, modern society has freed itself from any public influence of the various Christian confessions. But inherent in this movement is the simultaneous relegation of religion to a new function. Religion now becomes the cult of the private, *cultus privatus*. Religion is now understood as a matter of inwardness and feeling, a special attribute of the "personal." One expects from faith the preservation, protection, nurture, and upbuilding of personal humanity. If human relationships in public life are continually objectified and dehumanized, then one expects that faith will play guardian of the uniquely human, that which cannot and must not be objectified. The human soul becomes lonely in a world of commerce and exchange of goods. True humanity between "I and Thou" is nowhere to be found. Religion and faith must concern themselves with the lonely, unsettled soul, with the inner existence of modern man, an existence which has been called into question by the modern world. Personal suffering, personal happiness, and personal identity now become the concern of faith. It can no longer be demonstrated that God is the origin and goal of the world and of human society within the world process, but it can be demonstrated that God is the transcendental ground of existence, of the capacity to act personally and according to conscience. It is no longer possible to create room for God in the sphere of worldly knowledge and activity. Therefore the question of God must be asked in relation to the question of man's identity.

Here the Christian faith has great possibilities in modern industrial society if it can create for the internal life that which is missing on the outside: warmth, home, security, transcendence, responsiveness. It is interesting to note that even in the Marxist world with its reductionist concern for economics, a vacuum occurs in which the subjectivity of man is set free. It is a vacuum which the existentialism of Sartre invades[2] and which forces Marxism to revise its position with respect to the still-open question of personal life and its meaning.

A theology that is concerned with the personal has always assumed that the modern world has made man the lord and master of the world, that the gods of metaphysics are dead. Also the Christian God, insofar as he is worshiped as Lord of the world and Ruler of history, is for all practical purposes dethroned. Man has now assumed the role of the efficient cause of all things. Therefore, he is responsible for his world. The message from God, it is now maintained, must be directed toward the subject of this activity, and must answer the question about the humanity of this *Homo faber*. But this is only apparently the case, for modern man's experience of himself is won not only through the control of the world by technology, but also through being unburdened of the world by this same technology. Modern individualism is always a product of the rationalization, organization, and apparatus-bound character of the outward public life.

Therefore faith, construed as the religion of the personal, does not so much effect man's free lordship over all things and his responsibility for his world, but rather affords an inner unburdening and spiritual adjustment. The salvation of one's inner personal humanity merely effects a psychological balance in the midst of outward conditions which remain unchanged. The Christian faith colonizes that territory which society has, as a matter of course, already left free for individuality. It becomes, therefore, socially irrelevant. The personal decision of faith is challenged, not by the opposing decision of unbelief,

[2] Cf., e.g., A. Schaff, *Marx oder Sartre* (Frankfurt: Europa Verlag, 1964).

but only by constant confrontation with its own optional character. The confession of faith becomes a personal opinion not essentially different from the opinion expressed by a journalist. Christian love knows the neighbor only as the encounter with this individual or that individual, not, however, as the fellow man within political and social relationships. The sphere of the personal, in which faith now comes to life, is already thoroughly neutralized socially, even before faith arrives upon the scene. Industrial society is grateful if the Christian faith assumes these concerns. For it unburdens and stabilizes this society, but in no way disturbs it.

C ✦ *Christianity as the Religion of Fellowship in Society*

The second role, which the modern world can concede the Christian faith as a "religious" task, is that of promoting the fellowship life of man in society. To be sure, the romantic ideal of "authentic community" has been present in industrial society since its inception. But it long ago lost its revolutionary power and was integrated into the industrial system. Sociologists have often demonstrated that this age of ever larger organizations and economic complexes is, at the same time, an age of an increasing variety of special groupings in intimate circles. Within the larger system, informal groups, fellowships, clubs, organizations, free associations of free individuals spread and develop unimpeded. In these groups, the loneliness and isolation of man in the world is deterred. Here is nurtured that spontaneous, uncalculating cohumanity which is absent in the large organization. Already in the last century Alexis de Tocqueville observed this in America. "I see an incomprehensible mass of similar and identical human beings whose lives revolve restlessly about themselves as they attempt to create the little customary pleasures. Each one of them is drawn up within himself and shares not at all in the destinies of the others. Rather for him, his children and his special friends constitute the whole of mankind." Objectivity, standards of accomplishment, the claims of mankind are swept away in the circle of his friends, colleagues,

115

neighbors, and children. At home, in the choral society, at his club, and in the congregation, he is a "human being." Here he is *allowed* to be man. In this amorphous, private, unregimented vacuum, in these enclaves within the industrial society, the church is also expected to demonstrate its effectiveness. With her circles and fellowships, she can fashion a Noah's Ark for the socially estranged and creates an island of cohumanity in the rough sea of a society which John Doe cannot change. These fellowships lead a kind of underground existence in society. With all their intensity they are extremely helpful to society. They provide a compensation in the private dimension of man's existence for the destructive powers of society and for the public, planned, goal-oriented relationships of work, competition, and commerce. But this actually changes nothing with respect to the obdurate realities of alienation, accommodation, and depersonalization of man in society. Society is proffered only a dialectical counterbalance, so that man, oscillating between work and leisure, business and family, society and fellowship, public and private life, can endure the schizophrenia he creates.

D ✦ *Christianity as Religious Institution*

Finally, we must see that, at least in the Western world, the modern social order works to the advantage of the religious institution. It is precisely such a dynamic and progressive social order that stands in continual need of stable institutions. We would like things to stand firm. We would like things to run of their own accord without everything being continually called into question. This deeply rooted desire for orderedness and security arises out of the awareness of the risk that each man represents to himself and his counterpart. Man's institutionalization of his relationships with others is an attempt to give his temporal, pretentious, and changeable existence a permanent character. Therefore, he is not essentially opposed to, but, on the contrary, quite desirous of the church's institutions, which can create with some glamour a final haven of

116

certainty against the terrors of existence. His submerged consciousness of crisis creates in him the propensity toward a general, though non-self-involving acknowledgment of certain religious guarantees of his existence. The delegation of his decision of faith to the institutional church gives rise to the new religious attitudinal pattern of institutional noncommitment.

That which is "Christian" becomes socially self-evident within the compass of the other self-evident elements of society. One no longer needs to understand it; its presence is assumed. It has its effect upon man through its influence upon the milieu. There arises an anonymous Christianity, a Christianity incognito. That which is peculiary "Christian" is planted not only in the heart of the individual or in the fellowship of the many, but in the milieu of everyone. There it stands, firmly entrenched, scarcely able to move itself, much less capable of setting anything else into motion.

I have the impression that, in these new social roles—(1) nurture of a liberated and privatized personal existence, (2) creation of underground forms of intimate fellowship, and (3) noncommittal influence upon the social milieu—Christianity finds itself in a new Babylonian captivity. It is no longer the "crown of society" as in premodern times. But it has assumed for modern society the function of unburdening man. In this function it is a well-adjusted entity and institution within society. A new assimilation is achieved in these three ways and it leaves Christianity with nothing to say to the world other than what this world wants to hear.

If we now inquire about the new frontiers of Christianity in the industrial society, we dare not search for the future opportunities of Christianity in this form as such, but only for the future for which Christianity according to the will of its Lord exists and for which it must become effective.

2

A CHURCH FOR THE KINGDOM OF GOD:

CHRISTIAN EXISTENCE FOR THE
HUMANIZING OF MANKIND

A ✦ *Activation of Christian Hope*

If we want to know why Christianity exists at all, we must ask what future of God and man Christianity is called to serve through the witness of its faith. If Christianity has become uncertain of its stance within the new conditions of society, it must recall its hope in its own peculiar mission. If it seeks an exodus out of its old and new Babylonian captivities, it can acquire the necessary self-criticism and self-transformation only through activating the power of hope which arises out of its own origins. The difference and the creative tension between hope and experienced reality are always the driving forces of ethical and historical activity. If man lives immersed only in the present day, he knows only what is momentarily at hand. But if he lives beyond the present day, his present is qualified by the future through hope and fear.

In reflecting on Christian hope, we can discover that Christian faith is never identical with established religion in either old or new forms. Faith does not mediate to mortal man the eternal and immortal but, rather, the prospect of a new and different future from God. Therefore, it does not bring to man adjustment to the momentary situation and accommodation with the present, but a persevering readiness and a patient openness for the promised future. A Christianity that activates the power of its own hope will not imagine itself the "crown of society" and will not exhaust itself trying to create inner adjustment and unburdening for society. Rather, it will attempt to mediate to this economically dynamic society the dynamics of its own hope. In the Letter to the Hebrews, we read: "Therefore let us go forth . . . outside the camp [and this holds true for all camps], bearing abuse for Him [Christ]. For here we have no lasting city, but we seek the city which is to come" (13:13–14). "Lasting city" is the epitome of what both ancient and modern social orders have tried to offer man. Their old and new religions offer guarantees of this lastingness. But, on the contrary, Christians have this in common with Jews: a divine promise in their ears and, therefore, a restless hope in their hearts. This is what makes them strangers and pilgrims who can come to rest in no social order, but only in that future city of God, the Kingdom of their Lord. That is why for them, as the *Letter of Diognet* says, "Every homeland is foreign country, every foreign country, home."

The promise of their God and their hope is not directed toward a heaven of the blessed or a kingdom of pure spirit, but toward God's creation of a new humanity and a new heaven and a new earth. They are not, therefore, inwardly oriented, but outwardly. One should not confuse this peculiar life as a stranger and pilgrim with escapism, drop-outism, or otherworldliness. The Christian hope does not make man a stranger *to* the world or otherworldly, but, rather, alert and sensitive *for* the future. For the sake of the cross that stood on this earth, they are faithful to this earth through their hopes. They await from God a future for this earth and for the guilty and dying human beings on this earth. However, if this is true, then the expected future of God for mankind and the earth, the future in which Christians hope, moves into conflict with the present and experienceable forms of human and earthly life. Christians must recognize this creative tension between what they believe and what they see and experience while they yet persevere in patience and obedience. They can witness to their hope for the world only in connection with a creative contradiction of the pattern of this world which will pass away. This hope, established by Jesus' resurrection from the dead, can be not only comfort in all sufferings, but must also be understood and expressed as God's opposition to submersion in suffering, guilt, and death. This is why Paul calls death "the last enemy" of God and man, and expects that it

119

will be swallowed up by the life of the risen one (1 Cor. 15:26).

But if this holds true for this last and inevitable enemy which deems human life here as worthless, then how much more must this hold true for every little inhumanity that oppresses human life. If the Christian hope means through God the negation of the great negatives of life—guilt and death—how much more must it mean the negation of the many minute negatives of life. If faith is hope for the true and final humanization of man through the swallowing up of guilt by God's righteousness and the swallowing up of death by life from and with God, how much more must this hope for the humanity of man take up protest against man's inhumanity here.

The church is not here for itself. It is here for the Kingdom of God and the freedom of the children of God, and in this sense it is here for the world. Christianity is not here for itself, but for the coming of man's true humanity, which he can and should discover through Christ and in faith. Therefore, the church cannot be primarily concerned with its own security, influence, prestige, and recognition in society but, rather, it must be primarily concerned with the humanity of man and the humanizing of the social order. The goal of Christians in their prayers, thoughts, and sufferings should be the promised humanity of man, who writhes here in inhumanity. There is an old rabbinic saying about the suffering of Israel. "Every distress that Israel and the peoples share is a distress (that one should bring to God in prayer). Every distress that Israel alone bears is not such a distress." Should this not also hold true for the church?

If the hope of faith is now directed toward a real historical future of God for man, then as hope in God it can no longer draw back from the concrete movements of hope by relegating their concerns with attainable goals and visible change to another kingdom, confronting them with apathy and indifference, and in this way simply coexisting with them. Whoever hopes for the freedom of the children of God can stand critically but not with indifference over against the efforts to create a world more free. Whoever is sent through Easter into history with a great hope, can no longer be satisfied with an anxious affirmation of the status quo in the world, but is called to transform the world through suffering and obedience.

What relationship can the hope of faith assume toward these human movements of hope?

1) The hope of faith in God must oppose the vainglory in every movement filled with human hope for greater freedom and social justice. It must expose their uncritical naïveté. These reality utopias cannot exact from success-laden man a reconciliation with his existence. To those who insist that all is going well, it may be admitted that things have improved, but it must be denied that all is going well. The Christian hope must attack the germ of resignation in these movements of human hope. It cannot do this with the pessimistic motto: "Nothing will ever come of our efforts, man is incurably evil." Nor can it do this in the name of a comforting despair, but only in the name of its own "better promises" (Heb. 8:6). This labor of destroying the infection of presumption and of resignation is uncomfortable work and makes no friends, but it is necessary for the health of these movements.

2) On the other hand, the hope of faith must become a source of creative and inventive imagination in the service of love, and must release anticipatory thought that asks about the present possibility of man's life here becoming better, more just, freer, and more humane. If the Christian hope in the resurrection of the crucified one affirms that God gives comfort and promises righteousness to the guilty, life to the dying, freedom to the oppressed, and true humanity to the dehumanized, then this hope must also be alert for what is correspondingly possible in the present. It must investigate and seize newly emerging historical possibilities, so that they may better correspond to this future of the Christian hope. With tenacious patience it must search for those possibilities that

121

do correspond. It will not make a comfortable settlement with present circumstances like Sancho Panza. It will not tilt with windmills like Don Quixote. It will realistically recognize and accept the real and objective possibilities that bear some correspondence to the future set before it.

This does impede an unequivocal confession, but it characterizes a hope that not only wants continually to demonstrate its own good intentions but also wants to achieve something concrete. On the other hand, this does not preclude gratitude for the "given" as a gift of God. It means that gratitude uses the "given" for the mission of God, who gives it. Ultimately this is not in any direct sense labor for God's Kingdom. But it is obedience that seeks in the inadequate materials of transitory history that which bears correspondence to God's future, and it seeks this precisely in obeying and following the one on whose face the coming glory of God is manifest.

In turning to the concrete goals for which Christian hope can be activated in everyday life, we are presupposing the ministry of the proclamation of the Christian gospel. We cannot substitute for this some kind of anonymous cohumanity. Activation of Christian hope means that the hope of faith in the future which man discovers in God becomes real here in suffering from inhumanity and, wherever possible, in struggle against this suffering. Therefore, Christian social action will press for the overthrow of "all circumstances in which man is a humiliated, an enslaved, a forsaken and a despised being" (Marx), in order that this man may become a more abundant, upright, sovereign, and purposeful man. Here Christianity is confronted by the human problems posed by the industrial society. If we are not able to direct the industrial system toward humane goals, then man will perish in this system.

B ✦ *The Abundant Man*

The promised future of God's reign is directed not only to man's internal happiness, but toward that full humanity which is denied by poverty, hunger, illness, and suffering. Through industrialization it is now more possible than ever to achieve success in the struggle against hunger. Therefore, Christianity should participate in those social programs which strive for conditions in which hunger and poverty and illness cease for as many people as possible. In such participation, there are, in particular, two viewpoints that it can develop.

First, with respect to the distribution of the social product and the politics of capital investment, Christianity can become the advocate of those groups that have insufficient or no public representation in a particular society. It can further urge concern for a balance between consumption and capital investment. A society which limits itself to investing, sacrifices the present to the future. But a society which avoids the category "future" forfeits the power for farsighted investment. It sacrifices the future for the enjoyment of the present.

Second, it can become the advocate of those groups of hungry and destitute men who live outside the industrially developed society. For no man will be abundant unless all are abundant; no man will be satisfied if some lack satisfaction; no man will be happy until all are happy. The struggle against hunger and poverty through the forces of industrialization must be either universal and without distinction or it has not even begun.

C ✦ *The Upright Man*

In an economically dynamic and affluent society, in which prosperity for all is possible, we continually disregard the fact that man hungers not only for wealth, but every bit as much for acknowledgment. One can also be degraded and offended in the midst of prosperity and by the very conditions of gratuity. By sitting at table with tax collectors and sinners, Jesus elucidates what the acknowledgment of God's righteousness means for the unrighteous. Man is not only marked as worthless by external needs, he is made contemptible when humiliated by others and himself. Therefore, it belongs to the humanity of God to intercede on behalf of, and to honor the worth and the rights of, defenseless men.

The struggles of the underdeveloped nations and the demands of the labor movement have never been directed merely to the assuagement of physical need, but much more profoundly to the recognition of human worth and the granting of freedom and independence. Disregarding or failing to care for these needs can only lead to inordinate self-confidence and disappointment. Thus, to the slogan "Bread for the world" belongs its counterpart "Justice for the world." Unfortunately, until now the well-known prosperity programs and industrial leaps forward have been purchased at the price of enforced denial of rights, freedom, and independence. If we simply substitute economic or state bureaucracy for earlier and perhaps necessary domination of men by men, we have only a new kind of human subservience. But just as there cannot be human worth without an end to need, so there can be no happiness appropriate to human life without an end of both older and newer forms of subservience. Therefore, the building of the affluent society must coincide with the destruction of all dependency if, indeed, a more humane society is expected to emerge. The official myth of the Establishment would equate the satisfied slave of affluence with the "abundant man." But the abundant man can only be the man who holds up his head because of his intrinsic worth.

D ✦ *The Sovereign Man*

Paul and the Reformers always emphasized that the man who derives his honor and prestige from his own labor and accomplishment is degraded, dependent, and less than a man. He does not propagate free humanity in the world about him, but only the works of the law. This pride in one's own work contradicts the glory and acknowledgment that man receives by the free grace of God. And it follows that pride in one's own standard of accomplishment contradicts the true humanity of man. Paul exemplified this in his conflict with the Jewish legalism of his day in the fact that "a man is justified by faith apart from works of law" (Rom. 3:28). The Reformers saw this law of works operative in the laws with which the Christian church oppressed man and obstructed its own witness to the sovereign freedom of faith.

Man's self-enslaving tendency was also a theme of the nineteenth century. In the "Sorcerer's Apprentice," Goethe identified the quick transition from master to slave in which one appeals to the spirits only to be enslaved by them. With Karl Marx and Max Weber this "Sorcerer's Apprentice" pattern is emphatically stressed. "The offspring of their own minds have grown up taller than they. Before their own creation, the creators bow," wrote Marx.[3] The product of their hands becomes autonomous and begins to rule the producer. Science and technology and the processes they have set in motion are beginning to enslave the very ones who had intended to utilize them for their liberation from nature and fate. Management of his complex scientific "creatures" gets beyond the rational control of man. At first he is served by the machine. Then he ends up serving the machine. A man who is enslaved by his own industry is no longer human. If one takes account of a man only for what he produces or is capable of producing, this man lives without intrinsic worth. The message about the freedom of faith, the works of the law, and the unconditional acceptance of man by God shatters this enslavement of man by the works of his hands or the offspring of his mind. The man acquitted and unconditionally loved by God is the sovereign man, for he is free from glorying in or despairing over his own labors. He must be able to envision options over against the present forms of these processes.

Where possible this freedom of man must also find expression in the structures of justice in society. This means, first, that man must again gain the upper hand over the technical, economic, and military processes which he has set in motion. Who-

3 Karl Marx, *Die Frühschriften*, ed. S. Landshut (Stuttgart: Kröners Taschenausgabe, 1953), p. 341.

ever executes the kind of power that has fallen to modern man dare not assume the unconscious naïveté of children at play. He must learn to discern the consequences of his power and must reclaim alternatives to the use of this massive power. He must be able to see beyond his creations so that he can question the use to which he will put them. He cannot do this, however, as the slave of his own productive processes. Second, this means that human control must be exercised over the rapidly expanding powers of productivity, and those who exercise such control must in turn be subject to the control of a graduated system of civil courts. This would effect the necessary internal and external democratization of the scientific-technological power complex.

E ✦ *The Purposeful Man*

Finally, it becomes ever more apparent in the midst of our rising prosperity, that man's worth is not only undermined by suffering, lack of recognition, and works of the law, but even more by something scarcely tangible, and this is what we can only refer to as "nothingness," frustration, the disease of boredom. "We have fought a winning fight against hunger and poverty only to discover that we are facing perhaps an even tougher enemy—boredom," wrote Norman Cousins in *Selfhelp and Social Welfare*.[4] Even if we should manage to solve the economic and political needs of man, this does not mean that the misery of human existence is alleviated, but only shifted to another level. The lack of worth in human existence does not recede to the background in a successful program of prosperity and freedom, but is only now perceptible in the foreground: "Up from the jaws of death to the level of a life of boredom and superfluity."[5] Some men no longer face the negatives of life in concrete, directly assailable forms, as with the case of hunger, lack of freedom, this or that degradation. But the oppressive

[4] Cousins, *Selfhelp and Social Welfare* (New York, 1954), p. 44.
[5] Ernst Bloch, *Naturrecht und menschliche Würde* (Frankfurt: Suhrkamp Verlag, 1961), pp. 301f.

126

"nothingness" latent in these inhuman forms has in no way been eliminated from their life. It expresses itself in feelings of frustration, in the suffering of anonymity and loneliness, and has as its consequence, wholly incalculable and perilous attempts to break out into the absurd. More prosperity, more leisure, more justice does not lead men automatically to true humanity and self-realization, as one thought it would in the nineteenth century. On the contrary, these conditions confront man with an inner void and a surrounding nothingness with which he can scarcely cope.

It is entirely too simplistic to attribute these phenomena to the so-called anarchic conditions of capitalistic society. They are not the result of either capitalism or Socialism, but of industrialization. Economic explanations fail to make the problem intelligible, just as psychological or economic solutions fail to rectify it; psychotherapy adds little to either dimension.

Is it the melancholia of fulfillment which disappoints? What really disappoints us is the experience or foreboding of human existence itself as it arises or will arise out of industrial society.[6] Implicit here is the recognition that every system of hope disappoints as soon as it is realized, that in every breakthrough toward a more humane future, more is expected than any historical future can fulfill. Is it the negation and questioning of life by a death which makes itself felt as decay in the midst of a life which considers itself successful? Is it the still and silent presence of God, which makes itself felt as his absence?

I will not risk deciding this, but would like to emphasize that at this point all our social programs, declarations of independence, and humanistic designs encounter such a void that their courses seem to disappear into the sands of "nothingess." On the other hand, I think that the man of faith has reason to hope for the destruction of this "nothingness" by the God who creates out of nothing. He can therefore recognize the presence of this nothingness and accept the burden of suffering it. He knows that he together with all creatures is subject to this

[6] Raymond Aron, *Bergedorfer Gesprächskreis* (Protokoll Nr. 16, 1964), p. 8.

nothingness, but yet in hope. And in this sense his hope is a resurrection hope. It becomes universal where he, in solidarity with all waiting creatures, mediates to them this hope, which comes to life in patience.

Christianity has no future in the modern society if it does not bear witness to this society of that future which God has prepared for it. This is the future in which God is, and correspondingly a future of abundant, upright, sovereign, and purposeful humanity. After the perspectives on the future in society's hope-movements have disintegrated to the degree that they have succeeded in effecting their desired changes, this remains the only future that retains within it the fascination of real transcendence.

Christianity can struggle openly against these four forms of inhumanity, wherever it has opportunity to cooperate in sociopolitical activities in a developing society. When it does not have this opportunity, then through social criticism and conscious suffering and intercession it can become a public witness to the humanity it holds to be the only true future of mankind.

VII + God in Revolution

Behold, I make all things new.

Revelation 21:5

By focusing on the key words of this title, I hope to take up the theme of the Fourth Assembly of the World Council of Churches in Uppsala and set it within the horizon of our present-day experience of reality. The past seven years since the World Council's New Delhi Assembly have been characterized by the political upsurge and revolutionary engagement of young intellectuals all over the world. This is a provocation to the churches and a challenge to Christians everywhere. It is our task to respond to this provocation in terms of the changing world situation. This may, in turn, be the occasion for our posing a Christian provocation to society.

I do not want to begin this student conference with a well-polished theological discourse. Rather, I would like to open the discussion of the coming days with a series of theses. I do not intend to set before you a masterful theological soup which you should consume with relish. These theses are meant as an aperitif to whet the appetite. For theology is not only a matter of eating something, but also the shared task of first preparing it.

This was the opening lecture of the World Student Christian Federation Conference, July 23, 1968, Turku, Finland.

Thesis 1: *We live in a revolutionary situation. In the future we shall experience history more and more as revolution. We can be responsible for the future of man only in a revolutionary way.*

The threefold occurrence of the words "revolution" and "revolutionary" in this thesis seems a bit overdone. Since Vietnam and Cuba, and since the racial struggles in the United States and the student uprisings in Western and Eastern Europe, it has become a catchword and faded into a commonplace. And yet men are still not consciously geared to the new situation which the word "revolution" denotes. Christians and the churches seem to find peculiar difficulty in engaging this new revolutionary situation.

The milieu in which we live and think has become objectively "revolutionary." Three situations make this an especially poignant challenge for us. The predominance of white industrialized nations has allowed these nations to develop a system by which they are constantly growing richer, while the others are falling proportionately further behind. This has led to the anticolonial and anti-imperial wars of liberation in Asia, Africa, and South America and will lead to a global crisis in the coming decades. Liberation from economic exploitation is linked in these struggles with liberation from political dependence and from racial discrimination. The proletariat of contemporary humanity is not the workers of the progressive industrial nations but the peoples of the third world. It is here that Karl Marx's categories of alienation and of revolutionary hopes prove appropriate.

In the advanced industrialized nations themselves the capacities of production are outstripping the hitherto prevailing structures of production in capitalistic, national, and governmental bureaucracies. This is the technological revolution. The existing political, social, and legal ways of organizing production and distribution of products are no longer capable of progressive and equitable exploitation of new technical possibilities. This explains the increasingly dangerous tendency to make destructive use of technological power for the defense of the status quo.

In the universities we find signs of a coming revolution in education. Old institutions for molding middle-class citizens can no longer cope with the enormous surge of students. The mass of new students splits the universities at the seams. The old universities trained experts in the specialized knowledge demanded by a static society. Today we need universities where people can develop a critical and politically responsible consciousness. In the student protest movements, we have seen a revolt of man's political reason against its enslavement by merely technical thinking, of his moral reason against the exclusive use of "value-free" instrumental reason. The sciences are being recalled to their truly human possibilities and promises. They are to be enlisted for the realization of humanity. They can no longer be the slaves of a society which misses its genuinely human opportunities. Thus every science is questioned about its socio-political function.

In the future we shall experience history more and more as revolution. What is "revolution"? I understand revolution to mean a transformation in the foundations of a system—whether of economics, of politics, of morality, or of religion. All other changes amount to evolution or reform. But transformation in the foundations of a system becomes a genuine possibility only when previously unsuspected possibilities or powers are at hand. Only then does there emerge a critical consciousness in the present. We compare what is actual with what is possible and find a discrepancy between actuality and possibility. We realize that the future could be different from the present. We live today in a world of unrealized but quite realizable humanity. Now that it is really possible to eliminate hunger in the world and to control overpopulation, the systems which hinder the realization of these possibilities must be radically changed. Today real possibilities are flooding the existing institutions for realizing them. Hence, in the critical consciousness, the future as the fullness of possibilities comes into conflict with the constricting institutions of the present. And, by the same token, in the reactionary and repressive consciousness, the possession of the present comes into conflict with the new future. Because new possibilities are becoming increasingly more vast through science, technology, and education while political reason fails to grow in the same degree, we are entering into an accelerated revolutionary history. We experience reality as history, and history as revolutionary conflict between future and past. In the conflict between the "Party of Anxiety" and the "Party of Hope," on which side do we stand? This is the crucial question.

This revolutionary history has the tendency to become totalitarian. It will bring all spheres of human endeavor—from economic to moral, from political to religious—into the conflict of the possible and the real, the future and the past. Moreover, this revolutionary history has the tendency to become permanent. It will even extend beyond the new orders which prove capable of coping with the present. Therefore, revolution is not a limited transitional period but, rather, a new experience of time itself.

We are compelled to take responsibility for man's future in a revolutionary way. Involvement in a contemporary search for truth will mean discovering, as Gramsci did, that "truth is revolutionary." It will mean discovering that the world can be changed and that nothing has to remain as it has been. It will mean testing scientific theories by the imperative of transforming reality. The historical praxis which wants to realize a freer and more just humanity becomes the practical horizon of the development of theories. Scientific knowledge, then, is a means to the self-liberation of man from obdurate dependence only when it is employed in responsibility for a more humane future. To be responsible for history in a revolutionary fashion today means to find the unity of knowledge and action.

THESIS 2: *The new revolutionary situation has brought Christianity into a deep crisis of identity. Christians and the churches will rediscover their true self-consciousness only if they overcome their own religious alienation and their own hindrance to the free self-realization of man.*

"There is no theology of revolution," say our solicitous

132

bishops. And they are right. For the theology of revolution is certainly no theology for bishops, but a lay theology of Christians who are suffering and struggling in the world. On the other hand, it must be said that there will be no "theology of revolution" until there is a revolution in theology. As long as Christians refrain from acting in a revolutionary way, they have no right to make theological declarations about revolution. Neither does the church have a right to a "theology of revolution" in the world if it is not engaged in its own radical transformation. It is totally inauthentic for the church to speak and act against the economic alienation of man without struggling against the spiritual alienation which it itself propagates. We cannot say very much about the "new earth" as long as we do not realize that the heaven of religion has become old and repressive and that we need a "new heaven." "The critique of heaven is being changed into a critique of earth, the critique of religion into a critique of law, the critique of theology into a critique of politics," said Karl Marx. Today it is just the reverse.

Everywhere in the world we find an identity crisis of Christianity. "The old world is gone; the new has not yet begun," it is said in black and white, in American and European communities alike. Hence, in many places the churches are losing their monopoly of Christians. Many people are leaving the churches because it is only in solidarity with the oppressed and the revolutionaries that they can still live their Christian faith with assurance and integrity. But the Christian faith is also losing its mobilizing power in history. Many abandon Christianity because they can find in it no power of the future. They seek elsewhere the new man, the new community, and often even the new gods. Will the churches waste away and make place for a nonecclesiastical Christianity? Will Christianity die together with the predominance of Europe and the first industrial revolution? Or is there within Christianity a latent revolutionary potential, which we can discover, which we can bring to awareness and convert into social praxis? This, I believe, because of the 1966 Geneva Conference on Church and Society and along with the 1968 Uppsala Assembly, is the crucial question to which this conference in Turku should give an answer.

Without a self-critical movement of repentance among Christians, there can be no effective presence of Christians in the places of revolutionary decision-making in the world. It is therefore necessary to find resolute groups of people to carry the revolution into the established churches. The Christian faith relates itself to God and Christ. Yet its identity crisis lies precisely in the fact that it no longer knows with certainty for what purpose it exists. It knows very well where it comes from, but it no longer knows exactly where it is going. Therefore the future perplexes it. However, no one finds his identity simple through remembering his origins but, rather, in practical identification and engagement with the tasks of the present for a greater future. If Christians are to know again for what reason they are here, they must also rediscover who they really are. The present crisis leads some to flee into a golden past and to try to preserve it. Others retreat into a nonpolitical faith of the heart. Still others flee head on into direct action. They join revolutionary groups and then with astonishment ask themselves whether they are still Christians and why.

How can we break out of our own religious alienation from the reality of life to that freedom which knows what it wants? How can we penetrate through a criticism of traditional Christianity into that awareness of rebirth and to a new self-consciousness? Where is the "new heaven"?

It is the hope of committed Christians that the church can change. They are aware of the deep discrepancy between the hitherto realized form of Christianity and its unrealized possibilities. They suffer because faith is bound to anxiety in the face of the future. They are frustrated by the repressive character of ecclesiastical morality. They are thwarted by the authoritarian structures of church polity and by clerical manipulation. They are searching for a faith which is free and united with hope in the face of the future. They demand the individual responsibility of man in the dimension of personal morality. After the church has for so long narrowly presented the heavenly Christ in Word, sacrament and hierarchy, they seek communion with the crucified Son of man who waits among the hungry, the naked, the prisoner, and the refugee for the acts of righteousness.

THESIS 3: *The eschatological (and messianic) tradition of hope can give rise to a new birth of Christian faith in the revolutionary present.*

The modern world is a world full of open possibilities. Therefore the modern consciousness is future-oriented. Man no longer experiences nature as a fixed and completed reality. Modern science and technology have made nature the site for constructing the human world. We no longer view the structures of society as given by nature or by God, but know that because they are made by man, they can also be changed by man. People used to feel themselves personally responsible *to* these structures; today we feel ourselves communally responsible *for* these structures. They are no longer authoritarian structures, but functional forms of corporate existence. Consequently, modern man has become the lord both of nature and of his own history. He can be the creator of a more humane world, but he can also be his own gravedigger. "Future" means for him freedom and possibility and the opportunity for something new.

This new orientation toward a possible free and new future has brought our familiar religious concepts into a deep crisis and is the starting point for the modern critique of religion. Hence, faith in a God of the beyond and the religious bondage to the past are viewed as ineffective in the modern world. It is inevitable that this faith and this kind of religion will increasingly disintegrate.

Christianity can respond to this situation only by recalling its own inherent—if often suppressed—prophetic hope. This is the immanent revolutionary potential in Christianity. It is a hope directed toward God and his coming Kingdom. Therefore it cannot be reduced to hopes *in* future history. It owes itself, however, to the crucified Proclaimer of the approaching Kingdom and therefore enters *into* history. Though it was for ages viewed as a hope for the soul in heaven, the political relevance of this eschatological hope should be articulated by the use of the phrase "messianic hope." To be sure, there has been running throughout the actual history of Israel and the Christian church a constant struggle between a religious faith in the beyond, which leaves this world to its own devices, and a hope for the future, which accepts responsibility for transforming this world. But we find again and again among the prophets of the Old Testament and the apostles of the New a longing for something new. Israel forsook the Sun-god and his Pharaoh in Egypt and marched with the new God, Yahweh, out of religious and political bondage. Yahweh was a God of promise and of exodus, a God of covenant and of hope, a "God going before us," "into the future." The exodus was an event of religio-political liberation and is even today effective as a symbol of coming liberation.

Christians are known as "those who have a hope" (Eph. 2:12; 1 Thess. 4:13). In the crucified Proclaimer of the kingdom of freedom they see the old world crucified and the new world revealed. Therefore they lift themselves up out of humiliation by other men and out of resignation to fate in order to proclaim the coming God and his Christ, who will bring to an end the suffering of the whole creation. In the sacral-political world of antiquity, these Christians acted as revolutionaries of both heaven and earth. They scorned the so-called gods of the fatherland and refused to sacrifice to the Roman emperor-god. They were not satisfied with *Pax Romana* but eagerly waited for *Pax Christi*. Celsus, the famous second-century critic of Christianity, reproached Christians for causing a "tumult" (*stasis*) in heaven by refraining from sacrifice to the gods. This rebellious stubbornness has serious consequences in the anger of the gods. But as revolutionaries of heaven they simultane-

136

ously inflict the religio-political order on earth with confusion. They are therefore public enemies of the state and traitors to humanity. Neither Paul nor the early Christian theologians developed a "theology of revolution." Yet through their worship of God in the crucified Jesus, the Christians were certainly acting as revolutionaries. For by so doing they seized the nerve-center of the political religions and the religious politics of their time. Their theology was a revolution at that time even though they had no "theology of revolution."

Today, too, we must beware of formulating a program out of an effect which we do not control. Radical Christianity will have a revolutionary *effect*, but a revolutionary program would be just the way to neutralize it. The title "revolutionary" must, if at all, be given from outside; one cannot claim it for himself.

This stream of eschatological messianism may be generally represented by the word "new." The prophets proclaimed to the Hebrews in exile and captivity a "new exodus," a "new occupation of the Promised Land," a "new Zion" and a "new Jerusalem," and even a "new David." They blended into the message of the new future of Israel the as-yet-never-existing reality of a greater future: ultimate salvation and universal redemption for the whole creation. In the New Testament the apostles proclaim the "new man," the "new covenant," the "new song," the "new wine," the "new people of God" and in the end "the new creation of heaven and earth." This universal Christian message of the new is manifestly anchored in the expectation of the God who in the end says: "Behold, I make all things new."

The new future in this tradition enters into transitory history, as it were, in waves of anticipation. It appears first in the mission of the Christ of God, who personally incarnates the future of freedom among the unfree and in his resurrection opens up the future to everything which is dying. Then in the mission of the gospel's words of the future the sinner is forgiven, the Godless justified, and the humiliated given hope. Then the new future comes in the mission of the community of Christ, which, as the "new people of God" drawn from all nations and tongues, is the vanguard of the new humanity and the representative embodiment of freedom from the coercive powers of this world. Then it arrives in the new obedience of the believers, who in ordinary life refuse to conform to the scheme of this world, but anticipate the coming freedom. Finally, it comes in the "new heaven and the new earth" where justice dwells, where Christ's presence purges heaven of religious myths and powers and frees the earth from pain, sorrow, and meaningless death.

We find here a historical, future-oriented faith which brings together the new future, God's presence and the freedom of creation. Without doubt this historical stream of hope has been channeled and diverted in manifold ways in the past. We cannot easily call it up today in order to participate in it. Only through a critique of the repressive myths and the vain promises with which it is permeated can it become vital and effective. Yet I can mention no other core in Christianity in which there lies the potentiality of a rebirth of authentic faith in our time.

THESIS 4: *The new criterion of theology and of faith is to be found in praxis.*

The aim of Marx's critique of religion was the categorical imperative "to overthrow all circumstances in which man is a humiliated, an enslaved, a forsaken and a despised being." Not only for him, but for the whole modern age, ethical and political praxis has become the test of theories. Truth must be practicable. Unless it contains initiative for the transformation of the world, it becomes a myth of the existing world. Because reality has become historical and man experiences himself as a historical being, he will find a possible conformity of consciousness and existence only in historical praxis. This is the event of truth.

The Christian tradition of hope in the coming God and the new creation has not always adhered to this criterion of truth.

Even the Christian future hope was frequently speculative and narrated the events of the last times as if they were past history. But only the past can be narrated; the future has to be historically anticipated in word and deed. The Christian hope was also frequently merely consolation in the afterlife which God would guarantee. In this capacity, it served to unnerve historical life. But, on the other hand, we should not forget that eschatological visions were originally the visions of the Christian martyrs on their way into exile or the arena and thus related quite well to the practice of martyrdom. The critical question was framed by Walter Rauschenbusch: "Ascetic Christianity called the world evil and left it. Humanity is waiting for a revolutionary Christianity which will call the world evil and change it." Under the conditions of modern times, the eschatological symbolism of Christian hope appears to be mythical. But it dare not dream away any longer about an eternity beyond time. It must bring the hoped-for future into practical contact with the misery of the present. This is necessary not only on the basis of the modern historical world; it is also a demand of Jesus himself. He not merely announced the Kingdom of God, but practiced it in his love of sinners and publicans.

If students are discovering today that "truth is revolutionary," Christians are discovering that the truth of Jesus "makes them free" and demands to be "done," as the Fourth Gospel says. The Christian certainty of hope becomes practical in the transformation of the present. In the expectation of divine transformation we transform ourselves and the conditions around us into the likeness of the new creation. This is a possibility—the very possibility from which Christian faith lives. This possibility is realized in repentance, in conversion, in new birth to living hope and in new life which refuses to acknowledge Godless obligations. A messianic stream of renewal runs through history from the Christ of God who died in this world and was raised into the coming new world of God's righteousness. In him there are, and always were found, not only the inner repentance and liberation of the heart but also the reformations, renaissances, and revolutions of external conditions. For Christian hope the world is not an insignificant waiting room for the soul's journey to heaven, but the "arena" of the new creation of all things and the battleground of freedom. Christian hope dare not evacuate the present by dreaming about the future; nor may it compensate for an empty present by dreaming about the future. It must, rather, draw the hoped-for future already into the misery of the present and use it in practical initiatives for overcoming this misery. Through criticism and protest, on the one hand, and creative imagination and action, on the other, we can avail ourselves of freedom for the future.

Because the practice of the church is the strongest weapon of criticism of the church today, Christians will be judged by whether they live the truth of Jesus and verify their faith practically.

THESIS 5: *The church is not a heavenly arbiter in the world's strifes. In the present struggles for freedom and justice, Christians must side with the humanity of the oppressed.*

The church is for all men, say some. Therefore, it should remain strictly separated from political struggle. Since there are no unequivocal Christian judgments in politics, the church should religiously be in the service of all sides. This is the old ecclesiastical triumphalism in modern dress as offered by the representatives of organized churches to the contending parties. Here the church is always "the third power," a "neutral platform" for peace and reconciliation, a "place for meeting" and negotiating. *Sub specie aeternitatis* all worldly conflicts become relative and insignificant. There was a time when this mediating role of the church was occasionally in demand and was instrumental in promoting tranquillity. But today all ambiguous and abstract appeals for peace fall on deaf ears, as was demonstrated in the speech of Pope Paul VI to the United Nations. Struggling factions have become tired of appeals to their conscience and of verbose sermons on moral-

ity. They do not expect from the church any transcendent
wisdom to aid the resolution of their conflicts.

Yet, if Christians take sides in the political struggle, will
they not lose sight of God's love for all men? This is the
question from the other point of view. I do not think that
they need to lose it. The goal of Christian universalism can be
realized precisely through the dialectic of siding with the
humiliated. Let me amplify this. It is, in fact, the goal of the
church to represent that "new people of God" of whom one can
say: "There is neither Jew nor Gentile, neither Greek nor
barbarian, neither master nor slave, neither man nor woman
[and if we may proceed with modern relevance: neither black
nor white, neither Communist nor anti-Communist] for all are
one in Christ Jesus." The barriers which men erect between
each other to assert themselves and humiliate others are
demolished in the community of Christ, since men are there
affirmed in a new way: they are "children of freedom." By
undermining and demolishing all barriers—whether of religion, race, education, or class—the community of Christians
proves that it is the community of Christ. This could indeed
become the new identifying mark of the church in our
world, that it is composed, not of equal and like-minded men,
but of dissimilar men, indeed even of former enemies. This
would mean, on the other hand, that national churches, class
churches, and race churches are false churches of Christ and
already heretical as a result of their concrete structure.

The way toward this goal of a new humane community in-
volving all nations and languages is, however, a revolutionary
way. In this connection we quote the apostle Paul once again:
"For consider your call brethren, not many of you were
wise according to worldly standards, not many were powerful,
not many were of noble birth; but God chose what is foolish
in the world to shame the wise, God chose what is weak in
the world to shame the strong, God chose what is low and
despised in the world, even things that are not, to bring to
nothing things that are, so that no human being might

boast in the presence of God. Let him who boasts, boast of the Lord" (1 Cor. 1:26-31). Accordingly, the community of the obscure and weak is given the power of judgment over the high and mighty. So in the community of the crucified, according to the old prophetic images of the mountains being laid low and the valleys exalted, those who hunger after right-eousness are blessed and those who justify themselves are condemned. Thus the way of the kingdom of humanity into the world is prepared and only thus will all flesh see the glory of the Lord. Or to put it without images: The love of God and the humanity of Christ are partial to the laboring and heavily laden, to the humiliated and offended. But how can this be a way to the new community without barriers?

Martin Luther King, Jr., sided with the blacks and the poor. He organized protest movements and strikes. These actions were directed against the white racism and the capitalistic society in his country. But at the same time he was constantly concerned about the white people, unre-deemed and enslaved by their pride and anxiety. He mobil-ized the marches of the blacks and the poor, not for re-venge against the whites but for the redemption of black and white alike from their mutual racial estrangement.

The young Karl Marx also spoke not only of the aliena-tion of the exploited proletariat but also of that of the capi-talist exploiter. By withholding or robbing from another his true humanity, the robber deprives himself of his own human-ity.

Albert Camus described the humane principle of revolu-tion in this way: The slave revolts against his master. He denies him as a master, but not as a man. For his protest is directed against the master's refusal to treat him as a man. As master and slave, neither is a true man and neither can relate to the other in a humane way. If the denial of the master were total, the slave's revolt would bring nothing new into the world but would only exchange the roles of inhumanity. The humane revolution, however, is not out to turn the slaves into masters but to subvert and abolish the whole master-slave relationship so that in the future men will be able to treat one another as men. If the revolution loses sight of this goal, it becomes nihilistic and forfeits its fascination.   •

In this sense, Christianity's taking sides with the "damned of the earth" is a way to the redemption and reconciliation of the damned and the damners. Only through the dialectic of taking sides can the universalism of salvation make its entrance into the world. Any ecclesiastical triumphalism is, therefore, an immature anticipation of the Kingdom of God.

THESIS 6: *The problem of violence and nonviolence is an illusory problem. There is only the question of the justified and unjustified use of force and the question of whether the means are proportionate to the ends.*

Those who advocate nonviolence today are usually those who control the police power. Those who embrace revolutionary violence are usually those who have no means of power. This is a paradox. It is fully clear that the transformation of the conditions of power will come only through the use of power and the assumption of authority. The sole problem consists of the fact that power must be justified; else it is nothing but "naked violence." The use of revolutionary violence must be justified by the humane goals of the revolution and the existing power structures unmasked in their inhumanity as "naked violence." Otherwise, revolutionary violence cannot be made meaningful or appropriate. Unless every possible means is put to use, the revolutionary future is not worth committing oneself to, but if disproportionate means are employed, then the goals of the revolution are betrayed.

The criterion for action is the measure of possible transformation. We need skilled judgment to bring together the opponent, the means, and the end in such a creative tension that the hoped-for effect will come to fruition. It is senseless to encourage the radicalism of the right by short-lived revolutions. There is no point in "waking sleeping dogs" by simply stepping on their tail. It is also senseless to provoke by briefly contrived actions the massive use of counterviolence in the streets only then to announce how evil the opposition is. In the tempo of revolutionary impatience, which presses for ever-new actions, we need the "long-distance" wind of patience and the imagination for encountering ever-new situations. People must be able to combine what they *desire* with what is objectively *possible* and with what they can subjectively *accomplish*. This is a delicate art.

The humane goals of a revolution must not be brought into disrepute by inappropriate means of violence. There is also in the revolutionary movement a revolt of the means against the ends, as was seen in Stalinism. If these means are violent, it is always a question whether the postrevolutionary society can bring the violence under control. Who has ever known a dictator, a secret police, or a bureaucracy to abrogate itself? If the revolutionary goal is a more fully realized humanity, then revolutionaries cannot afford to be inhuman during the so-called transitional period. Already, on the way, we must directly begin with the future and make life truly human during the transitional period. Perhaps we can demonstrate for peace and freedom only by practicing peace and freedom here and now with more determination (H. W. Wolff).

It follows, therefore, that a revolution of the present for the benefit of a better and more humane future must not mold itself after the strategies of the world to be overthrown. Only with great restraint can revolutionaries enter the diabolical circle of violence and counterviolence if they are ever to conquer and abolish it as a whole. Revolutionary means must constantly be reconciled with humane goals, else the revolution threatens to end in terrorism and resignation. How are we to bring about the kingdom of nonviolent brotherhood with the help of violent actions? This is the inner aporia of revolutionary activity. Those who allow the law of the opposition to prescribe their own course are, in any case, not yet the new humanity. Any means may be appropriate, but they must be different and better than those of the opposition if they are to bewilder the opposition. Martin Luther King, Jr., spoke and acted from out of a dimension of truth which was not dependent on political power and the rules of its game. He was to a great extent immune against the anxiety and seduction of power. And precisely for that reason he became more threatening than the prophets of violence to those in positions of power. The atomic powers must be forced into guerrilla warfare; the poker players of power must be compelled into the chess game of reason.

THESIS 7: *The presence of Christians in revolutions can mean that revolutions are freed from the coercion of the law.*
Only with some circumspection and much self-criticism do I venture this last thesis. It is not meant pedantically but, rather, expresses a hope. Revolutions have a tendency toward legalism. In an understandable but also regrettable way, they are often dominated by a moralism by which they view themselves as good and the opposition as inevitably bad. They are of course right to criticize the evil of the opposition. This moralism awakens a new self-affirmation in their own camp as well as a previously unknown sense of solidarity with the comrades in arms; it is only right to appreciate these new-found values. But seldom is there much sensitivity for the ambiguity in even the best of human lives. To be sure, there may be a developed self-criticism in face of one's own mistakes. But this self-criticism does not prevent the Stalinistic fallacy of one's own achievements. Revolutionaries often resemble the old Puritans who took themselves with "deep seriousness" and forgot how to laugh at themselves. This is all quite understandable and perhaps even inevitable.

But I would expect from Christians, who believe in God's presence in the midst of revolution, that they would laugh and sing and dance as the first to be liberated in creation. In a very Christian student revolution in the United States I was deeply impressed that they could shake off the former compulsiveness and the old resignation and laugh at their opposition and themselves. They were "joyous revolutionaries." Even in martyrdom, a revolution can look like a procession of the liberated; then the revolution transcends itself. Jesus was no Zealot like Bar Kochba, nor a preacher of repentance like John the Baptist. He was called "a glutton and a wine-bibber." His disciples did not fast: together with Jesus and the outcasts, and in full view of the enemies. they celebrated the heavenly banquet of the righteous. Is this foolish? Do we have time for that in a revolution? The citizens of the Old World certainly considered it to be a definite piece of folly and it annoys the Puritans of our time. But I think this is the way that revolutionary movements can be redeemed from the coercion of the law and of good works. Faith in the God who makes all things new can only strengthen the historical renewals which are now becoming possible and must be realized. But it laughs at those who make themselves into demigods. Freedom *for* revolutionary action can be bound up in faith with freedom *from* the coercion of revolutionary action. Christians will be strange birds in the revolution. Perhaps they are something like the fools of revolution. They are deeply committed to it but also laugh about it and thus appear strange. They are deeply committed to it and laugh about it *because* they are the forerunners of a yet greater revolution, in which God will abolish even greater oppositions than any human revolution can envision. Any world-transforming act of justice, where it succeeds, corresponds to God's justice on earth. Nevertheless, it always needs to be referred forward to God's overcoming of this world in which even the best is still not "very good." The spirit of the final world revolution comes to life in every historical revolution. World-transforming love is sustained by world-surpassing hope. I think that in this way Christian faith can free man from the convulsions of anxiety and vengeance. I believe that at this point the deep earnestness of love for suffering man can be joined with the cheerful play of faith in God. To faith's practical initiatives for the world's future belongs also something like the mysticism of joy in the present God. The Christian God is no heavenly guarantor of the status quo. But neither is he the avenging God of the offended. In him is found that eternal joy which causes the whole creation to sing and dance. Marxism speaks of the transformation of work into free spontaneity. This is the transition from the "kingdom of necessity" into the "kingdom of freedom." This idea has a long history and is also alive in Christianity. Here it means the liberation from the law of works by faith, which brings forth the free fruits of love. In mysticism it is the idea of the transformation of labor conditioned by need into the play of freedom. Labor conditioned by need or by self-assertion is labor which alienates and humiliates man. Revolutionary work for another future of man is always dependent on what it wants to change and establish. What does faith mean other than already here and now in the midst of the kingdom of poverty and necessity to begin realizing the future of freedom, love, and play? Where this spirit of freedom reigns, of freedom not only from masters and exploiters, but also freedom of man from himself, where this spirit of festivity and laughing becomes infectious, there the revolution within the revolution can take place, the deliverance of revolution from the alienating forms which it assumes in the struggle. It was a student in Tübingen who transformed the saying of Che Guevara: "The vocation of every lover is to bring about revolution" into "The duty of every revolution is to bring about love."

147

VIII • Hope and Confidence:

A Conversation with Ernst Bloch

1

ERNST BLOCH'S "META-RELIGION"

Ernst Bloch's philosophy of hope[1] seeks to culminate in "meta-religion," i.e., "religion as inherited."[2] He believes he can show that the real substratum inherited in all religions is "hope in totality."[3] "Where there is hope, there is religion," and the effect of the eschatology of Christianity is to suggest that here the real nature of religion as such has at last come to light. "Namely, it has *not the static, and therewith apologetic, character of myth, but the humano-eschatological, and therewith explosive, character of Messianism.*"[4] To be

---

This article is a translation by James W. Leitch of the Appendix to *Theologie der Hoffnung* (5th ed.; Munich: Ch. Kaiser Verlag, 1965). It first appeared in English in *Dialog*, 7 (Winter, 1968), pp. 42–55.

[1] The main points of this critique were made in a public conversation with Ernst Bloch which took place at the invitation of the theological faculty in Tübingen on May 21, 1963. For an introduction to Ernst Bloch's philosophy, cf. W. D. Marsch, *Hoffen-worauf? Stundenbuch*, 23 (1963); J. Moltmann, "Messianismus und Marxismus," *Kirche in der Zeit*, 15 (1960), pp. 291–295, and "Die Menschenrechte und der Marxismus," *Kirche in der Zeit*, 17 (1962), pp. 122–126.

[2] *Das Prinzip Hoffnung* (Frankfurt: Suhrkamp Verlag, 1959), p. 1521 (hereafter cited as *PH*)

[3] *PH*, p. 1404.

[4] *Ibid.*

sure, every religious hope has the dubious appearance of holding out vain promises of a better future and thereby providing an alibi for the fearful who would leave the present in the lurch, but it can also be a treasury of forces that are hopefully active and effective in history. "The great religions of mankind often abused the will to a better world by soothing it with vain promises, but for long they were also its fairest field and, indeed, its whole estate."[5] Thus, if we would be the heirs of religion, and especially of Christianity, we must be the heirs of its eschatological hope. To this end we must trace religion back to the ontic foundation from which it arose. According to Bloch, the longing that gives rise to religion, the desire of oppressed creation for joy, for happiness, and for home, has its roots in "that dichotomy in man which is so pregnant with religion—the dichotomy between his present appearance and his nonpresent essence."[6]

This view of religion takes us beyond the customary explanation and criticism of religion in Marxism. If religion is the dubious treasury of hope resulting from the dichotomy in man, then a mere psychological and sociological explanation of it amounts to superficial explaining away. Religion, if it is hope and preserves hope, does not arise from fear, foolishness, and priestly deceit. But then Ludwig Feuerbach, too, with his theory of religion as wishful thinking and his reduction of man's heavenly double to the sensual coming of man to himself, fails to catch the essential note of hope in religion.

Feuerbach derived man's pictures of the gods from his own sensual presence as so far manifested—namely, from the abstract, nonhistoric species "man." Yet the "religious pictures of the coming kingdom, breaking the bounds of the existing situation as they do" ("Behold, I make all things new"), can-

[5] *Ibid.*, p. 1390.
[6] *Ibid.*, p. 1520. Cf. the very similar statement by Karl Marx: "*Religious* misery is at once both the *expression* of real misery and at the same time the *protest* against real misery. Religion is the longing of oppressed creation, the heart of a heartless world and the soul of soulless conditions. It is the *opium* of the people" (*Die Frühschriften*, ed. Landshut [Stuttgart: Kröners Taschenausgabe, 1953], p. 208).

not be reduced to this man who in his sensual givenness comes to himself by taking his gods back into himself. Thus Feuerbach inherited only the mysticism of Christianity, but not the Christian eschatology.[7] This mysticism of an immediate relationship between God and man apart from any historic mediation in Jesus of Nazareth was itself already a dissolution of the Christian faith.

Karl Marx took over Feuerbach's way of criticizing religion by means of a process of reduction, yet changed the sensual materialism of Feuerbach's anthropology into a historico-dialectical materialism of active man transforming his conditions. Man, like the sensual world around him, is "not a thing that is immediately given from all eternity and always the same."[8] "Man—that is the *world of man*, the state, society."[9] His nature is only in process of being worked out. Hence, for him the "criticism of heaven" does not become the blessing of earth,[10] but it becomes the "criticism of earth," the criticism of religion becomes criticism of justice, the criticism of theology becomes criticism of politics.[11] For him religion thus has its roots in the social conflicts of man with man and of men with nature. If we inherit it in Feuerbach's way, then the result is to establish man as the warrior who takes his history into his own hands and overthrows all conditions in which

[7] Cf. the very fine demonstration of this by Rudolf Lorenz, "Zum Ursprung der Religionstheorie Ludwig Feuerbachs," *Ev. Theol.*, 17 (1957), pp. 171ff. "It was from this mysticism that his philosophy of religion grew. It proves to be the result of a kind of piety which is not a legitimate possibility for Christian theology" (*ibid.*, p. 188). Alongside this source in mystical piety, to be sure, one would also have to point to Feuerbach's many quotations from Luther's Christology, from the doctrine of the *communicatio idiomatum realis*, and from the doctrine of the Lord's Supper.

[8] *Die Frühschriften*, p. 351.

[9] *Ibid.*, p. 208.

[10] As happens, following Feuerbach, in Rainer Maria Rilke, who in 1923, in a letter to I. Jahr, summed up the message of the *Duineser Elegien* as follows: "The attributes are taken away from God, the now Ineffable, and revert to the creation, to love and death. . . . All the deep and inward things of this world, which the church fraudulently relegated to the beyond, return again; all the angels take earth's part in songs of praise" (quoted by R. Guardini, *Zu R. M. Rilkes Deutung des Daseins* [1946], p. 21).

[11] *Die Frühschriften*, p. 209.

man is a humiliated and a contemptible creature. Thus the question of religion is not solved by a naturalistic coming of man to himself, but only by a revolution in society which brings a solution of the conflict between men and nature and the conflict of man with himself.

Ernst Bloch goes a step further: religion is hope, and hope is grounded in the ontic difference between what is and what is not yet, between existence and essence, between present and future—and this, too, both in man and in the cosmos. Man is a nonestablished creature and as such, one "which, along with his surrounding world, constitutes a task and a vast container full of future."[12] To hope belongs the knowledge that the life of the outside world is as unfinished as in the self which is at work upon that outside world. Thus religion, insofar as it is hope, has its ground in the process character of man and the world. *Homo homini Deus* ("Man is God to man"),[13] Feuerbach had said, thereby meaning I and Thou in sensual love. Bloch takes up this phrase in the sense, so typical of him, that the *Homo absconditus* of the not-yet-discovered and not-yet-successfully-completed future is the "God" of present man. All pictures of God and the future turn with increasing urgency around the human and cosmic incognito—the core of existence that is the hidden mainspring in man, and the world ground that is the hidden mainspring in the world—approaching it with ever closer and ever more human images of the beyond.

It is only where and when the ontic difference in man, his eccentric position toward himself, and the ontic difference in the world are resolved in the achieving of a home of identity, that religion as hope comes to an end because it is fulfilled. This means that for Bloch, "God" as an image and idol of man, is reduced not to the sensual present of man, nor yet merely to the estranged, antagonistic social situation

[12] *PH*, p. 135. *PH*, p. 285: "Both in man and in the world the essential thing is still outstanding, waiting, in fear of coming to nothing, in hope of succeeding."
[13] *PH*, pp. 1515ff.

of man, but to the "undiscovered, future *humanum.*" "*God*" is understood as a "utopian hypostatization of the ideal of unknown man." "The mysticism of heaven becomes the mysticism of the Son of man. The glory of God becomes the glory of the redeemed community."[14]

Thus in the same way as Feuerbach, Bloch has taken the Christian eschatology which had been disregarded—understandably enough in the light of the times—by Feuerbach and Marx, and reversed it. For Christian eschatology, the future of man, the liberty of the children of God, and the future of the whole expectant creation is disclosed and determined by the future and the promise of the risen Christ. The "unveiled face of man" which Bloch seeks is here illumined by the revelation of the glory of the hidden God (2 Cor. 3:18). For Bloch, however, the future of the risen Christ and the future of God is—methodically following Feuerbach's formula of reduction—"nothing else but" the future of hidden man and of the hidden world. What separates him from Feuerbach is the change from mysticism to Millenarianism, from mystical ecstasy withdrawing from the world to revolutionary subversion of the world, from Meister Eckhart to Thomas Münzer.[15]

This reversal, however, does not solve the problems in Bloch's philosophy of hope, but is, rather, the beginning of them. A theological conversation with Bloch cannot take the form of countering his philosophy of hope by appealing to our experiences of the absurdity of existence, for it might be that then the elements of Christian eschatology from which his *Prinzip Hoffnung* ("principle of hope") lives would also appear absurd. Nor can it consist in making an uncritical theological use of the *Prinzip Hoffnung*, for it might be

---

[14] *Ibid.*, pp. 1533ff.

[15] Cf. the very suggestive comparison made by Karl Mannheim between the mystical and the millenarian experience of time, *Ideologie und Utopie* (3rd ed.; 1952), pp. 186ff.: "For the absolute experience of the millenarian, the present is the point at which that which before was inward strikes out and all at once lays hold of the outward world in sudden transformation."

that then the specifically Christian aspects of Christian eschatology would be absurd. Rather, we have to ask ourselves and Bloch what elements in the Christian hope prove to resist being succeeded by the "meta-religion" of *Das Prinzip Hoffnung*.

For theology, too, the Feuerbachian formulae of reduction which he applies to Christian eschatology can be a possible watershed between God and idols, between faith and superstition, between the confidence that is based on promise and the utopia that is based on wishful thinking. Everything that can be shown to be idolatry of the human heart in the form of projections upward or forward must be explained as such, in order to make room for "the other." Only, nothing can be reduced to the man of the present or of the future which would abrogate the humanity of man and make him the god of his own self. Feuerbach's antireligious atheism can—in Feuerbach's own sense—be used in order to make man his own idol. It can also—in criticism of Feuerbach himself—lead to an "atheism for God's sake."

As regards the answer to the question of the resistance of Christian eschatology toward being succeeded by the *Prinzip Hoffnung*, Bloch himself comes part of the way to meet theology when in his philosophico-theological reflections he arrives at statements which, rightly understood, break through the fundamental closedness of the *Prinzip Hoffnung*. In using these statements to show the resistance of Christian eschatology, we would at the same time seek also the starting point for the criticism of Bloch's philosophy of hope.

2

HOMO ABSCONDITUS AND *DEUS ABSCONDITUS*

Bloch declares in Feuerbach's sense: "What men expressed in the hypostases of the gods was altogether nothing but *longed-for future*."[16] The "wholly other" aspect of God therefore

[16] *PH*, p. 1402.

appears in his philosophy as the "wholly other" of the not-yet-worked-out depth of man and the world.

Yet, in his treatment of the dialectical theology of the early Barth, he can say: "Only the *Deus absconditus* holds the *problem* as to what is the true nature of the legitimate mystery of the *Homo absconditus*."[17]

This last statement could be understood as follows: The problem which man presents to himself, his questionableness, his openness, his unfinishedness and hiddenness, is "held" (i.e., kept open and maintained), provoked, and grounded by the hiddenness of God, and finds its solution where and when this God who raises the question reveals himself. In Christian terms, the problem which man presents to himself in the hiddenness of his self and his true nature is "held," provoked, and grounded in the hiddenness of the future of the risen Lord, which encounters him in the promise of Christ and causes him to seek himself, his life, and his truth in hope and in breaking new ground. In that case, however, the hiddenness of God is not "nothing but" the hiddenness of man, but the hiddenness of man is then grounded in the hiddenness of God in his revelation, as a result of which this revelation becomes a revelation that points toward, and presses for, eschatological fulfillment.

The problem to which this points us lies in the question: What keeps man alive, keeps him moving, hoping, and pressing forward? What makes him an open question in his own eyes (as Augustine put it: *Quaestio mihi factus sum, terra difficultatis*—"I am become a question to myself, a world of difficulty")? What summons him out of his present home in the world to break new ground toward an unknown future? What is the reason why man can never achieve a sullen or cheerful harmony and satisfaction with himself and the world around him?

Bloch's answers to this question are not unequivocal, but as manifold as the cultural forms of human hope. Like G.

[17] *Ibid.*, p. 1406.

Benn and A. Gehlen, he can say: Nothingness, the *horror vacui.* "As such it cannot abide nonentity, but is actively related to the presence of a something."[18]

In the sense of pantheistic, left-wing Aristotelianism, he can say: The impulse and urge of the ground of the world and of existence toward self-realization—*eductio formarum e materia.*[19]

He can say: In the "darkness of the moment of experience" there comes a flash of something that thrusts us forward into an open future. In "boundless amazement" and in the shape of the "unconstructable, absolute question," the *eschaton* flashes upon us suddenly and in a "trice." "Every moment contains . . . potentially the datum of the consummation of the world."[20] But what is it that arouses this fear, this impulse, this hunger for being and identity, this urge toward self-realization? Bloch would take over the Aristotelian longing of matter for the entelechy of form, the Platonic and Neoplatonic *eros* toward the *eidos,* the Christian hope of the fulfillment of the divine promise by God—yet without any presupposed entelechy of form, without presupposed *eidos,* without the presupposition of a God of promise marching ahead of us. The ground of matter's longing must then lie in form-creating matter itself, the ground of the *eidos* must then lie in the *eros* itself, the ground of hope in hope itself.

The objects of hope must arise along with the urge of hope itself, so that the two continually supplant and mediate each other in historic and dialectical ways. Then, however, the "principle of hope" threatens to collapse upon itself. For either, the infinite hope transcends all the finite objects of hope which it projects ahead of us. In that case hope be-

---

[18] *Ibid.,* pp. 356ff.
[19] *Ibid.,* pp. 235ff. Cf. also Bloch's left-wing Aristotelian concept of matter in *Avicenna und die aristotelische Linke* (Berlin, 1952), by means of which he seeks to follow the footsteps of Karl Marx and overcome abstract scientific materialism.
[20] *PH,* p. 359.

comes the eternal, nonhistoric existential of man, and the life-process of the world becomes an endless process. This, however, would be an abstraction from real history. Existence in hope would become an abstract determination of the species "man." Or else the transcendent hope accommodates itself at some time or other to a utopianly defined object of hope and declares itself satisfied[21]—for example, with "socialistic achievements." In that case, however, it betrays itself.

Bloch is aware that when the images of hope are atheistically anthropologized by means of Feuerbach's theory of projection, these hopes are neither adequately explained, nor can they be put to fruitful activity for man. He himself raises the question, "What about the _vacuum_ which is left by doing away with the God hypothesis?" and inquires about the "space into which God was imagined and utopianly projected."[22] From the standpoint of method, something must be presupposed and must lie objectively ahead of us, if, indeed, the images of our wishes and hopes are to be possible of projection to such an extent as they have, in fact, been projected in history. He calls this "an open space, a vacuum," "the _open area of what lies before us_, the _novum_ into which the various series of human ends go on."[23] This "vacuum" is, for him, not a Platonic heaven of ideas, nor an Aristotelian hierarchy of forms, nor yet the presupposition of a God whose existence is agreed. As a "vacuum," it is for Bloch, in the first instance, a negative definition, i.e., the "vacuum" is the open realm which transcends all the images that seek to fill it. Yet that is not to say it is complete conceptual emptiness, but it means the open sphere of action

---

[21] The principle, "each according to his needs," can mean fulfillment of the ontic neediness of man in a totality of being. But it can also mean accommodation of his needs to the standard of what has been attained, "economy" of needs, forced satisfaction with, and reconciliation to, the reduction of needs to the surpassing of America in consumption per head. For this new exposition of the satisfaction of needs, cf. W. Leonhard, _Sowjetideologie heute_, II (1962), pp. 278ff.

[22] _PH_, pp. 1524ff.

[23] _Ibid._, pp. 1530, 1531.

which is still full of all kinds of possibilities, of heaven and hell, the kingdom and the abyss, the *totum* and *nihil*. It is the still open and unattained depth of man and the world, into which all hope's images reach out. The "realm of religious projection" is therefore no chimera, even though it has also no reality in the sense of being factually at hand. It is the realm that keeps moving ahead; ever and again uncomprehended and eluding our grasp, it is the open realm that beckons and excites. "The *homo absconditus* has consequently a sphere which remains ahead, in which, if he does not perish, he can tend toward his most fundamental manifestation in the world that is open to him."[24] It is the realm which lies "before us, in which the essence of man as also of the earth, the anthropological subject and the natural cipher alike, bloom to a utopian end, or, it may be, do not bloom to an end."[25] Where the God hypostases collapse via Feuerbach, this vacuum itself does not collapse.

Nevertheless, the question arises, What can this "vacuum" contain? If all the images of hope which Bloch adduces refer to the home of identity between the *Homo absconditus* and the hidden depth of the world, then it contains the open possibility of attained identity and the open possibility of frustrated identity between man and nature. But where does the alternative come from, which Bloch sets up between "all" and "nothing," and which this vacuum is supposed to contain? At every point in which he speaks like this, he refers to the distinction of "heaven" and "hell" in apocalyptic judgment,[26] demythologizes this apocalyptic and ethicizes its alternative in terms of militant optimism and the work of man in history, through which the alternative of all or nothing can finally be turned to good account.[27] But now, this means that in the "vacuum" of the open future we should really

---

[24] *Ibid.*, p. 1534.
[25] *Ibid.*, p. 1533.
[26] *Ibid.*, pp. 1532, 362ff., and frequently.
[27] Specially emphasized in *Philosophische Grundfragen*, I: *Zur Ontologie des Noch-nicht-Seins* (Frankfurt: Suhrkamp Verlag, 1961), pp. 55ff.

have to presuppose also a criterion by reference to which this critical decision takes place. For otherwise it remains unintelligible why the process of mediation between man and nature should have an end and goal at all, and why an alternative announces itself in the open realm of possibilities ahead and forces itself upon man in history. The alternative in question falls to pieces when the final separation between heaven and hell is certainly inherited from apocalyptic in the form of all or nothing, but not the third factor by reference to which alone the alternative arises at all, and which in apocalyptic is called the advent of the God of judgment.

In Bloch's possibly attained *totum*—in the "kingdom," as he calls it, thereby understanding a "kingdom without God"—man and the natural subject at last look upon each other with unveiled face. They are dialectically reconciled with each other as in Marx, in the "naturalizing of man and the humanizing of nature." They are not reconciled with each other by, and in the presence of, a third factor—as in Christian eschatology, through the divinity and Lordship of God. Hence, the question arises why they are compelled to find each other and be reconciled with each other in a dialectical identity of this kind at all.

For Christian hope, the hunger and the urge, the breaking of new ground and the readiness to face the future, have their ground in the hiddenness of the future of the risen Lord. Hence, this hope has an object ahead of it which is neither a thinglike existence upon which it can rest, nor complete conceptual emptiness, as in the vacuum which contains the *horror vacui* and the possibility of success, nor yet a mere cipher for hope itself. This object is seen as the promise of God and embraced in the confidence that counts on the faithfulness of the God "who raises the dead and calls into being the things that are not" (Rom. 4:17). It is the "God of hope" (Rom. 15:6), but not the "God hope," "*Deus spes*," as Bloch says. This God of hope, on whose promise and faithfulness hope counts, but who is not the hope itself, is a whole eternity ahead of the man who willingly faces the future in hope—to be precise, the eternity of his own death and of the judgment in which nothing that is can abide.

3

THE HOME OF IDENTITY AND THE KINGDOM OF GOD

Is the Christian hope of the Kingdom of God congruous with Bloch's "home of identity"?

Bloch's *eschaton*, which he calls the "home of identity," means man become "one in essence" with himself, with his fellows, and with nature.[28] In him the contradictions are therefore resolved (a) between man's Ego and his self, (b) between the individual and society, (c) between mankind and nature.

Now Bloch himself says of the "religious idea of the kingdom": "as little as the religious self is the same as the creature man in his givenness, and as little as religious security coincides with the self-satisfied incorporation of positivism into the empirical content of life, so little does the religious idea of the kingdom, as far as its intended compass and content are concerned, itself coincide entirely with any idea of social utopia. . . . It contains . . . an absolute in which contradictions that are other than social are to cease, in which the understanding of all hitherto existing relationships is altered."[29]

---

[28] This is in the first instance entirely in line with the teleology of Karl Marx: "This communism as perfect naturalism = humanism, as perfect humanism = naturalism, is the *true* solution of the contradiction between man and nature, and between man and man, the true solution of the conflict between existence and essence, between objectification and self-activation, between freedom and necessity, between the individual and the species. It is the solved riddle of history and knows itself to be the solution" (*Frühschriften*, p. 235). "Thus *society* is perfect oneness of essence between man and nature, the true resurrection of nature, the complete naturalism of man and the complete humanism of nature (*ibid.*, p. 237).

[29] *PH*, pp. 1410f.

159

The Christian "kingdom" is separated from the utopian king-doms by the new departure that is demanded by the explosive tendency of rebirth and transfiguration.[30] From this it neces-sarily follows that Christian eschatology—which counts on the "new departure," on the miracle of the resurrection from the dead, and on the new creation of him who calls into the present from the end, "Behold, I make all things new"—cannot be turned into a utopia, nor yet into the "principle of hope" of an immanent world consummation, by dint of nontranscendent transcending, but that rightly understood it also "explodes" the "principle of hope." This difference becomes plain when Chris-tian eschatology reflects upon its foundation in the resurrection of the dead and the annihilation of death by life, instead of on the human utopias in which it lived in the nineteenth century.

That Bloch has certainly an inkling of this despite his Feuerbachian formulae of reduction, becomes clear when we compare the conclusion of his *Das Prinzip Hoffnung* with the conclusion of *Naturrecht und menschliche Würde*.

His *Das Prinzip Hoffnung* concludes with the words: *"The real genesis is not at the beginning, but at the end,* and it commences to begin only when society and existence become radical, i.e., when they take themselves by the roots. The root of history, however, is man as he labors, creates, transforms the given facts and gets beyond them. When he has compre-hended himself and has grounded his life in real democracy without renunciation and estrangement, then there arises in the world something which appears to us all in childhood, and in which none of us yet was—home."[31] It is plain that by "real democracy" and "home" Bloch here means that "kingdom of liberty" of which Marx said that it begins only where the labor that is conditioned by need or by outward utility ceases, and that it thus lies only beyond the sphere of material production.

At the end of *Naturrecht und menschliche Würde* we are

[30] *Ibid.*, pp. 1411f.
[31] *Ibid.*, p. 1628.

told: "To be sure, a no longer antagonistic society will keep a firm grip on all our worldly destinies, and implies an absence of economic and political situation, a freedom from fate, yet for that very reason the indignities of existence emerge all the more painfully from the jaws of death to the ebbing of life in boredom and satiety. The messengers of nonentity have lost the plain colours they had in class society, and now wear a new, largely inconceivable dress."[32] Thus, at the point where society relieves man of his economic, social, and political cares and general production begins to regulate itself "automatically," there arises for Marx the "kingdom of liberty"; yet for Bloch, on the contrary, there emerge "more strongly than ever the real cares, the question of what is really not in order in life."[33] This means, however, that the "home of identity" cannot by any means be identified with what Marx called "real democracy," but that Marx's teleology can at best be a transparency through which to glimpse the "home of identity," which is still not attained even in his formulae for the future.

The Marxist conception of history, for which "the history of all society hitherto" is the history of class warfare, and therefore Communism is the "solved riddle of history and the solution of it," has reached its end where man's economic, social, and political contradictions and estrangements cease —but then the end is not yet here, for nonentity is not yet swallowed up in being. The Socialist revolution has then taken negative features of existence—economically, socially, and politically negative—and changed them into positives. But it has not taken the *nihil* itself, into which all existence threatens to sink, and abrogated it in an attained *totum*. Hence, the forces of negation then manifest themselves anew with inconceivable power—namely, in the "infinite pain of the negative" (Hegel). It no longer encounters us in iden-

[32] *Naturrecht und menschliche Würde* (Frankfurt: Suhrkamp Verlag, 1961), pp. 310ff.
[33] *Ibid.*, p. 310.

161

tifiable form as hunger, misery, and injustice, but in the intangible form of boredom, of life at an ebb, and of feelings of absurdity.

In this case, however, man does not yet come to himself, even here, but finds himself more than ever an open question. He finds himself a *Homo absconditus* at the very point at which, Godlike—and playboylike—he finds all things "become possible, fishing, hunting, cattle-rearing, criticizing," as Marx promised. The "total man," who according to Marx is produced by Communist society as its "constant reality," becomes the figure of a "man without attributes" (R. Musil), who drowns in his infinite possibilities because he nowhere finds necessity.[34] He becomes *Homo absconditus* in an as yet unheard-of radicality, because in the "absence of economic and political fate" there is no longer anything economic, social, and political which he could use as a foil to develop himself.

It may well be that this life can be expressed, to use Hegel's words, as love's playing with itself, only this idea sinks to the level of insipid edification when it lacks the earnestness, the pain, the patience, and the labor caused by the negative. This recognition that the Socialist revolution, too, is utopian in that, like all visions of "utopia," it seeks a society which, without conflicts, without history and thus without a future, is undisturbed and self-enclosed, and that therefore its expressions of harmony in terms of the essential oneness of man, society, and nature must change into expressions of being doomed to closedness,[35] may have induced Bloch to recommend to this society something "like a church"—"something which orders the mind and teaches the spirit, to live again and again like a church, in preparation and with a sense of direction,"[36] a steward of the messianic hope and an advocate of

[34] Cf. J. Moltmann, *Der verborgene Mensch, Das Gespräch*, 35 (1961).
[35] On this change cf. H. Jonas, *Gnosis und spätantiker Geist*, I (2nd ed.; 1954), pp. 156ff.
[36] *Naturrecht und menschliche Würde* (1961), p. 312.

brotherliness; "a churchly ship without superstition and under way."

But now, if there is to be such a thing as is here considered possible and also necessary—not, of course, the church as it has hitherto existed, but certainly a preserved and practiced form of Christian eschatology—then it follows that, contrary to Bloch, not all hopes turn to Marx, where they become rational,[37] but that even for a society of this kind in all its lack of history and in all its exposure to boredom for want of stirring situations, Christian eschatology has to maintain a constant question mark and keep the future open, in order that even there men will not "take life as it comes" (*in den Tag hinein leben*), but will "live for more than the moment" (*über den Tag hinaus leben*).

If, however, there is such a prospect as this, it follows, further, that the "home of identity" which is sought cannot exist already at the point where the contradictions cease in man, between men, and with nature, but really only at the point where death and nonentity will be no more. It is only where death "is swallowed up in victory"[38] that the real and ultimate nonidentity of man is overcome. The very fact that for Bloch, in the nonantagonistic society of Marx and Engels as he portrays it at the end of *Naturrecht und menschliche Würde*, death appears like the chill guest in *Don Juan* and disturbs the utopian harmony indicates the difference between the utopia of the Kingdom and the eschatology of the resurrection. All utopias of the Kingdom of God or of man, all hopeful pictures of the happy life, all revolutions of the future, remain hanging in the air and bear within them the germ of boredom and decay—and for that reason also adopt a militant and extortionate attitude to life—as long as

---

[37] *PH*, Preface, p. 16.
[38] In all Bloch's approaches to hope this phrase occurs again and again as a highest *fascinosum* (*PH*, Preface, pp. 15, 363, 1290, and frequently); *Zur Ontologie des Noch-nicht-Seins*, p. 62: "Dialectic thus describes the point of the sunrise in the point of its setting or in fact, the swallowing up of death in victory."

there is no certainty in face of death and no hope which carries love beyond death.

Bloch's "home of identity"—as was already the case also with the phrases about the "essential oneness" of man and nature in Marx—takes up the thought of "dialectical identity" as found in Schelling and Goethe. Whereas with Feuerbach we are in the neighborhood of the nondialectical view of an immediate identity of all antitheses in man, we find in Goethe, and in Schelling and Marx, the thought of a self-actuated, dialectical identity. It is the dialectical identity of centrifugal and centripetal forces, of impulse and need, of outgoing and appropriation, of activity and receptivity, of inhalation and exhalation.[39] When Bloch speaks of a "home of identity," of a humanizing of nature and a naturalizing of man, he obviously means this sort of identity, as in Schelling—an identity of mutual interpenetration in the living unity of giving and taking.[40]

This identity, however, is a dream identity—that of a life "which abhors death and keeps itself clear of destruction" (Hegel)—so long as it is not able to embrace and resolve the absolute contradiction of death and nonidentity. Hegel's dialectic, precisely in his early theological writings, is much wider,

[39] The thought of dialectical identity has been traced out in K. Bockmühl's excellent study, *Leiblichkeit und Gesellschaft: Studien zur Religionskritik und Anthropologie im Frühwerk von L. Feuerbach und K. Marx* (1961), esp. pp. 234ff. It is the "candid idea of the young Schelling," which Marx retains and applies to the criticism of Hegel's dialectic. For Engels, too, the goal of history "which our century is approaching" lies in "reconciliation with nature and with oneself." For Goethe, cf. G. Benn, *Goethe und die Naturwissenschaften* (1932), (Zürich, 1949), p. 25: "An idea that went beyond Spinoza, beyond his crystallized being. . . . his immobile ontology—beyond this to an identity which moved itself, a reality which became dialectical, a this-worldliness in which the transcendent activated itself." Cf. also E. Bloch, who uses phrases of Goethe's to describe his conception of the hidden driving-force of the "natural subject" (*PH*, pp. 782, 802). It arises also in the context of the problem of death: Communist readiness to die without hope, yet with the knowledge of a future resurrection of nature. "Communist cosmology is here [viz., in the problem of death] as everywhere the problematical field of a dialectical mediation between man and his work on the one hand and the possible subject of nature on the other" (*PH*, p. 1383).

[40] So, too, in Marx the "total man" is the man who stands on the well-founded earth, inhaling and exhaling the forces of nature (*Mega*, I, 5, p. 160).

inasmuch as—and as long as—it took its bearings from the dialectic of love and of the raising of the crucified. The eschatology of the resurrection of the dead does not speak of a "home of identity" as dialectically mediated, but of a "home of reconciliation" in new creation out of nothing.

4

EXTRATERRITORIALITY TOWARD DEATH AND THE RESURRECTION OF THE DEAD

The real problem of all thinking in terms of hope is posed by death, if what Bloch says of the latter is true: "The jaws of death crush all things and the gorge of decay devours every teleology."[41] But is the "principle of hope," with its prospect of the dialectical home of identity, itself a match for death, that greatest of "anti-utopias," or is it arrived at by denying the deadliness of death? Here the question arises once again, and this time in radical form, whether Bloch's home of identity takes up and resolves into itself the absolute nonidentity, or whether it is arrived at by shutting our eyes to nonentity.

In the chapter on "Hope's Pictures against Death," Bloch launches out onto the dark, uncertain sea of death, and concludes his voyage with the prospect of a point at the core of existence which is "extraterritorial" toward transience and death—with a utopia of *non omnis confundar* ("I shall not be wholly confounded").

In the mysterious darkness of the living moment, man approaches his core. "This most immediate factor in our being is at the same time its constitutive ground, the bare fact of our being."[42] This factuality in the Now of the living moment is dark, hidden from sight, nowhere given and objectifiable. It is immediate. This factual being (*Dass-sein*) which presses toward positive being (*Da-sein*) is the driving force in the

[41] *PH*, p. 1301.
[42] *Ibid.*, p. 1385.

process of development, the ground of development, and therefore the ground both of transience and of future. If it is the obscure core of existence which itself presses forward and surpasses every mode of its existence, then what we call transience and death must also have its ground in it. This driving, developing core of existence is therefore not subject to transience, since it itself constitutes the process of "dying and becoming."

Thus, in Bloch, the experience of the transience of all things and of man himself is given a new interpretation. Time devours all it brings to birth. Why? Because the genuine, finally successful birth has not yet appeared. Hence, this is not a transience which results from looking back sorrowfully upon the things that cannot last, but a transience which is borne in upon us because hope surpasses all its concrete forms. Time and transience, consequently, do not affect that which first gives rise to them. They do not affect the core of existence, which the process has not yet brought out.

The core of existence has not yet entered into the process and is consequently not affected by death. Where death is concerned, it is surrounded by the "protected zone of the not-yet-alive."[43] It is intransient not because it lies beyond development and decay in some eternal, timeless being, but because it is an as yet undeveloped urge. It is extra-territorial toward transience not because, like Plato's soul, it comes from another realm than the fleeting realm of appearances, but because it is related to an *eschaton* of attainment in which inward and outward, core and husk, will be one, and therefore life will be without death. Death lies only in that element of disunity in which being has not yet come to itself. Hence, Bloch can say that the utopia of *non. omnis confundar* allows every husk to be cracked by the negation that is death, but allows death only this power to crack open the husks surrounding the subject within. The core of existence is beyond the reach of death, and when this

---

[43] *Ibid.*, p. 1390.

core has been brought to attainment, it is more extraterritorial toward death than ever.[44] Then we have so to speak "neither core nor husk," but "everything at once." Hence, consistently enough, it is said of life here: "Wherever our existence comes near to its core, there permanence begins—not a petrified permanence, but one that contains newness without transience."[45]

This way of arguing with death manifestly makes use of the idea of the immortality of the soul and the transmigration of souls. It is not, of course, the old Platonic form of the idea, but takes over and alters the form which this idea had acquired in Lessing, Kant, and Fichte. The distinction between life and death as core and husk takes up the distinction between the ego, which in pursuit of its endless task discovers itself and becomes immortal, and the phenomena to which death belongs.[46] The alteration, however, is in the transcendental subject. It is no longer one that follows after itself in endless reflection, but one that endlessly surpasses itself in hope.[47]

[44] *Ibid.*, p. 1391.
[45] *Ibid.*, p. 1391. Bloch finds the really appropriate language of hope not so much in visions, ideas, utopias, and dreams, as in the "fleeting tonal structures" of *music*, in the "as-yet-nowhere medium of sound." *PH*, pp. 1289f.: "If death, conceived as the axe of annihilation, is the most stringent of nonutopias, it finds its match in music as the most utopian of all arts." "But imperviously, imperturbably, music really goes to meet death, with the intention—as a Bible word puts it—of *swallowing it up in victory*" (p. 1290). "The slow miracles of music are also the most profound, where their object is concerned; they stretch beyond time and have their goal beyond it, and consequently also beyond their own passing away" (p. 1289). "This does not mean a certainty of any kind in face of the most stringent of nonutopias, but it does mean an ability to deny its own field. . . . A freedom from pressure, death and fate is expressed in the as-yet-nowhere medium of sound—a freedom which has not expressed itself in definite visible form, and cannot yet so express itself. For this very reason all music of annihilation points to a core which, because it has not yet blossomed, cannot fade either; it points to a *non omnis confundar*" (p. 1294).
[46] J. G Fichte, *Uber den Unterschied des Geistes und des Buchstabens in der Philosophia* (1794): "Death is a phenomenon like all other phenomena: no phenomenon, however, affects the ego."
[47] Bloch calls it "the unkillable element of the consciousness of revolutionary solidarity." *PH*, p. 1381: "This consciousness means—in relation to the bearer of it—immortality in the person, in the sense of the immortality of its best intentions and contents." He regards it as the "soul of future humanity as the latter appears in advance" in the revolutionary consciousness.

Yet it still remains a doctrine of the extraterritoriality or immortality of the soul or the core of existence, even when the latter proves its existence not in contemplation and not in reflection, but in hope. This core of existence is not arrived at by withdrawing upon some transcendental impregnability and abandoning everything else to the realm of the insignificant, the inessential, and the transient, and thus by denying the reality of the history whose abysmal end is death; yet it does deny history and death by projecting itself into the realm of not yet and regarding the reality of life as a mere "husk" which it abandons to death.[48]

But is this to take seriously the deadliness of death? What sort of readiness for life and love of life arise from this utopia

---

[48] Cf. here Bloch's doctrine of that nonentity which enters into no dialectic and which no transforming countermove of courage and of militant hope can turn to being and to good (*Zur Ontologie des Noch-nicht-Seins* [1961], pp. 41–63). This is the "sheer nonentity," the "annihilatingly disparate," the "seed that dies and bears no fruit," in Hegel's terms, the absurdity of the Peloponnesian War and the Thirty Years' War, today that of the Fascist death camps and the atom-bombed cities. For Hegel this is something other than a creative difference, for Bloch something other than a Good Friday that leads to Easter (p. 60). This "mere negative" or "negative as such" remains absurd, insofar as ontologically it contains no dynamic not-yet and anthropologically cannot be abrogated in the countermove toward being by the "forces of antinonentity and of the utopian *totum*" (p. 56). Even Jews and Christians are not panlogical dialecticians in league with a friendly providence, that they should know what all evil things are good for. They are not the "all-for-the-best people" whom G. Benn contrasts with the "connoisseurs of the dark side." But they believe and know that *creatio* and *novum ex nihilo* is suddenly and unexpectedly there. The creation story does not present the existence of the world on the basis of not-yet-being, of the longing of matter and of possible being, but manifestly sees it against the background of the "darkness upon the face of the deep." Amid the barrenness and desolation of the "mere negative" there is suddenly *creatio ex nihilo*. The prophetic history similarly presents the prospect of salvation and of the new creation in the midst of being judged and swallowed up in nothingness, as *novum ex nihilo*. The sacrifice of Isaac and the desolation of Job, the end of Jesus on the cross and his being swallowed up in eternal death and hell, contain within them no dialectical positive. Only the new being that is suddenly there, startlingly and unexpectedly, amid such "sheer nonentity" is worthy of hope and trust. The latter are formulated in terms of the picture of "raising of the dead" and speak of salvation as "life from the dead" (Rom. 11:15). Maidanek and Hiroshima find no soothing dialectical answer, but the "earnest expectation of the creature" (Rom. 8:18ff.) becomes a cry to God in hope that the *creator ex nihilo*, who raised the forsaken Christ, will make such ends the start of his beginning.

of *non omnis confundar*? For, indeed, every picture which hope constructs against death results in a definite readiness to live or a definite refusal to live, be it apathy, be it ataraxia, be it the absolute fulfillment of our duty in regard to the material of the world or the militant optimism of world revolution—or be it the passion of the love that accepts death.

The Christian hope in the God who raises the dead and creates being out of nothing takes account of death in its radical deadliness, namely, in its roots in the *nihil*. Death is not one phenomenon among others, of which none affects the ego. Nor does life discover any point of identity which could make it extraterritorial toward death and immune from it. On the contrary, life can here be accepted as a life unto death—accepted in faith in the resurrection and hope in him who creates life out of death.

There is one identity which is maintained through the midst of the infinite qualitative antithesis of death and life. It is that identity in which resurrection is promised. Yet it does not lie in man, so that, in the core of his being at least, death cannot overwhelm him. But it lies beyond death and life in the event of the promise of God in which man can rely on the faithfulness of God. This identity is promised, and becomes a possible object of hope, in the dialectical point of transformation constituted by the resurrection of the crucified Christ. If it is perceived there, then the life that trusts in him can surrender itself to death, to the pain of self-expending and love, can lose itself and be gained precisely in so doing. The expectation of resurrection thereby gives to the life of love that future which it requires in order to be able to love, in order to be a love that "never faileth." Love always requires a little future.[49] It lives from the passion of hope, which Kierkegaard called the "passion for the possible." This passion for the possible is kindled by

[49] The words which Albert Camus puts on the lips of Pater Rieux: "It must, indeed, be admitted that the plague had robbed all of us of the capacity for love and even for friendship. For love requires a little future, and for us there was nothing more than moments" (*The Plague*, 1947).

the "impossible."[50] If this "impossible" is believed to be within the power of the God who raises the dead, then love has a hope beyond death and against death. It finds no end until the dead arise. It gains from this the power to "hold fast what is dead" (Hegel). But the reverse is also true: The future which is gained by the resurrection of Christ is truly recognized and truly accepted only in the love which expends itself even unto death.

Dolf Sternberger, in his review of *Das Prinzip Hoffnung*, has asked Bloch about this love that must arise from hope and accept death for the sake of life.[51] Faust, in his pursuit of the moment of fulfillment, knew nothing of this love. But when Sonja began really to love the murderer Raskolnikoff, she read him the story of the raising of the dead and stinking Lazarus.

Any hope against death which does not produce a love for life and a loving readiness to die surely always bears within it the seeds of resignation, for it relegates life to a supposedly extraterritorial core of existence. It gives death and pain only the husks of life to crack open—if we would abide by Bloch's picture—because they are already abandoned and left behind, because for that very reason they are empty. But does life not become hollow, when death gets only the husks which no longer contain anything or do not yet contain anything?

To distinguish life and death in the light of an extraterritorial core of existence results in a dualism of core and husk. To differentiate life and death in the light of the dialectical point of transformation constituted by the resurrection results in a dialectic of the fullness of life in hope and love, in self-expending and resurrection.

---

[50] Cf. L. Kolakowski's important reflections on the peculiar meanings of the "possible" and the "impossible" for the utopian consciousness (*Der Mensch ohne Alternative* [München: Piper, 1961], pp. 145ff.). Even Thomas Münzer had already spoken of the "courage and power to the impossible" and plainly considered the seemingly impossible to be the source of all possibilities (cf. K. Mannheim, *Ideologie und Utopie* [3rd ed., 1952], p. 186).

[51] Dolf Sternberger, "Vergiss das Beste nicht," *Frankfurter Allgemeine Zeitung*, April 9, 1960.

The Christian heretics and fanatics whom Bloch likes to quote among the ancestors of his thinking—such as Marcion, Montanus, Joachim di Fiore and Thomas Münzer—were all encratites, despisers of the body and the earth. They knew the hope which spiritually exalts men beyond death and the things of this world, which withdraws from the earth in mystic enthusiasm or destroys it in revolution. But they did not know the love which accepts the earth's pain and the suffering of obedience in love because it finds hope for the earth and for the body. It is against such enthusiasm that the Creed includes the statement about the "resurrection of the body."[52]

5

HOPE AND CONFIDENCE

Bloch has insisted often and emphatically, especially in discussions with Christian theology, that *"hope is not confidence."*[53] "No anthropological criticism of religion destroys the hope on which Christianity stands; it only takes from this hope that which would make it cease to be hope and turn it into superstitious confidence—the portrayal and deter-

---

[52] Cf. the difference between Thomas Münzer and Martin Luther in the doctrine of the incarnation. Thomas Münzer: ". . . that we fleshly, earthly men should become gods through Christ's becoming man, and should thus with him be God's disciples, taught and deified by God himself and his Spirit and wholly transformed in them, that our earthly life should soar to heaven" (quoted according to K. Holl, *Ges. Aufsätze zur Kirchengeschichte*, I [1927], p. 431, note 1). Cf. also E. Bloch, *Thomas Münzer als Theologe der Revolution* (München, 1921), Frankfurt: Suhrkamp Verlag, 1962, p. 238. Martin Luther: "Humanitatis seu (ut Apostolus Loquitur) carnis regno, quod in fide agitur, nos sibi conformes facit et crucifigit, faciens ex infoelicibus et superbis diis homines veros, idest miseros et peccatores. Quia enim ascendimus in Adam ad similitudinem dei, ideo descendit ille in similitudinem nostram, ut reduceret nos ad nostri cognitionem. Atque hoc agitur sacramento incarnationis." (*WA* 5, 128: "By the power of his humanity or [as the apostle says] of his flesh, which is exercised in faith, he conforms us to himself and crucifies us, making us no longer proud and unhappy gods, but true men, that is, miserable sinners. For because we rise in Adam to the likeness of God, so he descends to our likeness in order to bring us back to the knowledge of ourselves. And this is done in the mystery of the incarnation.")
[53] Cf. above all, the opening lecture in Tübingen, "Kann Hoffnung enttäuscht werden?" in *Verfremdungen*, I (Frankfurt: Suhrkamp Verlag, 1962), pp. 211ff.

mination, the senseless unreality, yet supposed reality, of the mythology of its fulfillment."[54] "Hope contains as such the risk of being frustrated: it is not confidence."[55]

What does Bloch here mean by "confidence" and what does he mean by "hope"? He describes "confidence" as superstitious, quietist, nonactivating, as the idea that salvation is guaranteed, as certainty of salvation without recognition of the category "danger" and therefore without a will to the experiment of life in the great *laboratorium possibilis salutis* of the world. He calls the Christian hope "confidence" in this sense, because it considers God and salvation to be established and because it considers the future to be established, dated, and fixed in its contents, so that neither anything new nor anything fundamentally evil can happen.

He thinks that in Christian faith, man is relieved of active hope and concern for the future, thanks to the providence of God and the atoning death of Christ, and that consequently it is only by means of consistent atheism that man can be burdened with the happiness and danger of his own history. He is thinking here of the Christian church which, under Constantine, took over the heritage of the Roman state religion and allied itself with the powers that be, and thus became the religious guarantor of existing—yet always inadequate—reality and the suppressor of potentialities. In "confidence" of this kind, hope is brought to accommodation with things as they are. He is also thinking of the struggle of the fanatics of Reformation days against the "easygoing flesh in Wittenberg" and against Luther's doctrine of justification—misunderstood to the effect that man can debauch himself "at Christ's expense" but is not drawn into the fellowship of suffering between the crucified one and the suffering of the whole sorry creation.

Confidence is not security. It is wholly unclear why Bloch calls Christian assurance "confidence," when what he really means is surely security, *securitas*. As applied to his caricature

[54] *PH*, p. 1523.
[55] *Verfremdungen*, I, p. 214.

of superstitious salvational positivism, the expression "confidence" is completely inappropriate, for confidence never means guaranteed knowledge about established facts, but always looking forward and taking stock of the future. On the other hand, the salvational positivism in question has nothing whatsoever to do with the assurance of Christian hope, but is, rather—as the example of a Marxism that has fallen into economic materialism shows—a form of disappointed hope. In this world, Christian confidence has only the call and promise of the God of the resurrection in its favor, and has therefore the world and death with all their possibilities and impossibilities against it.

It is consequently "hope contrary to hope" (Kierkegaard)[56] and a hope contrary to what is seen (Rom. 8:24); a hope where, according to our experience and to what we can conceive to be possible, "there is no hope" (Rom. 4:18); a hope of things which we do not see (Heb. 11:1)—because in face of death it sets its hope on the impossible, namely, on resurrection and life from God. That is neither pseudo-scientific certainty, nor yet mere empty wishful thinking. It has neither facts, nor auspicious tendencies on the part of nature, nor the immortality of human hopes and wishes in its favor; it has nothing save the faithfulness of God, who stands to his word of promise, who will not lie because he will not deny himself. If this assurance of Christian hope is grounded in the promise and mission of the crucified Christ, it does not regard the resurrection of Christ as a plain fact, but as an event that is the beginning of a process and gives ground for hope, an event that points to the future of the world and of man in the future of Christ. Hence it is no mere wishful thinking either, which would have in its favor only the optimism of the wisher and possibly also auspicious world tendencies. It has its ground—whether it speaks for or against our best experiences of ourselves and the world—in the *extra nos* of the *promissio Dei*.

For that reason it is not exhausted in human hopes kindled

[56] Cf. the quotation from Kierkegaard in *PH*, p. 1298.

by that promise, and does not collapse in moments of despair which anticipate their nonfulfillment. For that reason, to be sure, it can never come to terms with established realities any more than Bloch's hope can, but remains unreconciled until the fulfillment of the promise. When Christian confidence calls death "the last enemy" (1 Cor. 15:26), it thus affirms that it refuses to reconcile itself with death, as surely as the Christ by whom it is kindled did not remain in death. It is in this sense that we have to understand Blumhardt's saying that Christ is the protest against misery, injustice, sin, evil, and death. Nor does the Reformers' doctrine of justification assert that man is spared anything through the vicarious act of Christ, but it declares, as Paul Gerhardt put it in his hymn: "And as he breaks each chain,/Of death, sin, world and pain,/And as he bursts through hell,/I follow with him still."

The "category of danger," which according to Bloch a brave hope recognizes, is even more radically characteristic of Christian assurance. Bloch asks: What does the self-satisfied positivist know of the dangers of a hope which leaves the mainland and launches out onto the sea of possibilities in an uncertain world process that contains all and nothing? We may surely go on to ask: What does the man who hopes in Bloch's sense, the man in league with the auspicious tendencies of the world, know of the trials of the believer? The believer does not merely have the danger ahead of him in the open world process, but he stands already in the midst of it, because he is himself a danger to the danger. Where there is baptism, there is temptation; where there is faith, there is unbelief; where Christ is, there is Antichrist; where love is, there is death; where there is rescue, danger grows too; where the ultimate future of God is present in the world, there is crisis—a crisis, moreover, which involves both man's certainties and his wishes.

Bloch's hope is "disappointable," but it can also surmount its own disappointments because salvation and destruction

174

in the world process are not yet settled. It is in league with the as yet undecided character of the things in the world. The Christian assurance of the future, however, stands in the midst of the decision of the end itself, and is therefore in proximity to the cross. Hence, it cannot anticipate the possibility of its own disappointability, and take it into account, and itself in the spirit keep its head above the waters of the possible. It must accept the "cross of reality" in the "power of the resurrection."

Hope is not confidence, but confidence is also hope and constantly calls hopes to life. The Christian hope is not a utopia of faith, so that within the framework of a phenomenology of hopes it could be related to a presupposed world process and thus relativized as being "also a possibility." Rather, in this world with its processes and among men with their wishes, it starts its own process concerning the truth. Yet it does not for this reason go hand in hand with despair of temporal hopes, but itself constantly provokes and produces an anticipatory kind of thinking, a fantasy of love that pictures how there could be better conditions in the world and greater righteousness among men, because it is confident that the best of all and the righteousness of God is coming. For this reason it also provokes and produces critical thinking about the past and the present, because it knows of the crisis in which nothing that is can stand.

Thus the Christian assurance of the promise gives rise to resistance and new departures in face of a world that shuts itself up in self. Thus there arises hopeful thinking about men and things, the fantasy of love looking to open possibilities. The utopianly defined end of history in the phrases about the harmony of mankind and nature is surpassed by Christian eschatology and has its provisional and relative character disclosed. If, however, these utopias become surpassable, then they become variable and practicable for the fantasy of love, which is creatively engaged in finding how things could be better. Christian confidence must find the

175

strength for an iconoclasm that shatters the pictures constructed by utopian hopes—and this, too, not from resignation but because of the true wretchedness of the world and because of the future of God. In so doing it will give free rein precisely to plans and reflections concerning the future. It will be one with the *Prinzip Hoffnung* in refusing to put up with the given reality, with its supposed constraints and the laws of evil and death. Yet, neither will it put up with utopian sketches of the future, but will go beyond these too. It will go beyond them, not into empty openness but in the direction in which the promise of God points man where the misery of the creation is concerned.

Thus it will break open the closed utopian horizons, and in the utopian horizons which are open to all kinds of possibilities it will recognize and point to the essentials. In this way the eschatological hope becomes the driving force in history for the production of creative utopias of love toward suffering man and his uncompleted world, on the way to the unknown but promised future of God. In this sense Christian eschatology will be able to make room for the *Prinzip Hoffnung*, while, on the other hand, it will be constrained by the *Prinzip Hoffnung* to give a better and more sharply delineated account of itself.

IX ✦ The Future as New Paradigm of Transcendence

1
THE CONCEPT OF TRANSCENDENCE

"Transcendence" is a relative concept, for it concerns, whenever and wherever it is employed, a transcendence of something and for something. By "transcendence" we ordinarily designate that which surpasses the present and experienceable "immanence," that which moves to a beyond. By "immance" we designate that which impinges upon us, the present, the here and now. Just as the beyond is always the beyond of the here and now, so also the here and now is always the here and now of a particular beyond. Both concepts belong together, reciprocally defining each other and mutually relating to each other. The understanding of transcendence is always dependent upon the experience of a reality as immanence, and conversely, there is no concept of immanence which does not already imply on the other side of the coin, as it were, an understanding of transcendence. Between immanence and transcendence there is no dichotomy, but only distinction and relationship as we experience "the boundary."[1]

[1] I am taking over here the concept of "boundary" from Paul Tillich; cf. Gordon D. Kaufman, "On the Meaning of 'God': Transcendence without Mythology," *New Theology No. 4*, ed. Martin E. Marty and Dean G. Peerman (New York: Macmillan, 1967), pp. 69–98. For the definition of "transcend-

If something is experienced as limited and finite, there results at its boundaries the possibility of negation. Transcendence is defined, then, in negative terms as the in-finite and un-limited. If something is experienced as finite and limited, there results at its boundaries, on the other hand, the possibility of advancing into what is endless and boundless. Transcendence is defined then in analogous terms as that which is trans-finite.

Historically, the experience of the "boundary" has been quite diverse. But it was always this experience which first evoked the possibility of speaking about "transcendence" and "immanence." If we no longer have an experience of the "boundary," transcendence is denied and the possibility of speaking about immanence no longer exists. The difference which is experienced at the "boundary" then vanishes: everything is one and the same, and Yes is No.

It has been justly questioned whether or not the theological use of the concepts "transcendence" and "immanence" for the God of biblical history and for historical faith is meaningful (Karl Barth). If it is here simply a question of relating the two concepts in terms of the "boundary," then neither the aseity nor the subjectivity of God can be comprehended by the expression "transcendence." Whoever thinks of "God" only as transcendence for a definite immanence has thought of "God" as predicate but not yet as subject. He has thought of God for the sake of something else but not yet for the sake of God himself.[2] Nevertheless, it is appropriate to use the word "transcendence" for the relationship to God to

---

ence" and "immanence," cf. Gerhard Stammler, "Ontologie in der Theologie," *Kerygma und Dogma*, 4 (1958), pp. 143ff.

[2] Cf. this assessment of theology by Karl Barth with H. G. Geyer, "Gottes Sein als Thema der Theologie," *Verkündigung und Forschung* (2/1966), pp. 3–36, and Eberhard Jüngel, *Gottes Sein ist im Werden. Verantwortliche Rede vom Sein Gottes bei Karl Barth* (Tübingen: J. C. B. Mohr/Paul Siebeck, 1965). For the philosophical problem, cf. Dieter Henrich, *Der ontologie Gottesbeweis* (Tübingen: J. C. B. Mohr/Paul Siebeck, 1960). Cf. also Christopher Butler in *Vaticanum II: An Interfaith Appraisal*, ed. John H. Miller (Notre Dame: University of Notre Dame Press, 1966), p. 316: ". . . the eschatological dimensions of the gospel take us to the very heart of the whole theological problem of our day. We have all learned that one must take the Bible on

something else, that is, for his relationship to the world and to history. In this way it can express *what* God is and *how* God is related to the world and to man in his experience of the "boundary." To be sure, it cannot be said thereby *who* is to be called "God." In its history, Christian theology has persistently linked the historical tradition of the "name" of God and the history in which he became revealed with the present experience of the "boundary" and of transcendence: the *sacra doctrina* had been combined with the *prima philosophia*. We can disregard here the special theological question of the revelation, name, and history of God and turn to the question of the present experience of the "boundary" and of transcendence. "Transcendence" and "immanence" are involved, like the experience of the "boundary," in a history of their changing relationship to one another. If we inquire about this history, we encounter the "transformations of God" (Rudolf Bultmann). We presuppose that Christian faith owes its existence to the Word of Christ and ask only about that "boundary" at which it must be present today if it wants to do justice to the transcendence of God's presence. In this regard there are also "transformations of faith."

---

its own terms, and in order to give an exegesis of it one has to understand the mentality that operates in the Bible. . . . Now it seems to me that as one contemplates the eschatological moment in the Jewish-Christian teaching, one appreciates that . . . eschatology stands to history as in the Greek system of thought metaphysics stands to physics. On that analogy I rather like to talk, not about eschatology, but about 'meta-chronics.' 'Meta-chronics' stands to history as metaphysics stands to physics. It is the ultimate dimension of thought, apprehension, and understanding when you approach reality in historical categories." This is correct in reference to the transformation from the metaphysical to the eschatological concept of transcendence. But one must notice that in this process the understanding of immanence is also changed. The "chronological" understanding of time still stands in the jurisdiction of the ontology of past reality. An eschatological understanding of time overcomes the Greek god Chronos, who begets his children only to turn around and devour them, and understands historical time as continuing creation by the future God. If the "future" is linked with the transcendence of the Creator-God, the future becomes the source of time and history is experienced as hope. All good and evil memories of history are preserved in the power of hope. This is the hope in the consummation of historical anticipation and the hope in redemption from the agony of history—a hope which, in the incomplete condition of the Kingdom, exists under the conditions of history.

The following presentation and comparison of the models of transcendence is perforce simplified and too neatly typologized. It does not pretend to be an exclusive answer suspending further inquiry but, rather, an orientation in the present.

2
MODELS OF TRANSCENDENCE

A ✦ *Physics and Metaphysics*

Greek metaphysics emerged as a way of perceiving reality (*theoria*) from the ground of ancient Greek religious cosmology, as is reflected in the dictum of Thales: *Panta plere theon.* Metaphysical thought interpreted the manifold of experienceable reality in terms of its one primordial source or in relationship to its most comprehensive horizon. If, as Parmenides contended, the world has a spherical form, then transcendence is the outermost, all-encompassing periphery of immanence in its finite completeness. If the cosmos, as the Stoa later styled it, is the visible body of the invisible Godhead, then the divine and transcendent is thought of as the backside of everything worldly and immanent, which corresponds to divinity in the order of *logos* and *nomos*. Divinity is the transcendence of the divinely ruled cosmos, and the cosmos is the immanence of the invisibly divine. But where does the "experience of the boundary" lie?

Metaphysics is here the answer to the basic metaphysical question of all beings. Everything which exists is threatened by its finitude, transitoriness, and instability. Therefore, all beings strive for, and that being which is gifted with consciousness asks for, an infinite, immutable, and fixed being. "The world refuses to be governed badly. The rule of many is not good; one ruler let there be."[3] If immanence is experienced

[3] Aristotle, *Metaphysics*, ed. W. Jaeger (New York: Oxford University Press, 1957), 1076a. With this quotation from the *Iliad* Aristotle proposes a political concept of unity. Cf. Erik Peterson, "Der Monotheismus als politishches Problem," in *Theologische Traktate* (München, 1951), pp. 49–164.

180

at this "boundary" as finite, mutable, and threatened by chaos, then the corresponding transcendence takes the form of infinitude and immutability, of orderedness and oneness. Through participation in infinite being, finite being attains its transcendence, and in its correspondence this transcendence reclaims its immanence. "Physics" of finite being and "metaphysics" of the one ordering and prevailing being correspond to each other.

For many centuries the "metaphysics" of Aristotle was unquestioned as an adequate conception of transcendence. But his metaphysical conception of transcendence was valid only so long and so far as the "physics" of Aristotle was the convincing imprint of man's experience of the world and of his boundaries. The fundamental change in "physics," i.e., in the understanding of reality, has necessitated a corresponding transformation in the metaphysical understanding of transcendence.

B ✦ *Existence and Transcendence*

Modern man no longer understands himself in terms of the world and as a part of finite being. Without having completely lost this view of self and world, man nevertheless understands the world more and more as the field of the constructive possibilities of his spirit. The world is for him no longer a "house of being" and a home in which he dwells. Increasingly, it becomes for him the material which he investigates for conversion into his own use. Having once felt cramped inside the eternal orders of the cosmos, he now views himself as lord of nature, which stands over against himself. Indeed, the more the world becomes an object for man, the more he becomes in himself a world-transcending subject. As a result, he no longer finds transcendence in the outermost, all-encompassing periphery of the cosmos but in himself, for he has made himself the center of a world which is increasingly becoming his personal property for disposal as he sees fit. He no longer expects the heaven of metaphysics to unlock the physics of the earth for him.

Now his world is made accessible to him through his own transcending subjectivity. Consequently, in modern times transcendence is more and more experienced in the inner dimension of human existence, in man's transcendental subjectivity. Man can objectivize and utilize all things; only his own self transcends all of the objectifications of his spirit. Because the "boundary" between immanence and transcendence runs through himself, man comes to know this boundary in his own existence. Existentially he experiences finitude and infinitude simultaneously. He understands himself as God present on earth. Hence in place of the old correlation of "physics and metaphysics" the modern correlation of "existence and transcendence" advances to the foreground. This is manifestly evident in the historical effect of Cartesianism and Kantianism.

As a result of this change in metaphysics the whole traditional conceptualization of God has collapsed. Passing through the critique of religion, the critique of that naïve "metaphysics for the rabble" (Nietzsche), demythologization, and "atheistic" theology, it is becoming more and more irrelevant. Critical thinking insists that transcendence can no longer be expressed in objectifying language because the "objectivity" of the world has lost its old metaphysical framework. Only existentialist interpretation can form a significant alliance between the Christian tradition as kerygma and man's new experience of transcendence.

To be sure, men always have the feeling that God is dead if a trusted concept of God is lost. They readily speak of the "end of metaphysics" if they lose the traditional sense for transcendence. But these are only surface phenomena. What is at stake is neither the "death of God in modern times," nor the end of metaphysics altogether, nor even the age of secularization and atheism but, rather, only the metamorphosis of transcendence and the transformation of the boundary experience of immanence. The experience of transcendence, the experience of boundary and religion are in a general sense just as real as in former times. Only they are no longer to be found in those places where they once were.

C✦ Alienated Transcendence in the Areas of Unburdening in Modern Society

Today even the modern model of existence and transcendence has lost its formative power. Without doubt, man will continue to transcend nature both outside and within his own bodily existence, and through reflection intensify his possibilities for mastering the world. But instead of nature, there is revolving about him an increasingly impervious entanglement of his own works in social institutions, political organizations, and industrial enterprises, which in its own way constitutes a quasi-nature.[4] In place of the natural cosmos, which man ever more effectively colonizes and controls, there appears a new cosmos of his own objectifications which is consistently more difficult to penetrate and even more difficult to control. In this artificial cosmos of his scientific-technological civilization the old conditions, from which man freed himself, return in the form of the irrational coercion of his civilization: The opacity of destiny finds a new correspondence in the opacity of reticular bureaucratic manipulations; what once were natural catastrophes recur now in the guise of social and political catastrophes. The man who rules nature via society now becomes the slave of his own products. Man's creations become autonomous, "program"

---

[4] In what follows we are assuming the analyses of Karl Marx and Max Weber. For Marx there was the question: Why have external conditions become autonomous against men? Why has the power generated by their own life become dominant over them? Concerning the worldly asceticism of modern Puritanism, Max Weber says: "Since asceticism undertook to remodel the world and to work out its ideals in the world, material goods have gained an increasing and finally an inexorable power over the lives of men as at no previous period in history. Today the spirit of religious asceticism—whether finally, who knows?—has escaped from the cage" (*Die protestantische Ethik und der Geist des Kapitalismus*, in *Gesammelte Aufsätze zur Religionssoziologie*, I [Tübingen, 1947]; Eng. trans.: *The Protestant Ethic and the Spirit of Capitalism*, trans. Talcott Parsons [New York: Charles Scribner's Sons, 1958], p. 181).

themselves out of his control and gain the upper hand over him. Since the beginning of the industrial revolution, the question of the liberation of man from the predominance of his own work has become the theme of the philosophy which is related to action.

In this situation man enters again into a new experience of boundary. It is no longer the experience of his inner subjectivity transcending the objective world but the experience of his own impotence in a straitjacket of autonomous objectification and in a "closed society." The consciousness of transcendental subjectivity has, since the inception of the industrial world, become aware of its own impotence. Its own world becomes alien to it and it easily changes itself into the escapist form of romantic subjectivity. "At the core of this fantastic superiority of the subject (i.e., over the world) is hidden the renunciation of every active alteration of the real world."[5] The sudden transition of cosmic world-confidence into Gnostic world-dread in late antiquity has repeated itself in late Western culture.[6] The feeling of alienation through social thingification and the political impotence of the individual is growing, and out of these sufferings of man within his own world which enslaves its creator arise new ecstatic forms of seeking and experiencing transcendence. Where is there to be found a transcendence which does not alienate but, rather, liberates us from alienation?[7]

Through many of these new forms of religiosity and search for transcendence, men are seeking that freedom which lies beyond the domain of necessity and need. Moreover, the alienation, through which man becomes aware of the "boundary," is now understood not so much as alienation but more

[5] Carl Schmitt, *Politische Romantik* (2nd ed.; Leipzig, 1925), p. 227.
[6] In this connection cf. Hans Jonas, *Gnosis und spätantiker Geist*, I (2nd ed.; Göttingen, 1954) and *Zwischen Nichts und Ewigkeit* (Göttingen, 1963) ("Gnosticism and Modern Nihilism," *Social Research*, 19 (1952), pp. 430–452.
[7] Thus Roger Garaudy, "Vom Bannfluch zum Dialog" in *Der Dialog*, Garaudy/Metz/Rahner (Rororo acktuell 944, 1966), p. 91. Since that time this question of transcendence has been taken up by many Marxist thinkers.

as unburdening.[8] The old relationship of immanence and transcendence is reversed. The immanence of man's own world, which makes itself independent and confirms its own autonomy while structuring an increasingly more stringent entanglement around man, releases a free-floating transcendence of the soul which has become homeless in its own world. Because the modern subjectivity is no longer in a position to rule its own world, the inner transcendence of man becomes the play of an impotent escapism.[9] Ever since Romanticism, the "unhappy consciousness of the beautiful soul" (Hegel) has fled from the constricting, alienating, and meaningless reality of phenomena into the dream world of the beyond, into the unhindered realm of play where imaginary possibilities abound. Yet, it is precisely this flight from reality which has abandoned the social and political dimensions to inhuman powers. The abstract negation of the real world makes possible every sort of cynicism within the abandoned reality. Therefore, this new mysticism is frequently coupled with nihilism. These forms of modern romantic religiosity can be understood as epiphenomena of modern existential transcendence, for they actually owe their existence to the fact that the soul has been unburdened by a stabilized immanence. Immanence, then, is no longer understood as immanence of a transcendence, as characterized, actuated, and transformed by that which surpasses it. It becomes the basis which sets free transcendence's abstract realm of play. This means that the character which is ascribed to immanence and transcendence is also changed.

[8] This ambivalance between "alienation" and "unburdening" was first pinpointed by Arnold Gehlen: "Die Geburt der Freiheit aus Entfremdung" in *Studien zur Anthropologie und Soziologie* (Neuwied: Luchterhand, 1963), pp. 232ff.; previously in *Urmensch und Spätkultur* (Bonn, 1956).

[9] In the movements of the Hippies, of "transcendental mediation," of LSD-deliria and the like, I am able to recognize nothing other than such escapism. It is not necessary that one be puritanical in order to make a judgment about it. Here is arising, in fact, a new "post-industrial" religiosity, as Harvey Cox has rightly seen. Yet one should prefer, with Nietzsche, to "remain true to the earth," even when it threatens to become uninteresting.

185

In modern immanence where the production of food-stuffs is automated and the process of automation can be cybernetically controlled, "transcendence" has lost its job, as it were. It becomes the play of the unburdened spirit, free of necessity. The "realm of necessity" serves as the ground on which the realms of play, culture, and transcendence are constructed. Indeed, the more stable immanence becomes, the more unstable and open can transcendence be understood. Whereas transcendence had to be thought of earlier as a stabilizing factor of order—as "the highest star of being" (Nietzsche)—in a stabilized world, transcendence can be thought of precisely in its boundless openness, as the inexhaustible fascination of new possibilities and fantasies. The insight that in the modern world "the working hypothesis of God" (Bonhoeffer) is no longer employable has a negative ring only for the world of work, necessity, and compulsion. But if the "kingdom of necessity" is automated and is increasingly converted into regulated processes, it forfeits the interest of man. For that which does not offer resistance, so that its creative appropriation requires the pain of work and disappointment, can no longer be experienced as "real." Therefore the unreal, the sphere of the not yet realized, of the not realizable and absolutely absurd possibilities is increasingly capturing the interest of man and is experienced as "boundary."

In the realms created by modern society's unburdening of man there can thus be a new birth of the experience of transcendence. After extensive areas of love for one's neighbor have been socialized, there can be a rebirth of the uncalculating love of God. After God has been needed for so long in order to enjoy the world or at least to master it, it is yet by no means the case that God has disappeared from a world in which he is no longer "needed." The Augustinian inversion that we "need" the world in order to enjoy God has become much more apposite. Once economics has been automated and politics cyberneticized, theology can become a new theme of man specifically in the form of the eternal dialogue and play of man with God, and God with man. If the world is emancipated from "God," so also is God emancipated from his "helper in need" functions in the world and is free for himself. And as such we can reflect on and love him for his own sake. In a "post-industrial society" (Herman Kahn), industry becomes uninteresting and theology can become the deadly serious play of man in previously unknown form. For then doxology and nihilism will be immediately confronted with one another, with the mediating work on that which is finitely negative being eliminated. Without such mediation, man has to seek the forms by which he can exist between God and nothingness. Intimations in this direction are found in modern literature and art. In his culture, man lives by such anticipations of "life." In play, in festivity, and in humor, he liberates himself from the rational, goal-regimentation of work and from moralistic coercion in order to change present conditions and improve society. If there were no such anticipation of the kingdom of freedom, play, and cheerfulness, no matter how insufficient in form, man would not experience suffering from the negatives, nor would he feel the necessities of life as pain.

Nevertheless, in spite of what we have said, the kingdom of freedom based on the *unburdening* of the kingdom of necessity is an alienating transcendence. It is only a by-product of the kingdom of work and not yet its abrogation. If one understands it, however, as anticipation of the transformation of work into spontaneity, of morality into play, of emergency prayer into free worship, then the powers of world transformation can emerge out of it. Still, man experiences the "boundary" everywhere in finite negatives. Thus the dictum of Hegel against Schelling has lost none of its truth: "The life of God and divine intelligence, then, can, if we like, be spoken of as love playing with itself; but this idea becomes mere edification, and even sinks into insipidity, if it lacks seriousness, the suffering, the patience, and the labor of the negative" (*The Phenomenology of Mind,* Introduction). But in the end Schelling may triumph.

D ✦ *History and Eschatological Future*

With the decline in the efficacy of existence-transcendence models, there now lies at hand a new realistic understanding of immanence as *history*. In the ancient conception of metaphysics, history had no particular significance. It was the incalculable and chaotic. Only the cosmos, with its recurring orders and the rule of destiny, had transcendence. In the models of transcendental subjectivity, history gained the significance of personal decision and encounter. Today, social, technical, and political history becomes the field of mediation between man and nature. Only in this field does man gain his identity and only in the context of history's mediation does he comprehend nature. It is here that nature becomes nature for man. If the context of this mediation becomes autonomous over against man, then the interrelationship between men and their objective world will increasingly become the theme of history. The "boundary" of transcendence lies no longer only in the finitude of all things and beings and also no longer in human subjectivity which surpasses nature, but in the torpid, dead forms of his own objectifications and in the superiority of his own works over himself. In modern society, man's subjectivity and the objectivity of his works and relations appear so far separated that the products rule their producers and rationalized relationships exert a wholly irrational coercive force over men. This is a new "boundary" at which one inquires about transcendence. It is a transcendence over against a particular contemporary societal system. Therefore it is directed toward the "future." The present situation is experienced as a situation of antagonism between subjectivity and objectification.[10] This situation is characterized by the

[10] Cf. Günter Rohrmoser, *Subjektivität und Verdinglichung. Theologie und Gesellschaft im Denken des jungen Hegel* (Gütersloh: Verlagshaus Gerd Mohn, 1961).

impotence of the individual and the superiority of those conditions which he himself creates.

If this characterizes the historical present in its strife-ridden totality, then it is clear that transcendence can be found neither on the subjective nor on the objective side, but only where this antagonistic situation finds a qualitatively different, transforming, and new future. If the "boundary" of the present immanence is experienced in such a way that man is alienated from his world and his world is alienated from man, then transcendence is experienced where critical perspectives on the divisions of the present are opened up, where new possibilities for a meaningful incarnation of man and new possibilities for a humanization of his alienated conditions are manifested, in brief: where a future of reconciliation and transformation attains the upper hand over this state of affairs.

But it is not only the understanding of "transcendence" which is subjected to the modern fissure within consciousness. Today the understanding of "future" suffers the same fate. On the one hand, "future" in industrial society was identified with the progress and development of the present status quo. "Future" was objectified in the growth-rate of social products and the acceleration of the objective potencies of man. As long as the industrial system found itself in the process of construction, its objective progress exuded the fascinating spell of transcendence. It promised the vanquishing of man's dependence on nature, the fulfillment of human longing, the subduing of economic alienation, and also the kingdom of political freedom. But the modern "post-industrial," planned society defuturizes this kind of transcendental future. In the measure that the industrial society successfully completes its own edifice, its progress loses the fascination of transcendence. A planned and programed future has nothing more to do with transcendence.[11]

On the other hand, "future" was personalized and, as

[11] Cf. my article "Hoffnung und Planung," *Merkur* 208, XIX. Jg. Heft 7, pp. 609–622.

in Existentialism, became the inner extension of human existing, the openness of the heart and futurity of decision. Yet, this kind of personalization which develops from being unburdened from responsibility for present history owes its existence, on the other hand, to the objectification of the future. In this connection, the personalistic understanding of future as the possibility of existence is a product of the split in the modern spirit just as is the objectification of the future in the automatic progress of society.

In which sense, then, can "future" become a new paradigm of transcendence? It can become the new paradigm of transcendence only if it becomes the embodiment of the transcendence of present dissension and bondage in something qualitatively new. Future has the fascination of genuine transcendence if it promises something qualitatively new which stimulates the fundamental transformation of the "systems" of the present; if in it something different can be expected which leads to the basic transformation of the present, antagonistic conditions of immanence. This means in present-day language: if it becomes the occasion for the possibility of a revolutionary consciousness which seeks to transform an antagonistic into a nonantagonistic society and an unfree into a free society. Transcendence, then, in the manner of previous transformations of the concept of transcendence, is taken out of its substantival forms and put in the form of a verb. Transcendence becomes the embodiment of concrete, historical transcending of the concrete, historical "boundary." The substantive "transcendence" means, then, the space ahead of us in the open future where historical transformations take place. This implies that future as transcendence can no longer be understood as quantitative extension and development of the present, but must denote qualitative transformation of the history which is experienced in conflicts. The "wholly other" (Ganz-Andere) of transcendence, then, is conceived as the "wholly transforming" (Ganz-Ändernde) and the "going beyond" as the transforming of history from the direction of its qualitatively new future.

The power of the existing status quo which wants only to sustain itself, or through various reforms adapt itself to the times, is confronted with the powers of a qualitatively new future and with a fundamental transformation. Today "transcendence" is sought and in many situations also experienced at this "boundary" or "front" of present history. What for Marxism is the leap from the quantitative into the qualitative and from the kingdom of necessity into the kingdom of freedom, what for many others is the transformation of an unfree into a free, a repressive into a human society is thought of by Christians as the qualitative difference between history and eschatology and is anticipated in concrete faith under the conditions of history.[12] It is precisely here that new experiences of the "boundary" and of transcendence are found in the shape of political responsibility. And while these new experiences of transcendence in a political context do not supplant the old ones, they differ decisively from the experiences of suffering within the conditions of finitude or of man's suffering within himself.

3

THE LANGUAGE OF TRANSCENDENCE

In the models of metaphysical transcendence, reality was determined and ordered in definitions. The mode of viewing physical things combined the memory of eternal ideas with its act of perception. In the synthetic act of *theoria* the mind reconciled the changeable with the unchangeable, the appearing image with its true *idea*. The definitional concept became

---

[12] For this reason I believe that Richard Shaull employs the modern concept of "transcending" accurately. Cf. his contribution to the World Council of Churches Conference in Geneva in 1966: "Revolutionary Change in Theological Perspective," in Trutz Rendtorff/Heinz Eduard Tödt, *Theologie der Revolution*, edition Suhrkamp 258 (1968), pp. 117ff. For a different assessment by Heinz Eduard Tödt, see pp. 23ff. Nevertheless, one should not have historically leveled the concept of transcendence in the manner of Garaudy, but should have kept in mind the "qualitative transformation." It alone guarantees that history is not perfectible under the conditions of history and that revolution leads to "permanent revolution" if it does not betray itself.

the image of true reality. If transcendence is the most perfect reality, the concept of transcendence is correspondingly the definition of all definitions, the epitome of all concepts. The hierarchy of definitional and subsumptive concepts corresponds to the hierarchy of being.

In the models of subjective transcendence we find another way of defining transcendence. Here the reflection of the subject connects objective experience with its own trancendental conditions of all possible experience. Experience-able things are no longer bound up in *theoria* with their essential ideas. They are related in their mode of appearance to the perceiving subject. In this situation, objective definitions are replaced by relational concepts which express the relationship of things to the human subject. Correspondingly, transcendence can no longer be grasped in definitions but only in relationships to the inner ground of the subject.

In the model "history and future," cognition and language are once again changed. The perception of a thing or a relationship combines with the experience of its reality the expectation of its future possibility. Things are perceived in their history and linked with the sought and hoped-for future of history. Things do not present themselves in an earthly mode of appearance before the transcendental heaven of their fixed ideas. Neither are they apprehended merely in the reflecting light of the perceiving subject. They are perceived on the foreground of an open future of history in its significance for the whole of reality.[13] Language does not simply make statements but knows that in the very act of speaking about that which is, it is already grasping and transforming it in the open process of history. Wherever cognition and language become aware of their own historic-

---

[13] Cf. Th. W. Adorno, *Minima Moralia, Reflexionen aus dem beschädigten Leben* (Frankfurt: Suhrkamp, 1962), pp. 333f.: "Philosophy, in the only form in which it can still be responsibly upheld in the face of despair, would be the attempt to regard all things as they present themselves from the standpoint of redemption. Knowledge has no light save that which shines upon the world from the standpoint of redemption: all else exhausts itself in imitation and remains a piece of technique."

ity, together with the historicity of things, constative language becomes a critical language, for everything which is historical is accompanied by its own negation. On the other hand, this historical language becomes a performative language.[14] Insofar as it brings things in history to expression, it changes history and the things in it. Historical language must be clear, therefore, for which purpose it wants to bring things to expression and for which it wishes to transform them. For this purpose, the objective, generic concept of species is replaced by the dynamic concept of function, and the subjective concept of relationships is discarded for the concept of action and production. Room is also made for the concept of redemption which redeems a thing or a person from his fixity.[15]

4

REPRESENTATIONS OF TRANSCENDENCE

As the affinity between philosophical metaphysics and political theology in antiquity demonstrates, cosmological monotheism could correspond to political monarchism. To the extent that the polis was understood as human correspondence to the cosmos, such parallels are frequent. This is not inevitably the case, however, because human life often exhibits a delightful inconsistency. Nevertheless, there are affinities and alliances here. The passage which we quoted

[14] J. L. Austin, How to Do Things with Words, ed. Urmson and Warnock (London: Oxford University Press, 1962).
[15] Did Luther have something similar in view as he wrote on Rom. 8:19: "Aliter Apostolus de rebus philosophatur et sapi quam philosophi et metaphysici. Quia Philosophi oculum ita in praesentiam rerum immergunt, ut solum quidditates et qualitates earum speculentur, Apostolus autem oculos nostros revocat ab intuitu rerum presentium, ab essentia et accidentibus earum et dirigit in eas secundum quod future sunt. Non enim dicit 'essentia' vel 'operatio' creature seu 'actio' et 'passio' et 'motus' sed novo et miro vocabulo et theologico dicit 'expectatio creature,' ut eo ipso, cum animus audit creaturam expectare, non ipsam creaturam amplius, sed quid creatur expectat, intendat et querat" (Vorlesung über den Römerbrief 1515/1516, ed. Joh. Ficker [Leipzig, 1908], p. 198)?

above from Book L of Aristotle's *Metaphysics*: "The world refuses to be governed badly. The rule of many is not good; one ruler let there be," could have been understood as justification of an imperialistic peace politics. Often the hierarchical structure of the metaphysical world was understood as transcendent background of the hierarchical structure of the political world. Conversely, as is obvious in emperor ideology, the "one god" was represented through the "one ruler."

The modern form of "existence and transcendence," on the contrary, could no longer be represented in the old hierarchical and authoritarian structures of government. It is represented through the sovereign irreplaceability of every individual. Therefore the modern age no longer understands religion as the consecration of authorities in church, state, or society, but as the inner self-transcendence of every individual. As a consequence, the democracy of free persons for whom God is immediately present becomes the new representational form of transcendence. The divine crown rests no longer on the chief among the rulers but on the constitution of the free. Transcendence can no longer be represented "from above" in a secular way; it can be represented only as the network of the free relationships of free individuals. The relationship to God or the transcendent is no longer mirrored in the relationship to consecrated authorities but in the free acknowledgment of and respect for one's fellow man, in whom transcendence is present.

In the proliferating inner autonomy of the human world of specialization, this democratic form of representing transcendence obviously loses its power. Therefore, in the model of transcendence designated as "history and future," the representation of transcendence in the democratic network of interpersonal relationships is changed to new, revolutionary forms of transcending. In a society which is riveted to its status quo, this democratic transcendence, if it is not to fade into an empty, ideological sham, can be realized only if the oppressed and alienated groups in such a society are liberated and given an independent share in the shape of the society's future. Where fixed societies represent their transcendence in terms of their own fixity while excluding or outvoting others, true transcendence gains its representation in revolutionary groups that ally themselves with those who are alienated, oppressed, or simply frustrated. Precisely for this reason, revolutionary movements in such societies have about them the fascination of transcendence. However, where they resume the old hierarchical form of transcendence through party machinery, etc., they betray the new experience of transcendence. If revolutionary movements end in bureaucratic hierarchies of functionaries, they represent no progress over against the democratic forms of transcendence, but actually a regression.

5

THE FUTURE AS NEW PARADIGM
OF TRANSCENDENCE

Finally, by way of "experiment" alone, let us advance some reflections about a possible identification of "future" and "transcendence."

By "history" we understand here the experience of reality in conflicts. It is not simply the experience that everything is transitory. Neither is it simply the experience that all things find themselves in the river of time with the present standing between the no-more of the past and the not-yet of the future. Furthermore, it is not only the experience that man must ever and again make decisions. Rather, "history" is the impression that man together with his society and his world is an experiment and that not only he himself, but also his world, represents a risk. In situations of radical change and crisis he senses the constraint of Hamlet's "To be or not to be—that is the question." Involved in the experiment of history where the terrors of his failures always seize him, he must project visions of a successful solution. These visions also bear the character of being risks and projects. They must be authenticated through their critical power over against the present reality and through personal effort. They do not have the structure of objective "insight into necessity" but, rather, the structure of projection into what is possible with the intent of changing the present necessity. It is in this sense that the following statements are to be understood.

"Future" has not as yet anything to do with "transcendence" if it is itself only a matter of historical future. To be sure, a vision of the future can be projected only from within history. Therefore, it is just as transient as history itself. "Boundless transcending" is not yet genuine transcendence.[16] Nevertheless, as regards the intention itself one can distinguish the idea of a future of history from future history.

Only a future which transcends the experiment of history itself can become the paradigm of transcendence and give meaning to the experiment "history." The "utopia of the beyond" explodes all known world conditions. It is the ultimate and also the most fundamental experience of transcendence and is usually expressed in religious symbols. If one can speak of reality as history, one can also speak of an "end of history."[17] With which eschatological symbols such an "end of history" can be expressed in the midst of history and under its conditions is another question. But here we can say at least this much: A "future of history" cannot be a merely quantitatively new future but must be a qualitatively new future. The future must be identified with a transformation of the conditions of history itself. Only if the conflicts which cause man to experience the

[16] Here is a critical point in the thesis "Marxism is transcendence" which Jaroslav Krejci has advocated in "Ein neues Modell des wissenschaftlichen Atheismus," *Internationale Dialog-Zeitschrift* (1968), Heft 2, pp. 191ff., esp. pp. 197ff.
[17] Ludwig Landgrebe, *Das philosophische Problem des Endes der Geschichte*, in *Festschrift für H. Heimsoeth*, 1966.

present reality as history are abolished has future anything to do with transcendence. Only where these conflicts are transcended in the direction of their dissolution or reconciliation is something of this qualitatively new future present in history. Future prospects which do not meet these criteria reveal their psuedo-transcendency. They promise more than they can keep and impetuously exchange the fascination of transcendence for resignation.

But, on the other hand, the vision of a qualitatively new future of history can become the transcendent horizon which opens up and stimulates transcendence in a new historical future. If the relationship of history and eschatological future emerges in this way, then we encounter the relationship of difference and analogy. The future of history is something qualitatively different and new in the face of what is here experienced as history. But as future precisely of *this* historical reality it affects already here and now the experience and shape of history. In the qualitative difference, therefore, are correspondences, analogies, directions, and tendencies. They do not bring about the "new" in a different quality, but the vision of this necessary new departure influences the shape and also the suffering of history in the present.

In order to make the dialectic clearer, reference should be made to two prejudices and seductions. If the qualitative distinction between history and eschatological future is overemphasized, one falls into an abstract negation of the world and its history. The great failures in the experiment of history become, then, the circumstance for the meaninglessness of every event and action in history. The world is a "vale of tears." Radical evil dominates everything. The end is resignation. On the other hand, if the relationship of correspondence is stressed to the point of being the relationship of continuity, then transcendence is viewed as the essence of history itself, that is, perpetual disclosure of the future in the present and permanent movement beyond the momentary present. The end is likewise resignation, for every attempt at transcending creates anew a present which must be transcended. To what extent should that which is future be better than that which is present? A meaningful mediation seems to result only if the transcendence which is beyond history is linked with man's act of transcending within history; if in the midst of the critical difference one believes in the possibilities of correspondence, and if, conversely, in the possibilities of correspondence the qualitative difference is kept in mind. Then "systematic transcendental criticism" joins itself with "systematic immanental criticism," and the openness of a qualitatively new future is linked with concrete steps for bringing about a qualitatively better correspondence. The Christian faith understands both history and eschatological future to be linked in the Christ in whom this qualitatively new future is present under the conditions of history. Therefore, it speaks of the historical Christ eschatologically and presently finds in him the end of history in the midst of history.

The Christian faith does not supplant history so that history would become an indifferent matter to believers. Because the Christian can hope in the new future through faith in Christ, he begins to suffer in the unredeemedness of the present and realizes solidarity with all who suffer consciously or unconsciously in this unredeemedness. But neither does he become absorbed into history so that the future would become indifferent to faith. Because he can hope in this future, he begins to oppose the "scheme of this world" and the systems of the present and to change them. For a long time the Christian faith employed a metaphysical exegesis of the transcendence in which it believed through Christ. Later, that faith interpreted it existentially. But today it is realizing that Christ is present where the "boundary" of immanence is experienced in suffering and transcended in active hope. The more it interprets Christian transcendence eschatologically, the more it will understand the boundary of immanence historically and surrender itself to the movement of transcending. But the more it interprets this eschatological transcendence in a Christian way, that is, in consideration of the crucified Jesus, the more it will become aware that the qualitatively new future of God has united itself with those who are dispossessed, denied, and oppressed in the present. Furthermore, it will become more sensitive to the fact that this future begins not from above at the point of the progress of an "advanced society," but from below with those who have been sacrificed to this progress. This means that the Christian faith will have to integrate hope in an eschatological future and love which realizes solidarity with the oppressed. In other words, the future of the new being which brings history to a close is allied with the dialectic of the negatives in the historical present. The transcendence of the future of a "wholly other" begins dialectically in establishing those who, in a settled present and in static societies, are "the others." Precisely this combination is, for the Christian faith, the "power of transformation." So the power of God, who transcends history, is experienced by Christians in the midst of history.

X ✦ Hope and History

Many believe that Christian theology has become irrelevant. It has become introvert, orthodox, traditionalist, or personalistic. Occupied only with itself, it has lost contact with reality. In this wide field of difficulties, two experiences have created a new challenge to theology which can be met only through a reorganization of the theological system itself and a reorientation of the entire theological endeavor.

1
THE NEW TASKS OF THEOLOGY AND THE "THEOLOGY OF HOPE"

The first of these experiences is that in conversations with modern atheists, humanists, and Marxists, one always arrives at a point where one recognizes the deep schism of the modern age: in the past two centuries, a Christian faith in God without hope for the future of the world has called forth a secular hope for the future of the world without faith in God. Since the Christians, the churches, and theology believed in a *God without future*, the will for a future of the earth has joined itself to an atheism which sought a

"Hope and History" was given as a public lecture in connection with the Edward F. Gallahue Conference on Theology at Princeton, April 18, 1968. It appeared in *Theology Today*, October, 1968.

future without God. The messianic hopes emigrated from the church and became invested in progress, evolution, and revolutions. In the church only a half-truth remained. We have arrived at a moment in history that provokes the question: Should there now be a parting of ways in history, so that faith aligns itself with the past and unfaith with the future? I think that we can overcome this present dilemma only if Christians begin to remember the "God of hope," as he is witnessed to in the promissory history of the Old and the New Testaments, and thus begin to assume responsibility for the personal, social, and political problems of the present.

The other experience to which I refer is the emergence of something like "one world" for the first time in history. We have reached a situation where human beings can completely eradicate each other. It is thus the situation in which mankind will survive only in a new community. Therefore, today even the historical future will not be the continuation of the past but something new. In the past, human beings had histories in the plural but no common history in the singular. Today we have pasts in the plural: each people, each culture, each religion has its own past. But since in the future we will either perish together or survive in a new community, we have a future *only in the singular*. We have many pasts but only one future. Therefore, past and future today no longer appear in one and the same continuum. We have arrived at the leap from the quantities of history to a new quality of history. In a time in which the actual movement of history is beginning to reach the universal horizon of eschatology, our understanding of our responsibility in the areas of faith, politics, and ethics is still caught in the provincial thought forms of a passing epoch.

In my view, it was from experience of this kind that a movement, if it is a movement, emerged which has been called *eschatological theology* and which soon revealed itself as a project of a *political theology*.

Eschatology is here the *doctrine of hope*, the doctrine of the future for which one can hope, and simultaneously the doctrine of the action of hope which brings the hoped-for future into the sufferings of the present age. Theology as eschatology would wish to project the universal horizon of the future in which theology in history becomes meaningful and relevant. It does not wish to substitute eschatology for theology. The universal horizon of eschatology reveals the reality of the *world* as history, manifests faith in Christ as *practical hope* for the coming God, and thus qualifies herein the past and the present as the history of the future of God. This leads us to an understanding of the present as the *presence of the future*. The present becomes the frontier where the future is gained or lost. Traditional differences and conflicts become relative, if we can find the future together only in a common effort. Either we will all hang together now or we will all hang separately (Franklin).

The political dimension of theology emerges from the universal horizon of eschatology. The differences between a "theology of the word" and a "theology of culture," and the conflicts between a "theology of existence" and a "theology of world history" are relativized the more one recognizes that Christianity stands with all its powers in the dawn of the future and must therefore bring the "power of the future world" into the trouble spots of the present, personally, socially, and politically. In view of the universal horizon of the future, the church finds a new companionship with the social and political institutions of society. The difference between church and world becomes relative if both stand before that future which one traditionally has called the Judgment and the Kingdom of God. The lines of separation no longer go spatially through body and soul, spirituality and secularity, faith and politics, church and world, but are found temporally in all areas of life between the power of the past and the "power of the future world."

But which horizon of the future is wide enough to embrace the differences of the present and concrete enough to mediate them practically? Is Christian eschatology capable of it? What changes are necessary in an eschatology, traditionally oriented toward a salvation of the soul in the beyond, in order to be able to do justice to this task? Can we unfold a Christian universalism of hope which makes meaningful and relevant the political humanism of Christianity?

2

The peculiarity of Christian theology can be defined as follows: *Christian theology speaks of God historically and of history eschatologically.*

Christian theology speaks of God *historically*. It speaks of the "God of Abraham, Isaac, and Jacob," of the "Father of Jesus Christ," and unites the proclamation of God with the memory of historical persons.

It speaks of the "God of the exodus," as in the First Commandment, and of the "God who raised Jesus from the dead," as in the Easter kerygma, and unites with faith in God the memory of historical events. The hermeneutical starting point of Christian theology is therefore the concrete history witnessed to in both the Old and the New Testaments.

Christian theology speaks of history *eschatologically*. It proclaims the "God of Abraham" as the God of the promise in whom all nations will be blessed. It proclaims the "Father of Jesus Christ" as the one God of all peoples and as the future of every creature groaning in travail. In the making present of history, Christian theology anticipates simultaneously this one universal future for all men and all things. The all-embracing horizon of historical theology that gives meaning is "the end of all things" or "the future of history."

This unity of particular history and universality, of specific memory and all-embracing expectation, is a peculiarity which we find only in Jewish and Christian thought. As long as this dialectical unity can be retained and meaningfully represented, Christian faith is alive. If the unity breaks down, the Christian faith breaks up into a merely historical memory, on the one hand, and new experiences of the absolute and the universal, on the other.

The present crisis of the idea of God has come about because the old forms, in which the divinity of God had been understood and merged with the thought and the life of a particular time, have lost their self-evidence.

A first form of Christian theology was the union of the *sacra doctrina* (the biblical tradition) with *prima philosophia* (cosmological metaphysics). The cosmological proofs for the existence of God, in which the divinity of God and his presence were brought into an analogical relationship to the experience of the world accessible to everyone, have lost their persuasive power, since modern man no longer understands himself as a part of the cosmos, but has placed the world as material of his scientific and technical possibilities over against himself. He no longer lives in the house of ordered being but in the open history of a technical transformation of the world. The old cosmological-theistic worldview which spoke of God in relationship to the cosmos of the natural world is antiquated and is experienced as mythical by man, who has become the master of his environment. But it is naïve pathos of the Enlightenment to discard the *fundamental question* which was to be answered by the old world-view. Behind the cosmological-theistic world-views lies the real misery of man, which expressed itself in the manifold forms of the theodicy question: *Si Deus, unde malum?* ("If God exists, whence evil?"). The old worldview answered this fundamental question in the vision of the orderly and wisely steered cosmos and used the image of the divine cosmos in order to do battle against the pervasive threat of chaos. Even though this answer no longer persuades today, since we experience reality as history and no longer as cosmos, the fundamental theodicy question is still with us and is more pressing than before. For us it has no longer only its old naturalistic form, as in the earthquake of Lisbon in 1755. It appears today in a political form, as in the question of Auschwitz. But it still is to a large extent the comprehensive horizon of the question of God in which the theistic and the atheistic answers lock horns in battle. Thomas asked the question: *An Deus sit?* ("Whether God is?") on grounds of an explanation of nature and its evils, and he argued on the basis of the cosmological proofs of God against atheism. We ask the question: *An Deus sit?* on grounds of history and its crimes, and we must struggle with the question of God in historical knowledge and political action. Following the victory of science over the mythical world-views, the theodicy question and the debate with atheism in the context of this question lead us to the development of a political theology.

After the demise of the cosmological proofs for God's existence in the time of the Enlightenment, the psychological (Descartes), the moral (Kant), and the existential (Kierkegaard) proofs of God's existence began their victorious advance in Christian theology. Ostracized from cosmology by the natural sciences, Christian theology became anthropology. Here the claim of the Christian kerygma was joined to the question of human existence. While God could no longer be demonstrated as ground and Lord of the world, he was now understood as transcendent ground of one's being in the world. Here man's soul—his spirituality, subjectivity, personality, or selfhood—became the real referent of theological thought. This turn from theistic metaphysics of the world to the theological illumination of existence and language analysis is an important step. The misery underlying the illumination of existence is the identity question, the question of man as to his authenticity. The concrete initiative for the overcoming of the pain of this question, as inherent in *theology as anthropology*, can be regarded in the offer of faith as inner identity-experience, and in the offer of love as relationship to the neighbor, wherein personhood is fulfilled. The quest of man for his identity is here understood as the horizon of the question of God, and the debate with atheistic humanism goes on in the horizon of this existential question. If we take a closer look at the identity question of man, we will find, however, that it cannot be answered apart from the social, political, and historical particularities of man, nor apart from his social, political, and historical identifications, engagements, and commitments. After the individualistic view of man has become obsolete and in view of the debate with atheistic humanism, the identity question of man leads us toward a political theology. While the theodicy question for a just world cannot be answered without the justification of man in his personhood, man cannot find identity in himself without engaging his personhood in a battle for a just and human world.

As regards the basis of the fundamental question, there exists no genuine alternative between the cosmological and the newer anthropological theology. Man and world are mediated today in the realm of history, and that means in social, political, and technological history. Without humanization of the world, man will not find his inner identity, and without a solution to the identity crisis of modern man there is no imaginable solution to the social and political crises of the world. The theodicy question and the identity question are two sides of the same coin.

If we listen in this situation to the New Testament, a third dimension can speak to us, the dimension of primitive Christian apocalypticism. At this point, I am taking over the historical and systematic thesis of Ernst Käsemann: "Apocalypticism is the mother of all Christian theology." Käsemann does not mean thereby that body of ideas and writings we usually call "apocalypticism," but that peculiar questioning which combines the question of God with the question of the future of history. The eschatology of Paul, of the book of Revelation, and of primitive Christianity in general is propelled by the question whether or not God

is and *when* he would become God fully. This question
with its temporal component goes beyond the Thomistic
question: *An Deus sit?* The question of God is placed here
on the ground of historical experience and, defined in temporal
terms, turns into the question of his coming. It is the question,
first, whether or not the God of Jesus Christ is God and Lord
of all men and, second, *when* he would become this God fully.
The *ground* for this question is the contingent history of Jesus
Christ. Its *horizon* is the future of world history, as it is expressed in the symbols of the last judgment and the new creation. On the basis of the Christ event, Christian theology raises
the question of God as the question of the future of God in
which God will be God universally. Eschatologically directed
toward the future of God, Christian faith in the experience of
the world introduces the theodicy question: *Si Christus, unde
malum?* ("If there is Christ, whence evil?") and makes men
conscious of human suffering in view of the misery of man's
Godlessness and God-forsakenness Eschatologically directed
toward the future of God, the Christian message proclaims
the new man and thus leads man into an identity crisis,
that is, into conscious suffering in view of the misery of his
inability to recognize his true humanity.

Theology as eschatology tries to understand man together
with the world historically in view of that future which both
will find in the future of God.

Christian theology, therefore, is itself a historical initiative. It does not indicate what was and what is, but it tries
to change things historically through performative language.
It is historico-eschatological thinking about God between
cross and parousia. In the painful realities of history it
upholds the hope for God's future, and in the anticipating
reflection about this future it searches for realizable possibilities to overcome the misery of history. Christian theology is, therefore, even in its very language, according to
ancient terminology, *theologia viae*, but not as yet *theologia
patriae*. That is, it is still the theory of historical action, and
not as yet the theory of the *theoria Dei*, the vision of God.

3
THE "GOD OF HOPE": .
FUTURE AS GOD'S MODE OF BEING WITH US

If we understand the immanent reality of the world and of man historically, we presuppose that we view the transcendent reality of God eschatologically. Both emerge together: the understanding of the world as history and the understanding of God as the future of history.

From the God who reveals himself in the context of historical persons and events, everything that is, is referred to the future and is experienced in its historical openness. On the basis of the promises and the historical guidance toward fulfillment, the Old Testament spoke of the "coming God," who would bring his people out of captivity and exile and his creation out of chaos and misery into the home of his glory. Besides various spatial characterizations of his epiphanies in history, we therefore find in the biblical witness the temporal characterization of his promised future. Consequently, we must think through the "future" as God's mode of being with us. The future of his glory and his reign is not something accidental that must still be added to his eternity for the sake of completion. God is Lord in carrying out his reign. In the actual demonstration of his divinity he is "God with us" and with the world. The divinity of God will become manifest and real only in the coming of his unlimited reign.

The faith that God is God therefore necessarily embraces the hope that the future of his Kingdom will come in its full identity into the world. In the modern debate between the faith in the "God above us" and the faith in the "God in us" or "between us," a third position enters in, which speaks of the "God in front of us, ahead of us," the "God of hope" and the "God of the exodus." In the modern conflict between a theism that affirms "God is" and an atheism that negates

God, saying, "God is not," eschatological theology can say, "God's being, the Kingdom of his full identity, is coming." *God is* present in the way in which his future takes control over the present in real anticipations and prefigurations. *But God is not as yet* present in the form of his eternal presence. The dialectic between his being and his being-not-yet is the pain and the power of history. Caught between the experiences of his presence and of his absence, we are seeking his future, which will solve this ambiguity that the present cannot solve. By future ("advent") we do not mean a far-away condition, but a power which already qualifies the present—through promise and hope, through liberation and the creation of new possibilities. As this power of the future, God reaches into the present. As creator of new possibilities he liberates the present from the shackles of the past and from the anxious insistence on the status quo. Thus God becomes the power of the protest against the guilt that throws us into transiency and produces death, and he becomes also the ground of the freedom that renews life.

If we understand the reality of God in the temporal and the historical categories of the future, we must conversely also unite the temporal and the historical categories of the future with the God-idea. Our traditional understanding of time puts past, present, and future as the three tenses next to each other in terms of equal importance. In temporal terms, the eternity of God is usually expressed as his presence in past, present, and future: "Zeus was, Zeus is, and Zeus will be." This understanding of time balks against an overestimation of the future and finds God in the present and the past as well. In the New Testament this view of time is changed. In Revelation 1:4 we read: "Peace from him who is and who was and *who is to come.*" One expects to read: "and who will be." Instead, we find in place of the future tense of *einai* ("being") the future tense of *erchesthai* ("coming"). This gives the future a new dominance over the other tenses. Future is the "coming of God." Therefore, the future is expected from the coming God. What God was in the past and what he is in the present becomes understandable from the announcement of his ultimate coming. As the coming God, he is not only the future of the present but also the future of the past. We can therefore grasp history as the process of this future.

Even so, there remains a difference between eschatological theology which speaks of the "coming God," and teleological metaphysics and process philosophy, which speaks of the "becoming God" or of God as the *finis ultimus* ("the final end") of all things. As far as I can tell, process theology, on the one hand, speaks of the "becoming God" in the context of the dynamics of the world process. Eschatological theology, on the other hand, speaks of the "coming God" in the context of the dialectical dynamics, circumscribed by the symbols of *creatio ex nihilo*, *justificatio impii*, and *resurrectio mortuorum*.

1. *God and promissory history.* "The new is never completely new. A dream always precedes it" (Ernst Bloch). Correspondingly, the future of the coming God is never pure future. It is preceded by a history of promises and anticipations. Israel experienced the reality of God in its history of exodus, covenant, and promise. The Old Testament is a history book rather than a book of law and cult, since law and cult have been integrated within the covenantal history of the promises. What is a promise? A promise announces a reality which has not as yet arrived. But in announcing this future, the future becomes wordpresence. This distinguishes a promise from a mere prediction. If the promise brings the future into the present in the word, it compels the present to decisions. No one will see the land of fulfillment if he does not start seeking it. This distinguishes the Old Testament promises from Cassandra's oracles of fate. The Old Testament promises are historical because they open up a history through hope and exodus. But how are future and presence of God in the tension of this promissory history to be understood? I think that we can differentiate

here between a presence of God on the way and a presence of God at the goal of the way of promises. God is experienced as "fire and cloud in the exodus," and is sought in the homeland of his identity in which the exodus terminates. One can distinguish between the presence of the will of God in history and *as* history, and the real presence of God in the end of history and as its end. The historical epiphanies of God, of which Israel could truly speak, were particular and transient epiphanies. Therefore, memory transforms them into signs and promises of the ultimate and eschatological epiphany of God at the end of history. The future-oriented concept of the presence of God in his promises is not directed against the concrete religious experience of theophanies but actually preserves it in the "memory of hope." Because an ultimate future announces itself in a provisional past, hope exists in the mode of memory, and memory in the mode of hope.

If we understand history generally as promissory history, we discover a profound difference which is experienced time and again in messianic religious movements. It is the difference between hope and experience, between vision and reality. Israel set out to find the Promised Land "flowing with milk and honey," but it found Palestine where it was threatened by both internal and foreign foes. Jesus proclaimed—according to an ironic as well as profound dictum of Alfred Loisy—the Kingdom of God, but what came was the church. The French Revolution promised "freedom, equality, and brotherhood," but its progeny was the age of the bourgeoisie. The socialist revolution nurtured the expectation of the completely human society, but in effect produced a hierarchy of specialists and functionaries. The industrial revolution promises peace and humanity, but we find ourselves today in the midst of an irrational dynamics of civilization. All of this points to the difference in which we experience history. In fact, it is precisely this difference which propels history. On the one hand, hopes are greater than the fulfillment of reality, and history falls short of hope. On the

211

other hand, the new reality necessitates a new interpretation of hopes. We find this alternating process of realization and reinterpretation quite evident in Israel's history of traditions and, moreover, we should keep it in view in order to proceed with patience between the promises of history and the disappointments of history.

2. _God and Christ_. In the horizon of hope in the "coming God" we confront Jesus, his mission, and his history with the ancient messianic question: "Are you the one who is to come?" Thereupon we will discover that the messianic claim of Jesus lies in the prolepsis of his proclamation of the Kingdom In the antitheses of the Sermon on the Mount, in the Beatitudes, and in the call to discipleship, Jesus represents through his own presence and mission that not-yet-realized future of the Kingdom in which God is God. In that he himself announces the arrival of this future he brings eschatological freedom into the misery of the present. It is congruous with the eschatological proclamation of the historical Jesus that the Easter witnesses proclaimed the crucified one as the eschatological representative of God on the basis of his Easter appearances and found in him the focus of universal hope. Just as his proclamation could be repeated in the light of Easter, and just as Easter became the ground of a new hope on the background of his proclamation, so one could recognize in him the real anticipation of the future of God. With his mission and proclamation and the Easter event, the ultimate liberation of the world is set in motion and its end is confidently anticipated. If we see Jesus, his proclamation, and his history together in the concept of the "Christ event," we find in this event two perspectives:

In this event there lies a real _anticipation_ of the future of history in the midst of history. For this reason the early Christian community gave Jesus messianic titles and characterized his end with the eschatological expression "raised from the dead." The eschatological future of God, of life, of righteousness, and of the new creation occurred in history and under the conditions of history through him and in him. Therefore, memory of him can become the ground of world-surpassing hope.

Nevertheless, the early Christian community kept in mind the distinction between Jesus the Lord, and God himself. In the worship of the New Testament community one prayed only to God, never to Jesus the Lord. Rather, the Lord was called upon. We have access to God through the Lord, and can pray to God in his name. We again find this distinction between God and Jesus the Lord in the eschatological reflection of 1 Corinthians 15. God has delegated his Lordship to Jesus for a definite time and for a specific purpose. At the consummation of that purpose Jesus will return his dignity so that God will be "all in all." The meaning of these observations is that the finality of faith in Jesus as the Christ of God was linked with the provisionality of hope in God himself. The Lordship of Christ in a world of sin and death is the provisional and messianic realization of the ultimate Lordship of God. Seen from this perspective, the purpose of Christ's Lordship is to make room for the absolute Lordship of God. Thus we find in many parts of the New Testament an eschatological Christology, or, articulated in the formula of old church dogmatics, an eschatological subordinationism (Emil Brunner). Therein Christ becomes the precursor, the place-holder, and the representative of the coming God.

On the other hand, however, there is inherent in the Christ event a real *incarnation* of God's future. Eschatological subordinationism results only if from the particular presence of Christ one looks upon the universal future of God. If, conversely, one looks from the future of God to the presence of Christ, one finds in him the incarnation of God. I think we find this perspective again in the title "Son of God." However much Jesus' proclamation and the proclamation of the resurrected Lord are future-oriented, the church sees in his passion and death the offering up of the Son through the Father and the offering up of the Son himself. This is the

213

movement of incarnation, of obedience, and of love. Therefore, it is not sufficient to designate Jesus as the "stand-in"
and deputy of the coming God. For precisely in such a
capacity he is also already the incarnation of the coming
God. Eschatological Christology goes astray if it does not
become in the countermovement a *christological eschatology*. As the anticipation of the future of God, Christ becomes the ground of hope. As the preparatory Messiah of
God, he reveals God as the Father. The real anticipation
of God through Christ attains its abiding significance through
the trinitarian relationship of the Father to the Son and the
Son to the Father.

The *anticipation* of the coming God through Jesus and
in Jesus is comprehended in the symbol of the resurrection
of Jesus—"ahead of us." The *incarnation* of the coming God
in Jesus is manifest in the meaning of his cross—"for us."
The Christ who was raised "ahead of us" mortals as the
first-fruits into new life is the same as the Christ who "for
us" died the death of God-forsakenness.

It does not suffice to speak only of the prolepsis of the
eschaton in the resurrection of Christ. That is no help to those
who are living within the agony of history. Within the agony
of history the message of the resurrection and of life always
reaches us, as sinners and mortals, i.e., as men closed to the
future and unfree, in the form of the message of the Christ
who was, for us, offered up and crucified. Theoretically expressed: Just as the resurrection alone manifests the meaning of
the cross of Christ, so his cross alone makes the resurrection
meaningful for us. Resurrection faith can be grasped only as
faith in the crucified one. And eschatological hope can be
"hope against hope" only if it is born out of the redeeming
and freeing efficacy of the cross of Christ. For in the one
crucified "for us" and for our justification, hope in freedom
is not only portrayed paradigmatically before our eyes but
is actually mediated. Hope is not born out of enthusiasm but
out of love which liberates us from old bonds and opens up

214

new opportunities. Therefore, in a world of death and for-
sakenness the coming glory of God shines forth at first on
the face of the crucified Christ.

3. *God and the community of Christ.* With the acquired
christological or messianic concepts of *anticipation* and
incarnation, of resurrection and cross, we can consider the
mission of the community of Christ, of the messianic congregation in a corresponding way. Its word of the gospel
is the anticipation of the eschatological manifestation of
God in all areas of the world. It thus bears in itself the
character of promise. It is, in a hidden way, the anticipatory
epiphany of God in the world. "Where the gospel is proclaimed, the exalted Lord anticipates his manifestation in
his word uttered by man, he anticipates the future in the
announcement of himself as the coming one" (H. Schlier).
The gospel proclaims nothing other than that Jesus, the
Christ of God, was killed and resurrected for us. But that it
does this is already the beginning and anticipation of the
future of Christ and of the ultimate liberation of the world.
That such an ultimate liberation is already possible in history
through the faith-creating word is nothing less than a messianic
possibility. Correspondingly, the Christ event is represented,
and rebirth and reconciliation are made present in baptism and
the Lord's Supper. But that this is already happening is a possibility of the messianic time.

The memory that makes Christ present is, as such, the
anticipation of his future in hope. Because faith relates to
the reality of God only through word and not yet through
sight in the visible new creation, it is, as faith, hope. It is
the trusting beginning of the vision of God face to face.
The obedience of the faithful in the body and in everyday
life is an imitation of Christ, and as such is already the
anticipation of the resurrection of the body under the conditions of history and the anticipation of the kingdom of freedom in the possibilities of the present.

Finally, the community which is called together from

215

Jews and Gentiles, cultured and uncultured, masters and slaves can understand itself messianically as the representation of the new mankind. As the brotherhood of the Christ of God it is the vanguard of a world freed from Godlessness and inhumanity and, conversely, only where it is something like that is it the messianic community of Christ. Only when it freely chooses to make its own the groaning of the whole enslaved creation is the Christian community the sacrament of God's hope for the world.

4. *God and the creation of history.* With this we come to the furthermost horizon of eschatology, namely, the *eschatology of being.* Hope in the coming God leads not only to a messianic interpretation of biblical and of Christian history but must, if it is to be relevant, lead also to a messianic understanding of reality itself. A few intimations must suffice here. If we combine the idea of God with the idea of the future, the future assumes a creative character for time and for the whole of historical being. Out of the future spring new possibilities and out of these possibilities a new reality is created. In this sense history is the product of a creative process. To express it in another way: The future realizes itself in history and as history and yet always rebounds from its own realization in history and becomes again a not yet realized future of the whole of being.

All historical realizations of the future of being are ambiguous because they both realize and hinder this future of being. Possibilities are realized and at the same time also forfeited. Every historical reality has in itself the intention to be an enduring, eternal reality, for everything which is wishes to remain and not vanish. Thus we find everywhere in reality the tendency toward stabilization in cosmic orders against chaos. But no historical reality is already that prevailing eschatological reality; therefore, the prevailing reality transcends all historical realities and renders them once again historical realities. In the light of a messianic future we can thus conceive reality as historical tension between particularity and universality, between ambivalence and clarity, between incarnation and transcendence.

216

Reality is not a permanent cosmos and does not consist of repeatable orders. Neither is it a chaos. It is the historical process of the coming fullness of being. We can therefore rediscover in the intentions and tendencies of all beings in history something of what is called in traditional language "spirit." It is the agony, the motivating force, the tension of matter. It is the yearning, unfulfillment, anxiety, and suffering in matter itself. The unrest which man experiences in his heart wherever hope affects him is an unrest which he rediscovers in his body and in all beings. Everything which exists is burdened with transitoriness, but burdened in hope because it wants to be free. The formation of an eschatological or messianic understanding of being will necessitate (1) understanding nature historically and (2) understanding spirit materially and matter spiritually. The views of Teilhard de Chardin and Ernst Bloch point in this direction. To man's "restless heart" (Augustine) there corresponds a "restless world."

4

CREATIVE ESCHATOLOGY—POLITICAL THEOLOGY

How does the messianic mission of men for the future realize itself? In the perspective of messianic hope, the future, the Kingdom or the City of God do not simply lie in readiness in the future, so that one could only wait for this future and relate to it in conceptualization. Even though the Kingdom of God is God's Kingdom, it is also true that one must seek it in order to find it. Christian hope anticipates the future in the spirit of Christ and realizes it under the conditions of history. In that this future is anticipated in hope and obedience, it is itself conceived as in the process of coming. We are construction workers and not only interpreters of the future whose power in hope as well as in fulfillment is God. This means that Christian hope is a creative and militant hope in history. The horizon of eschatological expectation produces here a horizon of ethical intentions

217

which, in turn, gives meaning to the concrete historical initiatives. If one hopes for the sake of Christ in the future of God and the ultimate liberation of the world, he cannot passively wait for this future and, like the apocalyptic believers, withdraw from the world. Rather, he must seek this future, strive for it, and already here be in correspondence to it in the active renewal of life and of the conditions of life and therefore realize it already here according to the measure of possibilities. Because this future is the future of one God, it is a unique and unifying future. Because it brings eschatological liberation, it is the salvation of the whole enslaved creation. The messianic future for which Christianity arouses hope is no special future for the church or for the soul alone. It is an all-encompassing future. As all-encompassing future, its power of hope is able to mediate faith to earthly needs and to lead it into real life.

After the humanistic ethic of hope in the nineteenth century and its impotence in the catastrophes of the twentieth century, many in Europe and America developed an ethic of faith. That was justified, but it appears to me that today we should now develop a *new ethic of the hope of faith.* Together with Joh. B. Metz, I call it *political theology* in order to make clear that ethics is not an appendix to dogmatics and also is not only a consequence of faith, but that faith itself has a messianic context in which it becomes meaningful and that theology itself stands in a political dimension in which it becomes relevant.

For us the field of politics designates the extensive field of constructive and destructive possibilities of the appropriation and utilization of nature's powers as well as of human relationships by human society. Nature and human history come together in the process of civilization. In it there can no longer be a distinction between cosmology and anthropology. For man and nature, politics is becoming a common destiny. We take up the ancient concept of *theologia politica* or *theologia civilis* to point out the fundamental situation in which the God-question is raised and in which Christian God-talk must become relevant today. If it is correct that the old cosmological theodicy question about evil and misfortune has become today a political question, then the Christian faith in the creative righteousness of God and the liberation of the world out of its self-inflicted misery must become practically responsible exactly at this point. It is, on the other side, well known that the retreat of theology and faith out of politics into the private dimension has conceded the field of politics to Godless and inhuman powers. That faith which no longer seeks God and his righteousness in the world but only in the soul has allied itself with a practical atheism which seeks the world without God and righteousness, and with it has contracted an alliance of death, of the "death of God" in the world.

On the other hand, the theology of the believing "I" or of the esoteric I-thou relationship has reached its limitations because it is not in a position to come to grips with social and political institutions and organizations. But as soon as one emerges from the problem of realizing the "I" and of the question of identity, he can then see his "I" in connection with larger spheres. The identity question of man finds no solution without the recognition of the *call* of man to concrete engagement and to active self-renunciation for the sake of a greater cause. Man finds his inner certainty only when he finds certainty about the tasks for which he exists and in which he can exert himself. He who forgets himself in devotion to the mission of Christ for the liberation of the world will find himself. The New Testament community spoke of such calls in connection with charisms and virtues. They realized these in their time in the missionary proclamation of freedom, in the messianic community of free men, and in the new obedience for the sake of liberation out of bodily misery. If in our time politics is increasingly becoming the destiny and more and more threateningly the fate of man, it is necessary to develop a political theology of Christian virtues.

Political theology unites the old cosmological theology

and the new theology of existence in the eschatological understanding of history with the messianic tasks of men in history. Yet exactly at this juncture we must consider that it is unreal to anticipate and work for the future if this future does not come toward us. The future in which we hope is never identical with the successes of our activity, for our actions are as ambivalent as we ourselves insofar as we are historical beings. The future must come toward us in order that our activity be "not in vain," as Paul puts it in his chapter on the resurrection hope, against the paralyzing impression of the mortality and transitoriness of all things.

Revolutions which must bring a better future with force are aimed at the *reconciliation* of their attained reality with the hoped-for future. For that reason messianism, of which we spoke politically in reference to the liberation of the world from its misery, needs permanent reconciliation through the freedom of Christ.

Hope which mobilizes the renewal of life needs faith in order to find certainty. The liberating future of God enters into the possibilities and impossibilities of our history in a twofold way: as exhortation of redemption from the guilt-laden coercion, which binds us to the past and hurls us into transiency, and as demand for the renewal of life. The surplus value of the future over history manifests itself in hope's permanent surplus incentive and, with equal importance, in the redemption of the compulsion of the instincts. Without faith, hope cannot laugh, and without hope, faith cannot live and dispose of itself in the world.